WIDOWMAKER

Kimberly,

Thanks for interest in
th area of PTSD. I wish
you the best in your
program and hope the road
ahead is full of Good Orderly
Direction.

Drew Mortensen

Widowmaker

By Drew Martensen

To order additional copies of this book, contact:
Xlibris Corporation
1-888-795-4274
www.Xlibris.com
Orders@Xlibris.com
89322

CONTENTS

WIDOWMAKER, PART I

WIDOWMAKER, PART II

Widowmaker, Part I

"Even the bravest men are frightened by sudden terrors."
— Publius Cornelius Tacitus

CHAPTER I

Love, Mom

August 1967

I slowly open my eyes from a slumber as our plane begins a quiet descent toward the airfield at DaNang, South Vietnam. Four hours earlier our company of 200 grunts had been partying in Okinawa celebrating our departure from the good old USA. I look below at the rolling surf of the South China Sea which appears more like a vacation paradise rather than a war zone. Within minutes our plane drops onto the DaNang airstrip and I catch a glimpse of bomb craters and damaged planes along the runway. "Damn, we're really here," I murmur.

The captain announces over the intercom, "Marines, we're at your destination. I promise we'll be back to pick each and everyone of you up in thirteen months. May God be with you." Tearful stewardesses squeeze our hands and kiss our cheeks as we leave the plane giving me an ominous feeling about what may lie ahead. I walk out of the air-conditioned cabin onto the tarmac which is radiating heat like a furnace and quickly understand why our drill instructors worked us day and night in the scorching, snake infested back-woods of south Carolina. Jet engines scream, helicopter blades thump, sergeants bark orders, and tank engines roar rattling my eardrums. I hold my head high and proudly walk toward the receiving area.

My heart pounds as we board trucks and ride through the steamy streets of a city shaking with anxiety from nightly Vietcong rocket attacks. Prostitutes, pimps, and drug dealers call out, "Good dope, good boom-boom for Marine!" Dilapidated huts made of cardboard and bamboo line the narrow streets, looking like the houses we built as kids with poker cards. A Marine barters with two men wearing black pajamas and coolie hats holding out what looks like clumps of black tar heroine for wads of cash. We turn a corner and a voluptuous woman clad only in pajama bottoms hangs her clothes out to dry. Nearby, a group of kids beg an MP for candy while hollering the enemy leader's name, "Ho Chi Minh, no good!" An old woman shouts angrily and waves her fist at us, as if we had done something wrong. From the truck radio the voice of Hanoi Hanna, the Communist propagandist from North Vietnam pleads, "Please, Marines, give up the fighting, you can't win!" while groups of teenage Marines roam the streets armed with guns and knives. I wonder if this place is gonna' make the world safe for democracy.

At twilight our truck enters regiment headquarters. We grab our gear and rush into our sleeping quarters. A burly sergeant shouts, "Don't get too comfortable ladies but do enjoy your last night of peaceful sleep."

I toss my gear on a bunk next to a guy named Cars, whom I met just prior to leaving the States. His full name is Lee Carson but infantrymen, or grunts, are usually called by a shortened form of their last name. Cars is from a small hollow in Tennessee and lets me know he's proud of it. Cars calls everyone from the North "damn Yankees," and you'd think the South had won the Civil War. I like Cars because he never hesitates to say what he's thinking. He has a Southern accent, bushy mustache, sandy hair, and stands about 5 feet 8 inches. His features seem much larger than his 150 pound frame suggests. Cars is sitting on his rack singing a country ballad off key, "That no good drunken Injun, yeah, the Marine named Ira Hayes."

"Who the hell's Ira Hayes?" I ask in agony.

"You don't know Ira Hayes?" he quips. "He's the World War II Indian who helped raise the flag at Iwo Jima. After the war he had problems with booze and ended up dyin' of drinkin' too much. My old man told me a lot of guys were messed up after they came back, but nobody talked about it. He said they saw the beyond and returned with the thousand-yard stare."

"What's this thousand-yard stare?" I ask.

"That's when a grunt sees too much combat and they get this look about 'em like they're starin' at something far away."

"Yeah," I agree. "I guess my dad's brother had it when he came home on leave from the Big One. Dad said Uncle Jerry sat most of the day looking out the window like he had something real serious on his mind."

"He saw the bogeyman!" Cars says. "Old Man Death was out to get him but missed. That's when you get the stare."

"Where you goin' after you get back from the war, Cars?" I shrug.

"Tennessee. I'm goin' back there in 13 months after I do this temporary duty in the Nam, then I'm AMF—adios motherfucker, outta this Marine Corps Crotch." Then he continues singing that ballad Ira Hayes off-key—"That no good drunken Injun, yeah, the Marine named Ira Hayes."

I lie back on my cot listening to Cars and think about what our new duty station might be like. Those of us who arrived on the plane are heading for duty stations somewhere away from the Marine stronghold of DaNang, which is about 100 miles south of the Demilitarized Zone. The DMZ divides North Vietnam from the South. All the area 200 miles south from the DMZ is considered the I Corps and defended by U.S. Marines. The I Corps is a pivotal area, since the North Vietnamese troops travel through it to get to the central and southern regions of Vietnam where the U.S. Army is stationed. Two smaller cities north of DaNang are much closer to the DMZ: Quang Tri, 25 miles south of the DMZ, and Hue, about 50 miles south. The territories between these three cities have been hotbeds of enemy activity since early 1967. Drill instructors used buzz words like "Hill 881," "Operation Hastings," and "The Rockpile" to motivate us. They told stories of grunts who fought and died in these areas as legends for the rest of us to uphold and follow. I heard in boot camp that Marine casualty rates run at least 50 percent in these areas and that one in four Marines will wear his medals posthumously. The odds are fifty-fifty that I will get wounded, however, some battalions have casualty rates as high as 90 percent. They call them "Widowmakers."

"Think we might end up in a Widowmaker battalion, Cars?"

"Better hope not, 'cause there ain't no swingin' dicks that make it out of the Widowmaker. Anyway, there's only a couple of those Widowmaker battalions, and they're both up north along the DMZ doin' beach landings. We ain't headin' that way, we're goin' somewhere outside DaNang."

Cars and I bed down for the night next to a couple of guys we had met on the plane named Demarco and Matthews. We are alike in many ways: young, immature, head-strong, accidents waiting to happen. It's more important for us to fight in Nam than to have fought for deferments. Night sweeps over the regiment while we talk new-guy stuff. "Where you guys from?" I ask, puffing on a Lucky Strike.

"We're from east L.A.," Matthews replies. Matthews is small, with blond hair, freckles, and bright green eyes. He lies on his bunk with hands clasped behind his head, feet crossed, gazing at the ceiling. "We went to the same high school and joined the Crotch together and haven't been apart since. Hell, I'm closer to him than his girl. We're gonna get our medals and blow this hole, if the mosquitoes don't eat us alive first."

Demarco responds in a deep voice. "Yeah, we only got 13 months to do, then I'm gonna go back to school. Promised my girl and my family I'd do that."

Demarco is a big Italian with arms and shoulders that appear to be carved from a sturdy oak, and a neck as large as a linebacker's. His deep voice and gigantic size are tempered by his smooth olive skin. Demarco's Italian-Catholic heritage and large family are important to him. He speaks of eating fish on Friday, lying to the priest in Confession, drinking wine and eating hosts after serving mass, and going to summer school because some dumb nun was out to ruin his vacation. He wants to return to the States as a hero so his father can parade him through their neighborhood.

"Anyway, 13 months ain't so long," I say. "Hell, I did 12 years in Catholic school and still got welts on my ass to prove it."

A voice bellows from the other end of the long billet. "One night can be a lifetime in this place."

We turn toward the voice where a gaunt, dark-complected Marine is sitting on a cot slowly sliding a white cloth up and down the barrel of his M-16 like he's making love to his favorite girl. He's wearing faded jungle fatigues, gray ruffled boots from a long time in the jungle, and a green tank top. "I'm a short-timer," he says, tersely. "The shorter you get, the longer it takes each day to go by. Firefights seem twice as long and near misses really mess with your head. Each patrol takes forever. Wanna hear some more good news, newbies?"

Cars sits up and bellows, "It's a lick if you keep your eyes peeled."

The Marine continues giving full attention to the barrel of his M-16 "Unless you miss that one trip wire among a thousand blades of grass. I was with a Cherokee point man when he missed. Our eyes met just before a Malayan whip ripped him in half. Can you see as good as an Indian, new guy?"

Cars hammers, "I've been huntin' since I was five years old and I can hit a rabbit runnin' two barns away. My old man would beat my ass if I missed it. I didn't come here to play around, pal."

"Hell, yes!" Demarco yells. "I went huntin' one time with my uncle and we killed a bobcat. Tell you what, that thing could have attacked us, and I wouldn't be sittin' here right now."

"Sorry 'bout that but we kill tigers over here for dinner," he says, with a tight grin. "Where you newbies headin'?" he asks, in a low, even voice. "First Battalion, Third Marines outside DaNang," I respond, with pride.

The Marine stops stroking the barrel of the M-16, looks at me and bellows, "That's in bumfuck Egypt! I hope you have a good ride tomorrow 'cause the last truck outta' here hit a land mine and took five KIAs. That means five fuckers died. There wasn't much to send home either. Be smart and take a seat toward the back 'cause the front wheels hit the mines first. You also might want to cup your balls in your hands to protect your love life. I have three weeks to go then I'm AMF." The Marine places the M-16 on the cot next to him, lies back and lights a cigarette.

"Think I'm gonna' get some sleep myself," Matthews yawns.

The rest of us put our gear away and bed down for the night. I stretch out on my cot and think about what the Marine had said about the danger. I hear distant explosions that sound like a thunderstorm on a summer night. The reality of the explosions cause me to wonder if I made a big mistake by volunteering for Vietnam. Gunnery Sergeant, McKay, warned me about the danger before I left the States, but I didn't listen to him.

*   *   *   *   *   *   *

I had been on a weekend furlough in my hometown of Columbus, Ohio, partying with friends until I had to leave to go back to camp on Sunday evening. My friends drove me to the outskirts of Columbus where I hitched a ride from a Marine back to Camp Lejeune. We were drinking beer while traveling through West Virginia and the driver lost control of our car, nearly running off the road. A sheriff parked along the road witnessed the reckless driving. He pulled us over and charged my friend with DWI and arrested me for public intoxication. We had to stay in jail a couple of days, which caused us to be AWOL from Camp Lejeune. When we finally arrived back at camp, the guys told me I would probably get busted from lance corporal to private. There was a hitch, however. The Marine Corps was sustaining a lot of casualties in Vietnam and doing almost anything to get more infantrymen into the field, including dropping charges on guys with legal problems. I was so sick and tired of the spit-and-polish outfit at Camp Lejeune I endured for about a year that I decided to volunteer for Vietnam. That's when Gunnery Sergeant McKay heard of my decision and suggested I have a talk with him in his billet.

I had known the old gunny since my arrival at Camp Lejeune in early 1966. He had taken on a paternal role and seemed to have a special interest in what I was doing. A lanky 6-foot 2-inch, cantankerous, gray-haired geezer with a wrinkled face, McKay didn't mince words. He had been in the Corps for 25 years and had served in the infantry during World War II, Korea, and Vietnam. He was awarded the Silver Star for heroism in World War II, the second-highest medal this nation bestows, and was also awarded the Bronze Star, a lesser accommodation, in Vietnam. McKay had three Purple Hearts for wounds sustained in World War II and one Purple Heart from Korea. I remember walking into McKay's billet and how my backbone tightened to attention as I scanned the walls around his desk. Combat photographs with gold insignias reading Guadalcanal, Guam, Bataan, Tarawa, and Belleau Wood loomed from all angles of the room. A large poster of Chesty Puller in dress blues, the most decorated man in the history of the Marine Corps, hung on the wall above the gunny's head. To the right of Puller's picture was a black-and-white photograph of the flag raising at Iwo Jima, which wasn't at all like the publicized photograph I had seen in the past. In this photograph, six Marines with dirty faces and hollow cheeks were on their bellies pushing a small flag pole up on the side of a rocky hill. Their dark eyes were focused on the enemy, intense with fear and apprehension rather than brash courage.

The gunny stood up and walked over to the picture and pointed at it, exclaiming, "This is what the flag raising was really like! No heroes here. These are Marines wantin' to stay alive. Now what's this nonsense about you volunteering for Vietnam? Are you fuckin' crazy?"

"No sir!" I responded.

He frowned as he unbuttoned his shirt in a huff. "I want to show you something." He pointed to a large scar that ran from his collarbone down to his navel. "This happened at Guadalcanal. A lousy Jap sliced me with his stiletto just before I blew his head off. You ever see anybody lose his head, boy?" He asked with wide eyes. Then he pointed to a large scar near his elbow. "This is where a piece of shrapnel hit me on the arm. The guy next to me took the full impact. He ain't here."

The gunny surprised me by unbuttoning his fatigues and dropping them to the floor. He pointed to an ugly scar near his groin. "This bullet wound almost cost me my love life. I lost some good friends on that day in Korea whom I still think about." He hesitated for a moment in thought. "You ever cried, boy?" I was speechless. "Take a look at this." The gunny pointed at a tattoo on his left biceps.

I looked hard at the worn image of the past. It was a woman's face outlined in blue indigo and cast in faded crimson. She had long hair with three teardrops falling from each eye. The script below her face read "LOVE, MOM." "One night at Guadalcanal, I had a lot of time to think about dyin'. Thought a lot about my mom that night. Decided if I lived through the night, I would get a tattoo for her. Never knew how much she meant to me until that night. You got a mom, boy?" he paused. "Cause she's gonna miss you if you go through with this." The gunny's voice trailed off.

As far as I was concerned, I was listening to a war story which only challenged me to take the final step to experience what I had been trained for. The gunny's wounds were living proof that heroes *do* survive. Plus, all I could think about was getting out of Camp Lejeune. "Look gunny," I shrugged. "I joined this Marine Corps to fight, not to shine shoes in this pissin' outfit. I've had it with this place."

"Well, boy, can't say I didn't try. I've been watching your drinking, ya know, and I hope all that booze ain't doin' your thinkin' for you. Guess you're hell-bent on gettin' medals, but just remember, those medals aren't gonna mean anything if you come back in a body bag. Well, anyway, you got your mind made up, so take this with ya'."

The gunny handed me a scapula which is somewhat of a good luck charm but for Catholics it's a strong sign of faith. We believe if you have it on when you die, you go straight to heaven. I looked at the gunny and put the scapula around my neck saying, "thanks gunny-sir". Then he flipped me off by giving me the finger.

* * * * * * *

I lie awake on my first night in Vietnam thinking about McKay's warnings as explosions in the distance echo in my head. The combat zone is definitely getting closer.

The next morning passes quickly as we prepare for departure to our duty stations. By afternoon, eight of us board a six-by truck, which looks like a dump truck with two metal benches from the cab to the rear, and head out the main gates of DaNang into the countryside. We drive for about an hour heading south over narrow unpaved roads toward the battalion area. We pass through small towns, we refer to as villes, which are defended by the South Vietnamese Army, where the war seems non-existent. Drab buildings and bamboo huts are bedecked with lanterns and flowers, American and South Vietnamese flags, and banners bearing anti-Ho Chi Minh slogans. Peasants in black pajamas and conic straw hats, portage rice, pull rickshaws, and ride bikes alongside the road. Many of them raise their fist and curse angrily at us for having to make room for our truck. Pigs, chickens, and dogs blend into the masses. Children hold their hands out begging for candy and cigarettes. Between the villes are vast open expanses of rice paddies where farmers use water buffaloes to till the fields.

I feel excited about being in a foreign country when we reach a town called Loui Kim San, the final checkpoint before entering enemy territory. The driver of our truck pokes his big greasy face out the door and in a raspy voice says, "We got six miles of bad road ahead of us." He spits tobacco on the ground. "Five warm bodies got wasted here a couple days ago. They say you don't hear the one that gets you. I heard that explosion all the way back at battalion. Don't know how they could have missed it." He looks puzzled. "We think it was command-detonated by a VC squattin' on the side of the road acting like a good gook. So, you guys keep your eyes peeled for gooks on the side of the road or anything that looks unusual. Gimme a holler if you see anything." I grew as alert as a wild animal.

The driver guns the engine and the six-by surges forward. Demarco and Matthews are perched on top of the cab holding on for dear life, watching the road ahead. Cars and I sit on the metal truck bench with our balls cupped in our hands to protect our love life. It's like playing the game Russian roulette, and the stakes are for real. The not knowing drives me crazy. Would I feel anything, or would I just see a flash of light before everything goes blank. I start praying the Our Father harder than I had ever done in church. The diesel engine roars as the truck clamors along the dirt road. The metal dog tag around my neck etched with my branch of service, rank, and service number clanks against my chest. The dog tag will mark my body bag if we hit a mine.

Suddenly, the truck slows and the driver points at an 8-foot crater on the right side of the road. He yells, "That's where they got wasted!" I look at the bomb crater, envisioning bodies and bent dog tags strewn within the carnage.

"Looks like a howitzer round or an antitank mine," Cars says. "The VC were definitely into some overkill."

I wonder if we are going to make it to Battalion alive. We blindly move onward and, with each passing moment, I thank God. Just when I think I can't take it any longer, we clear a tree line and I see an American flag in the distance. It's the girth of First Battalion, Third Marines. "We did it!" Cars yells.

The battalion area appears a lone outpost with a diameter of about a half-mile. It's surrounded by a 10-foot-high dirt wall with sandbagged bunkers spaced 30 yards apart. In each bunker are two or three Marine guards peering at the tree line with binoculars. They are equipped with 60-caliber machine guns and Browning automatic rifles known as BARs. The perimeter of the battalion is strung with four rows of layered concertina wire as a first line of defense. Dispersed within the concertina wire are barrels of foo-gas, which can explode napalm to a radius of 50 meters. There are no trees, shrubs, or grass within a thousand-yards of the barren perimeter, and the light-colored dirt and sand blends into the natural wall of the compound, camouflaging everything.

As we drive through the gates toward Receiving, Marine guards are on full alert, their eyes as sharp as cat eyes. All the equipment is well organized for battle, and I try to memorize where everything is located. The 175mm howitzer, mortar encampments, and armored personnel carriers with specially mounted dart guns are strategically placed near bunkers. Spread throughout the area are barracks of different sizes made with wood foundations and tent-like sides of canvas. The roofs of the barracks are made of tin and protected by sandbags. Four-hole shitters and piss-tubes are set apart from the other structures in the open and shared by everyone. We reach the other side of the perimeter and I spot a couple of posts with a sheet of plywood nailed to them functioning as a screen for an outdoor movie theater. "Blue Hawaii" is written on a chalkboard next to the makeshift screen. Close to the movie theater, a platoon of hungry grunts are chowing down in a barracks-like structure designated as the mess hall. Another group of scruffy Marines are drinking beer in front of a sign which reads "Grunt Club—get it while you can." Near the club is an open area where garbage cans filled with water are elevated on posts. A long line of bare butts await their turn to take showers. It seems I landed on an alien planet.

The driver stops the six-by and sticks his head out of the window and boasts, "Looks like we made it. Good luck, new guys."

We deboard the truck and walk inside the receiving barracks where a company clerk stands behind a counter with an open screened gate, grinning from ear to ear. He's holding our service files and is ready to issue each of us field gear like he's probably done a hundred times before. He raises his thumb at Demarco as if he's measuring a steer and says, "Yep, you're an extra large. Here's some gear that would fit an elephant." He throws it at Demarco.

He then turns his thumb toward me saying, "You're a medium, killer. By the way, where should I send your gear when you're killed?" My heart pounds and my skin feels like it's being pricked by a thousand needles. The clerk is smirking behind that huge thumb he's holding up. I wonder if I should give him my father's name and address or just punch him.

Cars abruptly raises his middle finger at the clerk and blurts, "Fuck you, you bastard! Guess you get a bang outta welcomin' new guys to town, huh?"

The clerk chuckles saying, "I'm in the rear with the gear, so I don't give a shit." He tosses our field gear, M-16s, and ammo at us with vigor. "You guys are all goin' to Mike Company, Third Platoon. I didn't get a chance to give that message to the five new fuckers the other day, since they all got wasted on that road."

Cars interrupted, "Yep, we done heard about it."

"Well," the clerk's eyes sharpened. "I mean if those guys had made it through the road mines, then I'd have sent them to your new platoon. But doesn't matter whether they got wasted on the road or later in that crazy-ass platoon. That's why I asked where you want me to send your shit."

Demarco hikes up his fatigues and bellows, "What the fuck are you talkin' about, Marine?" It's as if Demarco is appealing to the clerk's sense of pride and honor as a fellow Marine. "I mean what the hell is this crazy platoon shit all about?"

The clerk begins closing up shop. "Look, this ain't the fuckin' Marine Corps that you've known over here, big guy. This is the Nam! You guys got a couple of days to get mellow before your platoon returns from the field to pick ya up. Enjoy the stay while you can and get truckin' straight down that road out front. It will get you to your platoon area." The clerk lights a cigarette, then slams shut the screened gate to the receiving room.

We grab our gear and walk out to the road, following signs that point to Mike Company, Third Platoon. Within a few minutes we arrive at our platoon area, which is made up of four squad billets each housing up to twelve men. We spend the evening organizing our gear, writing letters, and talking tough.

"Ain't nothing here to write home about," Cars says, lightheartedly. "I'm gonna be carrying my gear home with me when I'm outta here." "Yeah! I ain't heard a shot fired yet." Demarco shakes his head, enthusiastically. "This is gonna be a lick."

"I'll be takin' my gear home, too," I say, with confidence.

I gather a pencil and paper and write a letter home: "Dear Mom, I finally arrived at my duty station. It looks like a nice, easy spot to do my tour. Nothing happening around here but lots of sunshine. I really miss everybody. Can you send me some food seasonings for my C-rats?"

I glance up at the others and say, "I heard most of the action is happenin' up around the DMZ."

"Doesn't make a fuckin' difference to me, 'cause I'm looking forward to wastin' my first gook," Demarco says with confidence. I nod in agreement, but butterflies flutter in my stomach.

"Demarco," Cars grins. "All you'd have to do is look at a VC, and you'd scare him to death." Matthews and I laugh and give each other "five." "Well, that's all right, too, 'cause I'm just lookin' at gettin' my fair share of Kills for the Stars and Stripes." Demarco is serious.

"I think we'll all bag quite a few before it's all over." Matthews says in a quick even voice. "Whadaya think it's like to get shot at?"

"It ain't nuthin'." Cars says. "Remember when we had to crawl under the concertina wire in ITR and they shot bullets over our heads? Hell, I knew then I could hack it."

Matthews blinks. "Really! We used to go hunting and shoot at rabbits, just missing each other."

No one says anything. I work on my gear, trying to reassure myself I'm ready to go under fire. Night envelops the garrison and our voices taper to whispers as I drift off to sleep.

We spend the next day checking out the battalion area and adjusting to the blazing sun. We carry M-16s and wear flak jackets to look bad, unaware most seasoned grunts choose not to wear them due to the extra weight it adds to field gear. We learn from guys at the mess hall that our battalion's function is to protect the DaNang air field from rocket attacks. A huge expanse of rice paddies and jungle surrounding DaNang complicate this task. Finding the enemy, better known as "Charlie," in this vegetative environment is each platoon's responsibility. A total of 20 platoons are divided into five companies, which operate in or around our battalion area. The platoon we are assigned to has been in the bush for three weeks and are on their way back into Battalion for a short rest and resupply. By late afternoon, we return to our billet and begin organizing our gear while we wait to meet our new family. Finally, they arrive in the early evening and stand in loose formation in front of our platoon area for about a half hour awaiting orders. We sit on our cots and silently watch them through the screens of our billet. During this time, I am able to get a good understanding of the platoon leaders and the members of each squad.

The platoon, which consists of 30 Marines, is small, since full-strength platoons average 45 to 50 men. They probably have been taking casualties and not getting enough replacements. There are three squads of ten men and each squad is led by a squad leader who stands at the front of the squad. The squads are further divided into fire-teams of three or four men with another team leader. The small fire-team units are the heart and soul of the platoon. A Marine bonds more closely to the guys in his fire-team than he will to anyone. Back in the States, during infantry training while crouched in my foxhole, I could feel the same sense of apprehension and tension in my buddy that was in me. It was as though a sixth sense took over and I could tell whether he would stand by me in a life or death situation. It's through this extraordinary bonding that courage arises during battle and the deeper the bond, the more likely you would die for your buddy. I study the fire-teams within the three squads wondering which one I will be assigned to.

The first squad consists of seven riflemen plus a two-man rocket team. The rocket team is a valuable asset in battle because it can knock out enemy bunkers or armored vehicles when grunts can't get close enough. The rocket team is led by a guy the squad members are calling Minch, who is tall, jovial, and seems to be the focus of the squad. A 4-foot-long rocket launcher tube is strapped to his back. His partner is a short stubby guy who has several foot-long rockets attached to the top and sides of his rucksack along with all his other gear. The squad is led by a serious-looking Marine with a slightly gnarled brow by the name of Fuller. Fuller carries a grenade launcher, which looks like a sawed-off shotgun, slung over his shoulder. The grenade launcher is a nice asset to the platoon because it can fire grenades hundreds of yards into enemy positions. Fuller has two grunts standing near him indicating he might also be functioning as a fire-team leader within the squad. The other fire-team is led by a Chicano named, Roberto. He is a quiet type who carefully observes everything around him.

One of the black guys in his team, named Scott, asks Roberto if he is going to make them be really careful by digging a foxhole inside the battalion area. There is laughter and hissing from the rest of the riflemen in the squad. I assume Roberto is liked by the others but is overly cautious.

The second squad has a two-man 60-caliber machine gun team led by a guy named Taylor. Taylor is a muscular black guy who looks like the heavyweight champion, Cassius Clay. His ammo man is a huge black guy called Haus, who is well over 200 pounds and probably could hump everyone's gear. The machine gun team is another invaluable asset to the platoon during combat, because they can put out more fire power than a whole squad of riflemen. The only drawback is that the enemy usually focuses their fire power on the machine gun team first, attempting to quickly disable the platoon. A machine gunner's life expectancy during combat is only a few minutes, so the bond with his buddy is very tight. Another black guy stands next to the machine gun team by the name of Jessie. He is a rifleman carrying Claymore mines on his rucksack which are used at night to defend a perimeter, and two bars of a high explosive called C-4, used to demolish bunkers or caves. There are three other riflemen in the squad by the names of Carter, Layman, and Nichols. Carter is toking on a cigar and blowing perfectly round smoke rings high into the air. Layman has sandy hair and a handle-bar mustache that he keeps stroking as if deep in thought. Nichols is skinny, frail, and seems overburdened by the weight and size of his gear. The squad leader is a small, good-looking Marine named Phillips. He has blond hair and blue eyes and is intently focused on the other squad members. There is also a medic assigned to this squad who everyone refers to as Doc. The medic is without question the most important member of the platoon—his job is to save lives. He is the only one in the platoon who is overweight. He is probably pampered and given more to eat by the others.

The third squad is led by a guy named Red who looks like the all-American boy. He's also the leader of the two-man mortar team and carries a mortar tube across his rucksack along with several mortars. The mortar team is always placed securely in the middle of the platoon for protection so they can quickly set up the mortars and return fire on enemy positions. Red's aide is the smallest guy in the platoon whom everyone calls Killer. He's the platoon tunnel-rat. Tunnel-rats are the smallest and usually the meanest guys in the platoon. They have the temperament to crawl inside caves searching for VC, a job that most grunts gladly pass up. Standing next to him is a skinny guy named Caldwell who humps the field radio. Caldwell's most notable features are his crooked yellow teeth and his capacity to spit tobacco ten feet in any direction. There is also an American Indian who is the point man of the platoon. Point men lead the platoon through the bush and are responsible for avoiding booby traps and ambushes. He never smiles and is called Injun.

Three other guys stand in front of the platoon, obviously in charge of things. The company captain is a nice-looking older guy who looks to be in his mid-20s. He has a large muscular upper body which tapers to a narrow waist where a 45 hangs at his side. He confidently stands at the front of the platoon, and everyone calls him Cap. There is no brass on his jungle fatigues, thus preventing the enemy from recognizing his rank. Standing next to him is the platoon sergeant, another towering figure, who goes by the name of Tanner. They seem to be unwinding from long days in the bush by telling jokes.

One lone figure stands away from the formation. He is stocky with piercing blue eyes and scars above his eyebrows that remind me of a prizefighter who had fought too many wars in the ring. He takes a deep breath, sucks in his gut, and shifts his weight from foot to foot while hiking up his fatigues. He is big and arrogant in all his moves. His demeanor indicates he has probably been in-country a long time and I wonder how much action he has already seen. "Hey, Dusty," someone calls out. "What's the word?"

Dusty shifts his eyes at the platoon with a look of annoyance and responds in a Cajun drawl, "What's it to y'all?" The group hisses. "You know this ain't R&R. Y'all is here to pick up those fuckin' new guys. Fuller, go check the billet out for our new FNGs." He makes a vague gesture toward our billet with his fist.

Fuller laughs, slinging his M-16 around his shoulder and walks into our billet. "You guys part of the FNGs assigned to our pod?" He gives us a quizzical glance.

Cars nods, saying, "Yeah, couldn't wait to get here."

"Good, 'cause the fun's just startin'." Fuller looks stern, "By the way, the last six-by outta regiment didn't make it here."

Cars interrupts, "Yeah, we heard all about it."

"Outstanding," Fuller blinks. "But you really should've seen it! You'll have your chance, 'cause things have been heatin' up real good in the past few months 'round here. Only got tomorrow, then we're back to the bush. Dusty wants you four new guys to join us tonight over at the club. Whadaya say?" Fuller asks with a wild glance.

"Yeah, we'll see ya over there tonight," I quip.

Fuller responds, "By the way, this is my billet and you and this other tough guy are in my squad. You other two new guys are in Red's squad." Fuller points at Matthews and Demarco who are sitting on a cot next to me. "Can't wait to get a shower," Fuller says as he rubs sweat from his face and rejoins the squad.

Cars is muttering obscenities while arranging gear under his cot. "Cars," Demarco says, "you got to start making a better first impression." Matthews and I laugh but inwardly it bothers me that Cars was so mouthy to Fuller, especially since we are in his squad. Any time you challenge authority in the Marines you risk payback, which can be fatal in the Nam. Since I already feel close to Cars, I decide to try and ride the fine line between remaining friends with him and still obeying authority within the platoon. I hope he will learn to keep his mouth shut and follow orders.

Later in the evening, we stroll over to the club to visit with the platoon. We arrive at the small club and find it packed with about 35 guys sitting on makeshift picnic tables, smoking cigarettes and drinking beer. Everyone is telling war stories and laughing about things that had happened in the bush. We sit down and grab some beer from a cooler that is on the table. Through the cigarette haze, I notice Dusty sitting at a table across from us. He smashes an empty beer can on his head and yells at a guy sitting at a table in the corner of the room. Then suddenly, everyone dives to the floor. Cars and I are still sitting at the table trying to figure out what is going on. I hear loud popping noises coming from the wooden walls of the club, sounding like firewood cracking in a wood-burning stove. My new fire-team leader, Roberto, jerks me down shouting, "That's Old Man Death cracking his knuckles, guy!" I realize it's bullets popping through the wooden walls of the club and whizzing by my head.

"Charlie's really hot tonight. He's gonna pay for messin' with my club time." It's Dusty's voice.

The club goes eerily silent. After about a minute, everyone gets up and resumes laughing and telling stories as if nothing happened. I overhear someone saying a VC sniper must have climbed a tree in the jungle, and knowing exactly where the club's located, took pot-shots at us. I am trembling as I slowly pull myself up to the table. Dusty is looking at me and smiling. I am flushed and sweaty and can tell he is reading the fear that glues my insides together. I guzzle my beer and signal Cars to get out of the club. We make a beeline for the door, along with Demarco and Matthews on our heels. I vow not to return to the club again, even if it means not having another beer until I get back to the States.

Later that night, sitting on my cot, I think about tomorrow evening's departure into the bush. The time is fast approaching when I will be confronted by my own worst fears. I wonder if I will be able to keep my nerve under fire. Our recent encounter at the club fuels doubts about my being able to handle the pressure. I lie down on the cot and close my eyes, listening to the sounds of four-deuce mortars shooting flares into the sky, cracks of rifle fire in the distance, and occasional explosions. I doze off but with each unnerving sound my eyes snap open. The next morning Cars and I stay in our billet resting and trying to catch up on the sleep we missed. I have a feeling sleep is a luxury in the Nam.

In late afternoon, we prepare for our night departure into the bush. I am concerned about how my M-16 rifle will perform, since it has a reputation for malfunctioning in combat. I recall boot camp stories of how scores of Marines were killed during Operation Hastings a few years earlier because their M-16s jammed during battle. Many of the Marines were found dead in their foxholes with M-16s disassembled; indicating attempts to clear the weapon. I am obsessed with not letting this happen to me. Eyes closed, I put the M-16 on my lap and release the operating lever from the chamber and take apart the rest of the rifle by the count of 20. I reassemble it in the same amount of time. Good! A jam at night can be cleared in under one minute. The only variable is how much fear can I take without falling apart under live fire.

The day turns into night and the hours slowly approach midnight. Third Platoon Marines straggle into the billets for our 0300 departure into the bush. Corporal Roberto, who is designated as my fire-team leader, walks into the billet, deep in thought. He sits on his cot and methodically adjusts his combat gear. Everything is strictly business and by the book with him. Roberto walks over to our side of the billet and in a low, even voice says, "You need to do exactly what I tell you." His face narrows as he concentrates on Cars and me. "This place ain't like the real world. This is the Nam and anything goes. You *must* follow directions or you'll be history."

Cars grumbles, "Where we headin' tonight?"

"Nowhere special. Just out to the bush where Charlie lives. We need to be careful, 'cause there's no moon tonight. We're tail end, so we'll watch the rear. Drew, you'll be last in line walking the tail end. When we get hit, it's either from the point or the ass-end. Charlie's not particular, he'll take it any way he can get it. All right, let's get geared up. By the way, our fire-team will be carrying extra gear tonight for the rocket launcher and machine gunner."

Cars interjects, "What the hell we gotta carry their shit for? Hell, we got all our own gear to hump!" He points to our gear that is assembled on the cots. I cringe, hoping he will just keep his mouth shut.

"Look, Cars, better change your attitude, 'cause this is gonna be the least of your worries. So, let's get a lick on and quit the belly-achin'." Roberto walks over to his cot and starts gearing up.

I grab my clutch belt and strap it around my waist. It is laden with two canteens of water, a bayonet, one first-aid pack, a jungle kit, and six magazines of 6.72mm bullets. "Cars," I whisper. "What do you make of me being put at tail end? They outta be puttin' someone with experience at tail. This has gotta be one of the worst positions in the platoon."

Cars finishes strapping his ammo belt on. "Looks to me like we're gonna be the sittin' ducks tonight. They don't care about fuckin' new guys. Did you hear what he said about no moon tonight?"

"Yeah, he also said to be careful." I push six boxes of C-rats into my rucksack, followed by a poncho, an air mattress called a rubber lady, and handfuls of 7.62mm rifle ammo. "I wonder if the VC are out there tonight?"

The door of the hooch swings open and a tall black guy by the name of Scott walks in carrying a crate of ammo. "Hey, guys, I'm in your fire-team with Roberto, so we'll be seeing a lot of each other. Here, got some goodies for us." Scott drops the load on the floor next to us. "Okay, we gotta hump some extra ammo, so let's get it loaded up. You new guys each get two blocks of C-4, a 3.5 rocket, two Claymores, and one 100-round assault pack for the machine gun. Also, grab some grenades and willie-peters and hitch 'em up on the straps of your clutch belt. Come on, we gotta get a move on to get out of here on time."

"Great! I get to hump all this extra shit just for bein' the Crotches' ultimate weapon," Cars growls.

Scott grins, unaffected by Cars' comment. I interrupt, "What's this about being careful tonight that Roberto was talking about? I mean, where we going and what's up?"

Scott hooks grenades onto his shoulder straps as he speaks. "Lots of shit's been comin' down lately. Charlie's been messin' around a lot the last couple of weeks. Stay close to Roberto and me tonight, 'cause it's gonna be real dark. Just keep your cool, man."

I lower my voice saying, "Yeah, well why am I being put at tail end?"

"Don't know, but it doesn't seem right. Just don't be mouthin' off about it. That'll just get gungy Dusty on your ass. I can tell ya, he ain't no one to be messin' with. Get your packs on and let's fall outside."

I feel I can trust Scott. He's helpful and speaks from his heart. I will stay close to him and feel my way into the platoon. I can't tell what is coming down tonight or why I am assigned to tail end for my first patrol. I have a bad feeling about the way things are developing and sense something is going to go wrong.

We take turns helping one another on with our packs, which weigh about 70 to 80 pounds. A dull ache radiates from my shoulders into my back. It occurs to me that 70 pounds of TNT will detonate if I get shot in the right spot or step on a booby trap. I wonder if anyone has blown up like that.

We go outside and I see Demarco and Matthews in formation with Second Squad. Demarco's big face is pale with fear. I line up next to Cars which puts me last in the platoon. Scott and Roberto are on the other side of Cars. Dusty is in front of the formation with Sergeant Tanner and the Captain. Tanner turns on a flashlight with an emerald-green ray. He speaks in a low voice, "Word has it that Charlie's active tonight. There's no moon, so hold on to the guy in front of you. Don't lose contact or you're on your own! Point, take charge. Tail end, keep alert." I cringe.

It's 0300 hours when we arrive at the main gate. We pause a few minutes and then walk onto a dirt road leading to the jungle. Tanner turns the flashlight off and everything goes black. I grab Cars' shoulder in a vise grip and hold on for dear life. I raise my free hand to within an inch of my face but can see nothing. For the first time in my life, I experience what true blindness must be like. I walk forward hearing frogs croak, tiny animals rustling through the bush, my heart pounding inside my chest, and the men in front of me breathing laboriously from the weight of their gear. I turn my head and listen intently for anything behind me. There's only men breathing ahead of me—I'm sure of it. We walk into the dark abyss for about an hour when I sense the road narrow and wonder if booby traps have been set for us. "Drew, you're pinching my arm," Cars whispers. I release the tension in my fingers. Why did they put me at tail end? I'm new and can't really handle this position. I'm nothing more than a guinea pig positioned to alert the platoon with a squeal.

Roberto calls in a low voice, "Drew, keep alert to our rear! I think I hear something toward our right flank. Did you hear me? Drew!"

I can't speak. My voice just won't work. Finally, I ask, "What?"

"Fuck! Just hold on and follow!" Roberto barks.

The enemy might be nearby. I continue following Cars but I am capable only of putting one foot in front of the other. The hot, moist air begins to smell of rotten foliage and buffalo dung. I sense tree branches dangling in the still air around us. The air space itself seems to be closing in on us. I surmise the jungle is off to our right.

Suddenly, an incredible burst of gunfire erupts at the point of the platoon. I instinctively clutch my gut and squat onto my haunches. Sparks from rifle fire at the front of the platoon ignite the jet black sky. A grenade explodes and a brilliant white light rips through the night. For an instant I see the 30-man column kneeling with weapons pointed everywhere. To our right I catch a glimpse of human figures hiding behind a rice paddy hedgerow with large tree limbs dangling over them. The white light instantly goes out, leaving me with the visual image of enemy soldiers squatting behind the hedgerow.

The gunfire stops, then erupts into fiendish howls from wounded men. "God help me! Please!" someone yells. I cringe, because Marines aren't supposed to beg or cry. I just want them to stop screaming. Please, anything but the screaming.

Only a few seconds elapse when merciless gunfire again erupts from the point of the platoon and quickly spreads to the rear. I drop onto my stomach and point my rifle out toward the hedgerow. I push my helmet back off my face and look forward. The weight of my rucksack pins me down to the ground making it difficult to breathe. For the first time in my life, bullets start pelting the ground around me. Pow! Pop, pop, pop! Crack, crack, crack! Dirt sprays into my face and onto my back. My body quivers and convulses with panic. I look up and sense at any moment I will take a direct hit to my face. I bury my nose into the dirt wishing to be an ant that could crawl into a hole and hide. Then, as quickly as it started, the gunfire stops.

Once again, the silence is broken by fiendish cries and moans of wounded men. It is a man-made hell on earth. Infantry training never taught me one of the horrors of war is that men moan and cry. Unexpectedly, from the right of our squad comes a faint deceptive voice calling out, "Corpsman . . . Corpsman!" It has a distinct Vietnamese drawl to it. I am confused.

Fuller yells, "Doc, don't go out there! That's Charlie out there!"

I realize we have enemy off to our right hiding in the hedgerow not more than 30 meters away. Now, two or three voices are bellowing:

"Corpsman . . . Corpsman . . . Help . . . Corpsman!" It is a frightful turn of events designed to lure our corpsman out for butcher. Everyone is fair game. "Watch out to the rear!" Roberto roars.

I spring to my knees, turn a half-circle, and point my rifle into the abyss. I hear movement directly to our rear. My body is trembling and my brain is as useful as a dead battery. The enemy was moving in! Instinctually, I point my M-16 in the direction of the sounds, switch the selector to full automatic, and squeeze off two short bursts of automatic fire. Roberto yells, "Fuck! You just gave our position away! Use grenades or a bayonet!"

I can't see an inch in front of my face but need to act fast. I drop my rifle and grab a grenade that is hooked to the strap of my rucksack. I pull the safety pin and realize the grenade is still attached to the rucksack. I stop breathing. An overwhelming feeling of stupidity hits me as I realize how my death will become a boot camp story on how some fuckin' new guy kills himself. I throw the pin down, unsnap the grenade from the rucksack strap and hurl it into the abyss. I dive to the ground, covering my head. "Ca-BOOM!" The explosion sends a shock wave over my back. "Who the fuck threw that grenade?" Roberto yells.

"I did."

"You better know where you're throwin' that,' goddammit!"

I've made two mistakes Roberto is aware of. The first was giving our position away by firing my M-16, and the second was not having a target when I tossed the grenade. How could I have forgotten such basic principles? At least he doesn't know I pulled the pin from the grenade while it was still strapped to my chest.

All hell breaks loose as the VC to our right open up on our position at the rear of the platoon. Bullets hit all around me. I squeeze the trigger of my M-16 and hear "click, click, click." I had forgotten to insert a new magazine after expending my ammo on the last short burst. Third mistake: always keep your rifle loaded. I fumble, pulling a magazine from my clutch belt, push the release lever of my M-16, discard the old magazine and replace it with a new one. I squeeze the trigger with a short burst of automatic fire. Fourth mistake: in my confusion, I forgot to switch the selector back to semi-automatic. Frustrated, I switch the selector back and squeeze off a round. Then, all the firing trails off.

Out in the hedgerow to my right, I hear the swish of an enemy body being pulled along the ground. The Marines at the point of the platoon are scurrying around trying to help the wounded. The moans and cries continue. Please, just make the crying stop, I pray.

"Drew," Cars whispers, "sounds like the VC's haulin' ass."

"Yeah, I hope so. This is a nightmare." The anticipation of combat is over and it is more horrible than I could have ever imagined. I lie on my belly with my heart beating like a sledgehammer, trembling from head to toe. The whole firefight lasted about two or three minutes but it seemed like a lifetime. I am now bonded to Mother Earth like an animal under attack who is granted life one millisecond at a time, depending on where the next hiding place or hole is located.

Roberto snaps, "All right, we're gonna slowly crawl forward toward the point. Keep low 'cause there's no tellin' if Charlie's still out there. Drew, keep an eye to the rear. Let's go!"

I crawl forward on my elbows, keeping close to Cars. There is no forethought in my action. Boot camp training makes more sense to me now. "Tench-hut! Forward march! Right face!" Yeah, all that bullshit training made a real monkey out of me. Now, I know why.

I look to my rear as we inch forward and don't sense danger behind us any longer. The enemy has vanished. I see the emerald-green ray of Tanner's flashlight on the path ahead of us. The platoon tunnel rat, Killer, is kneeling next to Cap with the field radio on his back. Cap has the handset up to his ear talking to headquarters. Muffled radio talk is barely audible. "Charlie-four, this is Mike-three, over."

"Mike-three, this is One-three, we read you."

"Yeah, One-three, we need a dust-off. We got four down and a cool LZ. My coordinates are 277026, over."

"Roger, Mike-three, we're on our way." The metallic crackle of the radio fades into the steamy jungle.

We crawl past Killer and Cap to the front of the platoon where the wounded are lying on the ground. Several Marines cradle them in their arms while Doc works feverishly to bandage their wounds. Some of the wounded have their shirts off and blood covers their upper bodies. One guy has his pants off with wounds on his legs and ass. He shrieks in agony. I look at his face and realize it is Matthews. My God, it's really him! I remember that Demarco and Matthews were positioned close to the point where the intense action had taken place. I want to run over and console him but can't make myself do it. The blood, the cries, the moans, all keep me at a safe distance. Then, I realize that Demarco is lying next to him. He's on his side with bullet wounds in his shoulder and chest. His huge body isn't moving. His face is pale and his eyes are closed. Demarco's too big and strong to die. I hear the corpsman say, "This FNG's history, Cap.

Killed on his first fuckin' mission." I recall how he wanted his father to parade him through the neighborhood as a war hero but instead, a military funeral will pass through the streets of his hometown.

There is nothing more to do but move forward. We crawl on our elbows until we reach an area where a small rice paddy dike intersects the road. We stop for a few moments and word comes down for us to fan out into the jungle and set up a defensive perimeter. Light is peeking through the trees as we encircle the landing zone and set up positions. I drop my rucksack to the ground and lay my head back on it to rest my sore shoulders.

"Not so fast, guys," Roberto interjects, "get those E-tools out and dig two foxholes. Don't want to get caught out here in the open, do you? Charlie usually shows up when you least expect him."

Scott and I jump up and start digging a foxhole. Cars and Roberto move to the right about ten yards and dig in. Scott is tearing the ground with his E-tool as he speaks. "Roberto has a reputation of being really careful. He always makes us dig-in whenever we stop for more than a few minutes. He believes that the more careful you are, the more likely you will live through this hell hole. I don't personally believe that shit. I think if your number is up, you're fuckin' history. Just like those guys over there. Hell, it could have just as easily been us, if we had drawn point. I say, fuck it!"

We finish digging our foxholes and I hear the approaching medevac as it begins its descent to our position. The blades of the chopper clap loudly as it lands on the road to our rear. It touches down only long enough to pick up the wounded and dead, then takes off in a windstorm over the trees. Unexpectedly, Dusty walks to our foxhole and peers down at us with his hands on his hips.

"I hope you new guys enjoyed your first night patrol," he says. "We aim to please at One-three." He laughs, enjoying his position of dominance. "Y'all know we ran into Second Platoon? They were comin' in from three weeks in the fuckin' field. Can you believe that? Their point man ran flat-ass into our point man. What was his name? Oh yeah, Demarco. Yeah, that wap Demarco didn't know his ass from a hole in the ground, so he blowed the fuck out of Mr. Dip-shit, the point man from Second Platoon. You're lucky we picked you for tail end instead of point. It'd been your ass wasted instead of that wap, Demarco. How'd y'all like Mr. Charlie out there on the dike messin' round with our heads? Yeah, he really knows how to screw with ya. I know some gook ville that's gonna get some payback for this shit. Oh yeah, we're gonna get some good payback real soon. Whadaya say, Scott?" Dusty smirks, tight and mean.

Scott picks up his rucksack and fumbles around like he is looking for something, trying to avoid eye contact with Dusty. "Yeah, I could use some payback," he says, in an unconvincing tone.

"Sure you could, Scott. We all could, couldn't we? What's your name, boy?" Dusty forces a grin while glaring at me with half-crazed eyes. "Drew, my name is Drew. Sure we could," I say, not knowing exactly what he meant.

"Well, we'll see about that, Drew?" Dusty looks toward the jungle and shrugs. "Hell, boy, you keep bringin' us luck like this, and you ain't gonna get outta here alive. Y'all keep your heads down, ya hear!" Dusty walks off toward another foxhole, glancing back at us.

Scott shakes his head and lights a cigarette. He takes a deep breath and blows a straight line of smoke into the air. "You know, that Dusty's crazy as a bedbug. I mean, gone plain fuckin' dinky dau. He's been in country about eight months and been wounded twice. One more wound and he gets a free ride home. Problem is, he says he likes it here and doesn't want to leave. Last time he got hit, it messed his head up. Don't ever cross him, Drew, 'cause he'll blow ya away. I mean, plain and simple, this cookie likes to kill, and he doesn't care who it is! Just be careful around him."

I reach into my rucksack and pull out a box of C-rats while thinking about Scott's warning. All I'll do is stay out of Dusty's way and things should be okay. Anyway, now is a good time to celebrate being alive with a present from Uncle Sam. I ease my fingers down into the small box of C-rats and pull out a candy bar and a four-pack of Lucky Strikes. Where else can you get free cigarettes but in the Nam? There's also pound cake, applesauce, and small napkins I can use as toilet paper. I reach deeper and pull out a can marked "ham and limas." There are no good food bennies in this batch of C-rats. Using the P-38 can opener that hangs from my dog tag chain, I carefully open the metal container.

As I sit in my foxhole eating C-rats, I think about the real reason I have to wear dog tags is to identify the dead. I really don't like the dog tags, but I can't make them go away any more than I can make what just happened go away. Demarco is dead, Matthews is maimed, and there is something very different about me. I don't quite know what it is, but nothing is how I thought it would be. The moans, the cries, the yells all continue to echo within my mind. It seems everything I had learned in boot camp isn't worth spit. Then, there's Dusty: The platoon has a sergeant and captain in charge, but when the shit hits the fan, it appears everything is run by a two-striped lunatic corporal. Thirteen months is beginning to seem like a very long time.

I look up through the trees and see a beautiful bright blue sky where a 747 jet is heading back to the States. I think about my mom and how she couldn't bring herself to go to the airport when I left for Vietnam. Now, I really miss her. I reach into my rucksack and pull out a pencil and paper. I consider the reality of my situation, but can't bring myself to tell her the truth. "Dear Mom and Dad," I write. "Well, I finally arrived at my new duty station. The guys here are really great, and it's nothing like I thought it would be. Sometimes boot camp can't teach you everything. Mom, I'll have a surprise for you when I come home. I hope you like it."

I think hard about Gunnery Sergeant McKay's warning before leaving the States. I promise if I survive Vietnam, I will get a tattoo that reads "Love, Mom."

CHAPTER II

The Face of Death

Late September 1967

It's been three weeks since the night ambush when Demarco was killed and Matthews and three other Marines were wounded. Roberto tells me to put that night and those guys out of my head, because thinking too much about lost friends will only weaken my fighting spirit. Survival hinges on staying focused on the task of killing Charlie before he has a chance to kill me. Each day brings new challenges of learning squad positions, operating procedures, and getting to know the platoon members. Over the past few weeks, we have engaged in several firefights but our platoon hasn't taken any new causalities.

Today, like many other days, begins by waking up in a two-man foxhole at the break of dawn. Cars had the 0200 to 0600 watch and is in a grumpy mood. I cut the lid off my C-rat can and sprinkle steak seasoning my mom had sent to me over Beans and Dicks. I envision eating a New York strip steak. Cars tears a clump off a block of C-4 about the size of a small marble, drops it into an empty can and lights it so we can heat coffee. I smell the fresh aroma and wonder if Charlie is getting a fix on our position. We spend about a half hour chowing down and cleaning our weapons before heading into the bush. Cars is bitching the whole time about how Tanner could have ordered combined teams of four-man foxholes instead of two, allowing us more sleep. The word is passed down that we are going to hump toward a ville where Charlie has been known to hang out. It amazes me how the gooks live a dual existence by allowing Charlie to enter their villes at night and Marines during the day.

Our squad is walking tail end as we approach the small ville of about 15 hooches located on the edge of a cliff. Nichols, our point man, is inching along a rice paddy dike about 50 meters from the ville. He comes to a halt, causing the duce-point and the guy behind him to bunch up. Suddenly, a sharp "rumph" rips through the humid air. A dust cloud forms at the point of the platoon and someone shouts, "Medic! Medic up!" Cars and I are at the rear of the platoon and drop into the rice paddy. We lean against the dike to use it as cover. Fuller passes back the word that Carter, Nichols, and Layman hit Mr. Frankenstein, a trip wire connected to a grenade stuck inside a spool of barbed wire. He says Nichols took most of the blast and might lose a leg, but Carter and Layman had minor wounds, enough to give them a ticket to the hospital in Japan and some R&R. He tells us to guard the rear so a medevac can pick up the wounded.

I nervously scan the trees behind us, knowing Charlie likes to attack while we tend our wounded. After about ten minutes, I hear the thunder of a chopper descending on our LZ. It flies over the trees, hovers, and touches down in a vaporous windstorm. Doc and a few other Marines from point squad carry the wounded men onboard the medevac. The chopper quickly lifts and shoots forward over the treetops. As the sound trails off, I realize I didn't know the wounded guys very well. I hadn't shared a foxhole or even talked much to any of them, but still I feel a sense of loss. It's sobering to become aware that survival in a platoon is like being an animal in the middle of a herd depending on safety in numbers and dumb luck. As the herd dwindles, the chances of getting killed increases.

I sit in the foul sewage of the rice paddy, batting bugs off my face and wonder how Nichols missed seeing the trip wire. He was a good point man with more than eight months' experience in the bush. Obviously, no place is safe to walk. Could the villagers have known where the booby trap was located? This is one of the few dry dikes leading into the ville that is regularly used by them. I notice some gook farmers, who had been laboring in the rice paddy before the explosion, walking quickly toward the ville. They walk past our perimeter area and Sergeant Tanner and Dusty grab three women from the group and begin badgering them with questions. Tanner tells two Marines to tie the women's hands behind their backs. He gives the rest of us orders to follow in a staggered column to the other side of the Ville. I can't figure out what's going on but reluctantly follow keeping one eye on our rear and the other on the point where Tanner and Dusty are using their M-16's to smack the backsides of the women to move forward on the booby trapped path. Once we reach the other side of the Ville, Dusty starts pushing the women with his rifle toward the edge of a cliff while Tanner follows close behind. The women yell, "No! Numbah-ten, Murines! Bad! Numbah-ten, Murines!" The women begin crying and their long black hair falls forward covering their faces. They keep calling out, "Numbah-ten, Murines." Two of the women are probably in their 60s, and the third looks to be in her 20s. Tanner hollers, "Bitches!" and smacks the women in the back of their heads. Then, he makes them kneel at the edge of the cliff, facing over the abyss. Everything appears to go into slow motion. With their hands tied, he places his big jungle boot in the center of each woman's back and kicks them off the cliff. I can't see them falling, but I'm able to hear grunts and moans as they tumble down the hillside. They are either badly injured or killed.

I'm in a state of shock and disbelief. Cars looks at me and says, "We can't let those sons-a-bitches get away with this." We throw our weapons down and walk over to Tanner.

"What the hell is going on?" I say, clenching my fist. "Why did you do that?"

"They didn't do anything to deserve that!" Cars growls.

Tanner's eyes are red. He places one hand on his 45 and points his other at us saying, "You new guys better keep your mouths shut or you won't get outta here alive!" There is a long pause as he glares at us. I suddenly feel as though I'm the enemy.

Dusty walks toward us with hunched shoulders. He stops inches from my face and yells, "This ain't the fuckin' real world, asshole! Y'all better get your shit together before it's too fuckin' late. Now y'all know what payback is." Dusty stares at me with icy blue eyes. He turns, lights a cigarette, and walks away with Tanner.

I'm in shock and very confused. This unconscionable attack against defenseless women can't be justified under any circumstances. I keep repeating to myself, Why? Cars and I walk silently back to our position along the dike. I am still stunned about what had happened when Killer, Calahan, and a fire-team leader from third squad named Corporal Stafford approach us. I'm thinking, now what? Stafford does the talking. "You guys better learn to keep your mouths shut or something bad might happen to you. What I mean is, when there is one of those crazy firefights, anything could happen. Some stray bullets may end up coming your way. Cars, you bitch too much! You better start listenin' up and get with the program. You guys could start pullin' a lot of LPs and walkin' point if you're not careful. I hope we've given the two of you something to think about. Welcome to the Nam, new guys." The three of them turn and walk away.

The message is clear Submit or be destroyed. I am trying to figure out a way to deal with these new threats when the order comes down to search-and-destroy the ville. "Zippo time," hollers the machine gunner Taylor.

"Let's get some!" the tunnel-rat, Killer, responds.

Cap, Dusty, and Tanner are smiling like they are about to attend a party. Everything is happening so quickly, I go along feeling it would be wanton suicide to do otherwise. Cars and I get on line with the rest of the platoon and head into the ville. Everyone pulls Zippo lighters out of their jungle fatigue pockets in preparation to set fires. The villagers begin yelling to one another and running out of the other end of the ville as we close in. Cars and I follow Scott and Fuller toward two of the hooches on the fringe of the ville. "Go in and check the hooch out for hidden caves," Fuller yells to Cars and me. "This whole ville's run by Charlie. There ain't gonna be a hooch left when we get done. Let's go!"

Fuller and Scott go in one hooch while Cars and I carefully walk into another. The dirt floor of the hooch is covered with bugs and smells like a barn. A couple of chickens in the far corner of the hooch flap their wings and fly out the door nearly scaring us to death. Once my heart settles down, I continue surveying the hooch. Near the opposite side, there are two straw mats on the ground that serve as beds for the gooks. Against the wall, behind the mats, is a stone altar with a statue of the Buddha surrounded by white candles. There is a fireplace to the right with a small table in front of it. Trinkets and cheap religious ornaments adorn the interior. Flies and bugs are crawling on everything, and I wonder how anyone can call this home. Suddenly there is a commotion coming from nearby hooches as the Marines around us begin destroying everything. Cars joins in by overturning a table and bench. I grab the straw mats and throw them in the fireplace. We both grab the trinkets and pictures, toss them to the ground, and stomp on them. This is my first act of vandalism and a sense of power sweeps over me and I feel it's all justified. Cars grabs the Buddha and hurls it against the stone front of the fireplace, shattering it. "No caves in here!" he shouts. "Let's get outta here and finish the job."

"Yeah, this is one bug-infested house," I say. We walk outside and see fire and smoke engulfing all the hooches. A group of about 40 gooks stand in a line about 200 meters away at the edge of the jungle watching the carnage. Many of them hold their hands up to the sky in prayer while their homes crumble.

"That'll teach 'em to string booby traps out for us!" Fuller hollers. Dusty is standing next to him smiling.

Cars and I flick our Zippos and ignite the straw walls of the hooch. I feel like we have a license to do whatever we want. Within seconds the fire rushes up the sides of the hooch and engulf the structure. Once the hooch crumbles, we go through the rest of the ville searching out hidden food sources and enemy caves. We throw smoke grenades into large clay vats of harvested rice that were hidden underground. Years of Vietnamese toil go up in smoke. Dusty tosses an Instamatic camera to me saying, "Hey, new guy, take some pictures." Thirty minutes earlier I had been sickened by the carnage. Now, I'm recording our mission as a trophy. Dusty fires warning shots over the heads of the gooks, and I take pictures of them scattering into the trees. Then, Dusty tells us to gather our gear and abandon the ville. No one seems to care much about giving the ville back to the VC, since the only thing that really matters is getting payback for the guys who had been injured. In the aftermath of our shallow victory, we slowly march off toward distant rice paddies in search of the ever-elusive Charlie. Today, I feel more a part of the platoon.

We hump through the boonies the rest of the day without further incident. Toward evening, word is passed back that we are going to set in on the fringe of the jungle near a suspected North Vietnamese army hideout. The NVAs are well-trained and well-equipped troops, sent down from North Vietnam to help the local VC guerrillas. Our plan is to attack the NVAs in the early morning in hopes of catching them off-guard. I am teamed with Scott, Cars, and our fire-team leader, Corporal Roberto. We start digging foxholes and, as usual, Roberto expresses caution. "Let's dig these holes deeper in case Charlie wants to give us a surprise visit tonight in return for that ville we wasted earlier. After that, break down your rifles and clean 'em up. Don't want to get caught with a jammed rifle during a firefight."

Roberto is so cautious he gets on my nerves. He relies on hypervigilance to stay alive in the jungle and is driven to extremes in everything he does. Whenever we set in for more than a few minutes, he makes us dig foxholes. He never lets his guard down, always surveying the terrain for a possible enemy ambush. He distrusts civilians and holds his rifle ready to fire when he is around them. Roberto's quiet time is usually spent writing letters or holding a picture of Saint Francis in prayer. He is from a border town in Texas and speaks little about his Mexican-American family and friends. He is recognized by the platoon as the model grunt because of his self-discipline.

I sit crouched with Roberto at the front of the foxhole scanning the perimeter. "Roberto, can you believe this sunset?"

Roberto looks at the orange sky for a long while before he replies. "Mexico had sunsets like this," he says softly. Roberto seems to be drifting into a melancholy mood which is uncharacteristic of him. "My padre would sit on the front porch and talk to us about goin' back to Mexico. My sister and I listened to Padre talk about what life had been like in old Mexico." Roberto pulls a picture of his family from his wallet and hands it to me. "This picture was taken in Texas," he says with pride. It was a black-and-white picture of Roberto and his sister standing next to his parents. His dad has a big belly, a curled mustache, and is wearing a sombrero. His mother has beautiful long black hair and is wearing a colorful long dress that touches the ground. They are standing in front of a gas station with highway signs around them. "This is where my padre worked after moving here from Mexico."

"Why did you leave Mexico?" I ask.

"We never had much money when I was a kid in Mexico, but we had a farm near the mountains. There was a town nearby where everyone gathered at night after dinner. All the men walked in one direction around the town square while the girls walked the other way. That's how my padre met Mama. Some day I would like to go back to Mexico and build a house up in the mountains."

"How did you end up in the Nam, Roberto?" I ask.

"It was hard to get a decent job after I graduated from high school. I didn't have the money to go to college and get a deferment. What choice did I have but to fight? Why did you come here, Drew?"

"I fight so that my kids won't have to grow up under communism," I say, remembering what I had learned in boot camp about the war. "It's not just because of the gooks that we're here. The Communists are taking over everywhere, and before we know it, they'll be on our shores, too." A sense of self-respect sweeps over me.

Roberto didn't respond. I look up at a sun-scorched sky and feel momentarily removed from the war. "I never thought this country had any beauty to it, but this is absolutely incredible," I say. I see clearly for miles as the sun casts an orange glow over the rice paddies and trees. Enormous elephant grass lines the rice paddies while water buffalo roam the fields giving the landscape a prehistoric appearance. In the distance, Vietnamese peasants wearing large coolie hats till the rice fields. There are plumes of smoke from the many hooches where mama-san is cooking rice and fish for supper. "Do you miss your family?" I ask.

"My padre wants me to return with medals," Roberto mutters.

"You got a girlfriend, Roberto?"

"You ask too many questions, Drew," he snaps. "Thinking about home will get us into trouble out here." Roberto's tone tells me he is back to business as usual.

I look across the horizon and see black, ominous thunderheads moving quickly toward us. Within minutes, an unseasonably cool breeze blows in with the approaching front and darkness envelops our position. A crouching figure makes his way toward us from the CP at the center of the perimeter. "Hey, guys, it's me, Fuller. There's a big storm headin' toward us. Cap says it's a typhoon comin' in from the sea with winds more than a hundred miles an hour. This might be a rough night, huh?"

"Think those NVAs will be out patrollin' tonight?" Roberto asks.

"No way. They'll be buttoned down like us," Fuller says, with certainty. "You guys make sure your foxholes are deep enough to protect you from falling trees." Fuller glances up at the trees and moves on to another foxhole to pass on the word.

Roberto starts giving orders as a brilliant flash of lightning illuminates the surrounding jungle, followed by a roll of thunder. "Scott, you and Cars dig a foxhole next to us and make it deep in case the trees start fallin' around us. Okay, let's get movin'."

"Roberto, can we have a quick smoke?" I ask. It's always dangerous and against the rules to smoke at night, because light can give our position away to the enemy. However, most of us develop good techniques to smoke cigarettes without being seen.

"Go ahead," he says reluctantly. "Smoke one, but I better not see a speck of light."

I reach deep into my rucksack and grab my poncho. I pull the poncho out and slip it over my head, making it into a small tent, and squat into the foxhole. Raindrops begin tapping my poncho like mice running on cardboard. I make sure there are no openings for light to escape and carefully cup a match in my hands and light a Lucky Strike. I inhale deeply and sit up pulling the hood down over my head, keeping the cigarette concealed around my midsection under the poncho. "Good," Roberto said. "I didn't see a thing." Roberto scoots down into the foxhole and follows the same procedure to energize the luminous dial on his watch with a flashlight.

"What time is it?" I ask.

"It's 2300 hours," Roberto responds. "This storm is really heatin' up and it will be a full-blown typhoon in a few. I was in a hurricane that blew across the gulf and hit the coast of Texas a few years ago. Trees were uprooted and frame houses crushed like matchboxes. Most of the people that were killed were either struck by flying debris or thrown through the air and found miles away from their homes. Do you think our foxhole is deep enough?"

I look up at the trees that are already bending and swaying in the howling wind. Fear of dying begins to build in me. It reminds me of a close call I had with death a few nights ago. "Don't know, Roberto, but it can't be any worse than what happened the other night."

"Yeah, you were out there with Fuller that night, huh?" Roberto's eyes are focused on the swaying treetops.

"I still don't know if the explosion that got that amtrac driver was command-detonated? What do you think?" I ask.

"I think Charlie knew you guys were out there on the listening post the whole time. That's the thing about Mr. Charles, he's so cool, he'll just wait for the right moment. How did you see it last night?" Roberto asks.

"Well, I didn't like the looks of things to begin with. You know, being out on an LP on top of that hill in plain sight of God and everybody. Charles would have been blind to have missed us. Fuller and I crawled out after dark and lay flat on the ground 'cause there was no cover. I'm new, and I've never been on a listening post without some kind of cover. We were calling in radio checks every half hour, waitin' and listenin' for something to happen. I had the feeling that Charles was close by."

Roberto interrupts, "Cap had called in amtracs to re-supply us. Charles must have heard them coming, too," he smiles.

"Mr. Charlie waited till that first amtrac was almost up the hill when he detonated the mine," I say.

"So you think it was command-detonated, huh?" Roberto questions.

"What did you say?" I ask. "This rain's gettin' noisy as piss. What did you say?"

"Was it command-detonated, I said?" Roberto repeats.

I raise my voice. "Yep, it had to have been. The guys in the second amtrac said they saw Charlie running from the scene just about where Fuller and I were lying. I didn't hear or see a thing until the explosion.

That first amtrac came up the road and got about 30 yards from us when it hit the mine. There was a huge flash of light and I could see the driver shoot out the top of the amtrac like a rocket. He must have flown 30 feet into the air before falling to the ground. Scared the hell out of Fuller and me. We figured out that Charlie could have taken us out at any time, but was waitin' for bigger game. That seems to be the thing about command detonations—Charlie's totally in control of the situation. He'll blow up whatever he wants, whenever he wants. I wonder if the driver of that amtrac survived the explosion?"

"Probably not. Those NVAs have got some more payback comin' tomorrow for sure. That's if we make it through this typhoon tonight. I've never seen it rain this hard since bein' in Nam." Roberto is concerned and puzzled.

It's about midnight when mountains of rain pour down on us without mercy. I am lying forward, peering over the edge of our foxhole as the water level quickly rises to my chest. "Start bailing the water out with your helmet!" Roberto hollers. I furiously begin bailing water out of the foxhole only to have it fill up again.

"Roberto, we aren't gonna' be able to keep the water out!" I yell.

"I am not leaving this foxhole!" Roberto protests. "This wind's more dangerous than Charlie. We're dead meat out there in the open. We'll have to just stay here until the storm passes." Roberto eases down neck deep into our water-filled foxhole. Cars and Scott are sticking their heads out of the foxhole next to us looking like drowning rats. Within minutes, the full brunt of the storm hits. The wind blasts through the jungle screeching like a demon, forcing huge trees to bend in half. The omnipresent rain is falling in horizontal, then slanting gray lines, and when lightening flashes, millions of raindrops turn to bright silver; and at other times, blankets of rain turn into hail blowing across the perimeter like a snow storm in January. Lightning flashes electrify the air causing the atmosphere to flicker and glow an ominous orange between bursts. Explosions of lightening hitting trees make my heart pound with each deafening thunderbolt, and I scoot farther into my water-filled foxhole. I decide not to get out of my hole for fear of being blown into the air. I understand why primitive people create their gods around the forces of nature.

"Boom!" Sparks explode from a nearby tree as it breaks in half and falls to the ground with a deafening thud. "Boom!" With the next flash of light comes the sight of what looks like a human figure hunching beside a tree. I can't believe what I am seeing. Could the figure actually be a man moving about in the middle of the typhoon? Who could it be? Are my eyes playing tricks on me? The last lightening strike didn't sound like the other ones. It had a solid thud sound like a grenade or a mine.

I look to my left and see Scott and Cars still snug in their foxholes not more than 10 yards away. Roberto is at arm's length, peering up at the treetops. I wonder if I should alert them to what I am seeing? I scan the perimeter for some evidence to support my vision. It is hard to make out anything for certain. The wind is blowing everything at right angles and nothing seems natural. Flying rubble clutters the perimeter. The lightning illuminates everything followed by seconds of infernal darkness where my imagination tries to re-create the scene. I suddenly realize this is a perfect time for Charlie to overrun our positions. Could we actually be under attack and not even know it? There is another flash of light followed by "boom!"

"Roberto! Roberto!" I grab Roberto by the shoulder, shaking him as I bellow. "Did you see that last flash? Did you see him in it? Somebody's out there!"

Roberto becomes alert like an animal being preyed upon. He sticks his head out above the foxhole, glancing in all directions. Rain pelts his face as he studies the situation. "Can't see much and with all this rain, I can't tell what's going on?" he yells as he eases back into the foxhole. "Where did you see him?"

I point to the large tree where I had seen the human-like figure. The tree is nearly bent in half by the force of the wind and the gigantic branches are parallel to the ground. "There! There's where I saw him, along the side of the tree."

"I think I see him!" Roberto's eyes widen.

"What should we do?" I plead.

Roberto thinks out loud. "Can't throw grenades 'cause they'll end up almost anywhere. We didn't place Claymores around the perimeter 'cause of the storm. Can't use rockets, mortars, or our grenade launcher. I'm beginning to think Charles is one up on us tonight."

I continue surveying the area around the tree where I had seen the figure. "Think we should go to the CP and tell Cap?"

"No, not until we're sure Charles is up to something. I mean he might be as scared of this storm as we are and he's stayin' put. One of us should crawl out and see what's goin' on."

I feel my heart sink. I quickly respond, "We need to make sure Charles is really there before we do anything. I ain't for goin' out there unless we have to. I'll crawl over to Scott and Cars' hole and tell them what's up." I didn't wait for Roberto's answer. I slither over to their foxhole as the wind howls around me. "Cars! Scott! There's something moving around out by that big tree." Their eyes widen. I point to the tree, saying, "Look! See, there!"

"Yeah," Scott says, "I think I see something moving beside that tree. Can you see it, Cars?"

"Maybe, but I'm not sure. If somebody spots Charlie, open up with tracer rounds, then the rest of us can open up on where the tracer rounds hit. I say we sit tight until the storm passes."

I feel relief and say, "It beats crawling out there to that tree to check it out. That's what Roberto wants me to do."

"Yeah, that's Gungy! We're not taking the risk. Tell 'em we're sittin' tight," Scott says.

"Sounds good to me." I crawl back and tell Roberto our plan.

"Okay," Roberto says. "This storm seems to be lettin' up anyway. Charles is in a world of shit if he stays out there when this storm passes, 'cause we'll blow him the fuck away." Roberto says, with a smirk.

Over the next hour, the threatening wind transforms to a low howl. The treetops sway in light rain and the raging thunder is in the distance. We begin bailing the neck deep water out of our foxholes. I keep a close eye on the tree where I had seen the dark figure, but am still unable to identify anything for certain. The mosquitoes hover around us, a sure sign that the rain is coming to an end. "Roberto, think it's time for some sweet-stink?"

"Yeah, get the repellent out before there ain't nothing left of us. What time you got?"

I pull a Timex out of my pocket, cupping the luminous dial in the palms of my hands under my poncho. "Looks like 0430. We got about an hour 'til daylight. Hey, Fuller's coming over from the CP."

Fuller's eyes are red and swollen as he kneels beside our muddy foxhole. I wonder if I look as bad as him. "We're gonna be moving out down the path by the big tree. Cap says it will run us smack into the ville where those NVAs are supposed to be hiding out. You guys are tail end. Phillips will be walkin' point with his guys."

Roberto interrupts, "I think we saw some movement out by that big tree during the storm. Charlie could have an ambush set up somewhere down that path. I say we take a different route into the ville."

"No way, Roberto. Charlie thinks we'll be stayin' put for a while 'cause of the storm. Cap thinks we can catch 'em by surprise by using that path.

Get your gear ready, 'cause we're movin' out in a few." Fuller moves on to the other foxholes.

I slowly gather my sopping gear and check the operating lever of my M-16. Covered with mud, Cars and Scott crawl to our position. "Sounds like Cap and Dusty want to play John Wayne this morning. I haven't slept a wink," Cars snarls. "If they have their way, we won't ever get back to the real world."

Roberto responds, "Sorry 'bout that, Cars, but you ought to at least try actin' like a trained killer 'cause it ain't gonna' get any better."

"Cars," Scott joins in, "you outta' get with the program so we can re-up after we get back to the world."

"All right, cut the chatter," Dusty demands, as he approaches our foxhole holding a 45. He kneels, resting his arm on one leg and nonchalantly waves the 45 in my face. "Here's the scoop," he says, with a mean grin. "I'm walkin' point with Phillips and his squad. You guys will be tail end." He keeps pointing the 45 at me. "Chances are, we're gonna get some up ahead on this trail. When the caps start bustin', y'all hustle forward 'cause we're gonna assault 'em. Those NVAs won't know what hit 'em." He laughs and finally shoves the 45 into his holster. Dusty stands and joins Phillips, who is walking toward the big tree that leads to the trail of the enemy ville. I watch intently as they pass the tree but nothing happens. I wonder if my imagination had been playing tricks on me.

It's a dead-silent morning, charged only with heat and humidity. I feel dogged when I stand up shouldering the weight of my gear while little gadgets of death dangle and clank as I climb out of my foxhole. Tense psychic energy is everywhere, like what I remember feeling as a kid when I got really scared at night. I put one foot in front of the other, trailing about three feet behind Roberto's silhouette. We walk very slowly for 15 minutes covering about one-quarter mile. The tree limbs are more visible, indicating daylight isn't far off. We stop and I drop to one knee to take a quick break. I lean forward resting on my rifle and think about what might be happening at home. It's just turning night and Mom and Dad are probably watching "Ed Sullivan" with my sister and three brothers. A friend might call and ask my parents if they had heard from me. My girlfriend, Gayle, might stop by to tell Mom she misses me. All I want to do is hold her in my arms.

My fantasy abruptly ends when Roberto turns to me and whispers, "Be careful! I think the point man has seen something up ahead in the bush." It's very quiet and dark, a good time for Old Man Death to make an appearance. I listen intently for something to clue me in on what is going on at point. The seconds tick away like hours. Finally, Roberto stands and briskly moves forward. I quickly pursue his silhouette. We lock into a fast pace and I keep my eyes fixed on the green utility towel wrapped around his neck. Roberto stops again. I follow suit and wipe sweat from my brow. There is a ten-second lull followed by a quick forward burst and another halt. We continue moving forward, stalking the enemy. I sense we are close to having contact with Charlie. The surrounding jungle foliage begins to clear, indicating the entry to the ville. Pow! Pow! Rat-tat-tat! Boom!

"Forward!" Roberto shouts. I reluctantly run forward. The sharp, piercing gunshots rip through the jungle, cracking tree limbs a few feet above my head. I slow my pace hoping the shots will stop by the time I reach point. Bursts of gunfire ricochet off trees and whistle through the air. Roberto points to the left toward another path and yells, "There's Charles!" I look down the narrow path and catch a glimpse of an NVA soldier jumping over a five-foot hedge. "Let's fuckin' get him!" Roberto yells. I feel a heightened sense of awareness as I consider actually killing someone. We take off down the path while hearing sporadic gunshots in other areas. The NVAs must have divided up and taken off in different directions to throw us off. The platoon has split up and is chasing after them. We reach the area where the NVA soldier had jumped over the hedgerow. I part the bushes and can see him making a beeline toward the jungle. I raise my rifle to fire but, at that instant, he darts into the trees. Roberto and I quickly maneuver through the hedgerow and run to the edge of the trees where Charlie escaped. A surge of energy radiates through me and I feel the raw power only a battle chase can produce. "Where did he go?" I ask, feeling confused.

"I don't know! Let's spray the area with fire." Cars, Scott, Roberto, and I quickly get on line and cut loose with four M-16s on full automatic. For about five seconds a roar of bullets hammer the trees where Charlie had disappeared. We freeze, wide-eyed, looking into the jungle which is now shimmering and smoking with falling debris. "Did you see fuckin' Charles jump over the hedgerow? That thing's 5-feet high!" Roberto says, in amazement.

"Where do you think he is?" I ask.

"He's probably all the way back to Ho Chi Minh City by now," Scott says, laughing.

"Do you want to go into the jungle and chase him?" I say, feeling my adrenaline begin to rise again.

Roberto is peering into the tree line when he answers, "No, all the shooting has stopped. I think we ought to head back to the platoon and figure out what happened. Dusty will probably call in arty on those fuckers."

Cars says, "Yeah, for all we know, this could have been another cluster fuck."

Roberto counters, "If it were left up to you, Cars, we wouldn't stand a chance of winnin' this war."

"Yeah, that's right, but I'd be alive to talk about it. At this rate, all of us are gonna be history." Cars is blowing off steam from all the tension of the firefight. As we walk back toward the ville, Cars continues muttering to himself. I stay at tail end, glancing back to keep an eye out for Charlie. I'm also angry and tired from the long night of terror followed by this futile chase through the jungle. Many firefights end with nothing more to show for our efforts than frazzled nerves. However, I'm not going to let Roberto hear me complaining because it will get back to Dusty and increase my chances of being assigned to more high-risk positions.

We get back to the clearing surrounding the ville and Roberto starts giving orders. "Okay, dig some holes and get in 'em. Clean your rifles but make sure somebody keeps an eye out for Charlie. I'm gonna head over to the ville and see what came down."

Once Roberto leaves, Cars remarks, "This is bullshit having to dig a foxhole every time we stop for a few. You don't see anybody else having to do this shit. Roberto's buckin' for sergeant if you ask me."

We continue digging our holes as Scott responds. "I get sick and tired of this shit, too, but there ain't nothin' you can do about it except bitch, bitch, bitch, Cars. You honkey pogue. You're about as far from being a trained killer as they get."

Cars throws his E-tool down saying, "Yeah, I'll tell ya what . . ." He suddenly stops talking when Dusty and Roberto walk toward us. It's odd that Dusty is accompanying Roberto. Dusty's walking fast, swinging his rifle in cadence with each step, hunching his shoulders as he always does when he gets excited or angry. We stop digging our foxholes as they approach. "Now what!" Cars whispers.

Dusty is belligerent. "Okay!—Drew!—Cars!—you guys come with me. You new fucks have gotta see this one." Cars and I jump up, grab our rifles, and follow Dusty down the path to the ville. I have no idea what Dusty is up to, but it can't be good. As we approach the ville, I see Tanner and Cap standing alongside the path about 20 meters ahead of us, looking down at something and talking. After a few more steps, I see they are looking at a mound along the side of the path. I focus my eyes on the dark mound, trying to make out exactly what it is. As I get closer, it becomes clearer what I am looking at. Tanner and Cap are chuckling and giving each other "five." I peer down along the path and realize I am seeing a pile of broken bones and bloody flesh. It's a huge heap of lifeless bodies that forms a grotesque monster with many heads and arms. I squint my eyes and look again at the bloody mess. Bloody arms, legs, feet, hands, and heads stick out of the pile. I feel dizzy and begin to sway. Lifeless eyes dot the pile and mouths are stuck open in silent screams. I want to gag from what smells like an open sewer. I reach for the end of my utility towel and put it over my nose.

"Well, well, boys. What the fuck do we have here?" Dusty is hooting and smiling. "You see this guy's head?" Dusty raises his foot back and kicks one of the heads sticking out of the pile with full force, splashing blood into the air. "Yo! Hard fuckin' head." He kicks it again and again, obviously trying to amputate the head from the rest of the body. He points his 45 at the neck area and pulls the trigger—Bam! He once again kicks the head and it flies into the air. "Wow! Did you see dumbfuck lose his head? That'll teach Mr. Charlie to mess with our platoon. I want you new guys to get acquainted with Old Man Death. See, this is how y'all are gonna look if ya don't get with the fuckin' program." Dusty jumps on top of the pile of bodies and starts springing up and down. "Yo! Ride 'em cowboy!" He pounds his feet down hard, smashing the flesh beneath him. Sucking chest wounds hiss, spitting blood into the air, coloring Dusty's jungle boots bright red. Tanner pulls an Instamatic camera out and starts snapping pictures. I keep my utility towel up to my nose to stop from puking. Dusty continues jumping up and down on the corpses and yelling like he is at an amusement park on a thrill ride. "Wow-wee! Yeah, buddy! Take that, fuckin' Charlie!" Dusty pulls a bayonet out and starts stabbing the bodies after each jump. "Swish, swish, swish." The corpses' lifeless eyeballs glistened in the sunlight. "Get a good hard look 'cause this is what the fuck it's all about, boys. This is the face of Old Man Death," he hammers. "Get used to him and learn to laugh and curse him. Curse him and y'all stay alive. Fear him and y'all get wasted." Dusty jumps down off the corpses and wipes his boots off on some of the bodies. He strolls away with Tanner and Cap like they are taking a walk in the park.

Cars and I stand motionless staring at the heap of bodies. This is the first time I've seen the face of the enemy. It's frightening to realize these guys were alive only moments ago. Human life blasted off the planet like nothing more than grains of sand. The story of what this war is really like will never reach home, because the truth is just too unbelievable. How does anyone get to the point that he mocks God? How can anyone do what Dusty did today? The brutal reality grates at my insides as I stare into the face of death.

"Drew," Cars' voice is low and somber. "Let's get back to our pod and get some rest." We turn and walk back to our foxhole where Roberto and Scott are eating C-rations.

"Where you guys been? What's goin' on?" Scott speaks out of the side of his mouth as he eats C-rats.

"I'm not sure what happened," I say. "There were a bunch of dead NVAs up there on the trail. They were piled on top of one another in a bloody heap. Dusty went crazy kickin' the shit out of 'em. What's bein' a fighter got to do with all this, Scott?"

"Drew, you honkey pogue—you ain't ever heard about boonie rats in the Nam?" he asks amusingly.

"I know about bein' a grunt or a fighter."

"That's real-world shit ya learn in boot camp. Over here, if ya get like Dusty, you become a boonie rat. Somebody that doesn't give a rat's ass about livin' or dyin'. Dusty's a number-one boonie rat. If you stay around here long enough, you'll see what I mean."

I reach into my rucksack and pull out a box of C-rats containing a can of ham and limas. I exclaim, "Hey, I got some beans and motherfuckers." I open the can, stare at the gooey mixture, and begin to slowly eat the concoction. Then, I begin thinking about what I am becoming in this wretched place. Something evil grabbed hold of me today. I feel my spirit of patriotism and belief in just causes slowly slipping away. I have moved a step closer to being a boonie rat in the Nam.

CHAPTER III

Rite of Passage

Early October 1967

Cars and I are still being watched closely by Dusty and his right-hand man, Fuller. They have pegged Carson as a troublemaker who likes to challenge authority within the platoon. I am seen as having questionable killer instincts because I have a soft heart for the Vietnamese. Dusty takes every opportunity to put Cars and me in high-risk positions. He has been assigning me to walk point on patrols, however, I've become a good point man, since mistakes are fatal at this position. Cars has been assigned to humping the field radio, one of the first positions the VC try to take out during firefights, since the radio is our only link to getting help. Cars is always complaining about being RTO. Both of us are assigned to listening posts, or LPs, at night when we aren't on patrol. We have to crawl out to a designated spot in the open and lie there as the first line of defense against attack.

On this particular day, Dusty designates me as point man for the platoon. I'm cautiously guiding all the grunts through an obstacle course of booby traps, ambush sites, and other assorted horrors. We have penetrated beyond our most distant patrols and are working a VC-infested area near a free-fire zone known as no-man's-land. We approach a small ville situated at the fringe of the free-fire zone hidden deep within the jungle, which is known to have many booby traps strung around it.

I carefully inch forward as beams of sunlight streak through the lush jungle canopy illuminating the path ahead of me. Dense undergrowth spews an overpowering scent of wild plants into the humid air. The dead silence is broken by twigs snapping under my jungle boots, signaling that I have successfully avoided a booby trap.

"Drew!" Scott blurts. "Did you see that snake back there?" I kneel down on one knee taking my eyes off point and survey where I had just walked. "Man, that's a boa lying alongside the path! It's at least 15-feet long! Can you see him, Drew?"

I can't believe I missed something so obvious. It could have easily been a booby trap and we would have all been history. I glance into the foliage but still can't see the snake. Scott is wide-eyed, still pointing behind me. "See it?" he says. "See it?" I peer at the growth along the path, but everything blends together into clumps of moss, weeds, and creeping bugs. My mind whirls for a moment as I realize we are not only fighting the VC, but have been thrust into a world of the weird and bizarre, living alongside the fiends of the animal kingdom. Creatures I had known only through books are now a part of my everyday existence.

Fat, blood-sucking leeches lunge at our legs in rivers and streams. If you're lucky, you can remove them before they gouge into your skin. Gecko lizards form colonies and make strange-sounding squawks throughout the night. Huge water buffaloes inhabit most areas and are aggressive toward us. Tales of tigers and apes attacking Marines pass through platoons. Monkeys and gibbons occasionally bark like dogs at night. Hoards of flies, mosquitoes, and ants swarm onto any warm-blooded creature.

Snakes slither everywhere, including one of the most deadly snakes in the world, the Bamboo Viper. The small, green reptile belongs to the family, Viperidae, and is known to Marines as the One-Two Snake, or Mr. No-shoulders. The snake's bite is known to inject powerful venom which drops the victim within two steps. The VC like to tie these deadly serpents to the opening of caves to guard against Marine tunnel-rats. Mr. No-shoulders is especially suited for this task since he is small, has a keen sense of smell, and is sensitive to temperature changes and vibrations. His eyes, specialized for night hunting, can open wide like barn doors to let in the least trace of light, or they can close into narrow slits when the light is bright. The memory of those eyes still sends chills down my spine from a close encounter a week earlier.

Our squad of eight guys had been wearily humping through the boonies one morning when Dusty decided it was time to set in for a rest. We were around lots of bamboo where Mr. No-shoulders likes to make his home so I should have been more aware of my surroundings. We formed a small circle looking out toward the tree line where we could see Charlie in case he attacked. We were resting and it seemed to be a good time to take a dump near some bushes about 20 yards away. I walked out to a spot which was visible to the others, and pulled my jungle fatigues down around my ankles squatting into what we referred to as a gook-squat. I let loose with a bang, and heard some hoots and hollers coming from the guys. Then, I glanced down between my legs and froze. Not more than twelve inches from my nose, and staring directly into my eyes, was Mr. No-shoulders. His slender, green, smooth body was motionless. I moved my head slightly and could see his pupils enlarge as my shadow moved across his field of vision. Don't move a fraction! I knew I had startled him because his eyes were fixed as if he were ready to strike. He slithered forward about a foot and grotesquely bent his head back in an offensive move. Suddenly, an E-tool shovel severed the serpent's head, flipping it into the air, blood splashing everywhere. I was so frozen with fear, I didn't hear Dusty walk up beside me to relieve himself. Spotting the snake, he slashed it with his entrenching tool. He roared with laughter as he chopped up the snake.

As I recalled the close encounter with the snake, I feel a sharp pain on the back of my neck. I intuitively smack my neck and a small spider rolls down my sleeve. I wonder if it's poisonous. Maybe I'll get a free ride out of the bush.

"Drew, forget about the boa. Get movin'!" Scott hammers.

"This place is a damn zoo," I mutter. "I still can't see the boa. At least he isn't Mr. No-shoulders, huh Scott?"

"Yeah, he almost got you last week," Scott snickers. "Get yourself together. We got that ville up ahead and this place is loaded with booby traps."

I walk cautiously, knowing each step might be my last. As we approach the ville, I consider getting a Vietnamese to walk point for me, because the villagers usually know where the booby traps are located and will certainly avoid them. I have to take advantage of anything if we are going to make it beyond the danger zone of this ville. Every Marine patrol that ventures into no-man's-land takes casualties. Puff The Magic Dragon, an AC-47 Gatling gunship, works the area at night when we're gone, spitting hellfire on every inch of enemy territory. B-52s periodically drop their payloads during the day leaving huge craters throughout the jungle. No-man's-land is infested with VC.

I hear voices up ahead and can finally see the jungle beginning to clear away into the front of the ville. I walk very slowly and motion others to move forward. Roberto, Cars, and Scott catch up and we crouch together in a circle and look into the ville. "Okay," I say, "I'll rush in first and grab that old man and get him to walk point. The rest of you cover me."

Roberto cautions, "If anybody runs from us, blow 'em away! Where's Dusty?"

"He's back at tail end," Cars whispers. "He'll be here didi mau because you know he can't wait to fuck things up."

I burst forward screaming, "Dungli! dungli! That's right, nobody fuckin' move!" Nearly 20 women and children begin screaming and holding their hands out in prayer. We had taken them totally by surprise, but their screams could alert the VC. I quickly grab one old man out of the group to walk point.

Dusty runs into the ville shouting, "Shut those gooks up! Shut 'em up, I said!" The guys start hitting the women with the sharp end-piece of their rifles called the flash-suppresser. We feel our actions are justified since the ville is so close to the free-fire zone. "Drew," Dusty growls, "get that papa-san up front with you and let's move out! The rest of you guys put the women and kids in a hooch. Get movin' before the VC get a chance to organize!"

I use my rifle to push the old man to the other side of the ville. "Didi mau, papa-san," I order. He obeys, moving quickly through the ville. We enter the jungle and sunlight disappears, creating a genuine spook-house. The old man suddenly slows his pace, and I'm hoping that papa-san wants to stay alive as much as me. I push him forward again with my rifle. He high-steps and weaves around the underbrush like he knows every inch of the terrain. I follow his every step. He leads me safely through the danger zone around the ville and I wave him off.

Papa-san bows in reverence. "Marine, numbah-one! Marine, you numbah-one son!" he says. He has large, dark eyes and a thin, pointed beard. Papa-san's skin is dark and wrinkled, and he has no front teeth. Brown beetle-nut juice drips from his mouth. Oddly, he is missing part of an ear. He weighs only about 100 pounds, probably existing on rice most of his life. He looks about 60 years old and has already lived well beyond the life expectancy of most men in Vietnam. He seems like a decent human being, but like so many other Vietnamese, he is caught in the middle of an indiscriminate war. Now, we will leave his ville and the VC will take over.

"Whadaya think, Drew?" Scott is scanning the thick foliage around us.

"Don't know, Scott. That papa-san was sure nervous. Charles has gotta know we're here, especially since those women were screaming so much. I feel Charles nearby."

"Yeah, he's just waitin' for the right moment," Scott whispers. "Here comes Dusty."

Dusty's shoulders are hunched and his face is taut. "Drew, take us into the jungle straight ahead for a couple of clicks. Then, do a 160 and head back to the ville. Keep your eyes peeled 'cause we're in a free-fire zone, so shoot anything that moves. I'll be right behind you guys."

Dusty duck-walks behind Scott and disappears into the jungle. I move forward four to five steps at a time, stoop onto my haunches to survey the bush for possible ambush sites. It's impossible to know anything for certain, because the jungle is full of deception. Plants and trees create a steamy outdoor greenhouse percolating in the hot sun. Millions of leaves hanging from vines, trees, and bushes create a parasitic garden for insects, birds, and animals. Each variegated pattern is a perfect jungle camouflage for the VC. Light winds send ripples across green flora making everything seem alive and ready to jump out at me. I hold tightly onto the trigger of my rifle.

My next instinct is to examine the immediate terrain for booby traps. I look closely for thin wires and clear nylon lines extending low across the trail which trip short-fused grenades. This is the type of booby trap Nichols hit last week. Another horror of the jungle is clumps of moss and fern unnaturally arranged to conceal a toe-popper, a small explosive device designed to take off toes, or a bouncing Betty, which is a pressure-released mine set to flip into the air and explode at crotch level when tripped. Larger batches of foliage can be arranged on a straw mat to cover 10-foot-deep punji pits. Malayan whips are rigged to trip at chest level, slamming a bamboo-spiked pole into your midsection. Worse yet, an antitank mine, rigged to detonate from the pressure of a man's weight, can easily take out a whole squad. Complicating the task are the hundreds of wait-a-minute vines and thorny bushes that stop us in our tracks causing a grunt to call out, "Wait a minute!" while he untangles or cuts himself loose. My visual inspection of the area can take only a few seconds, so I learn to rely on a sixth sense to get me through the unknown.

I continue inching ahead at five-step intervals for about an hour. My gut and leg muscles ache. Sweat pours into my sopping jungle fatigues and mosquitoes are thick around my face, I sometimes inhale them. I squash liquid between my butt cheeks and a foul odor oozes up from my fatigues. I don't want to be bagged like this.

"Drew," Dusty calls, as he approaches from my rear. "Do your 160 and head on back! I can't believe Charlie ain't hit us." He sounds disappointed and I wonder if he wants me dead. I head back toward the ville maintaining the same stealthy posture all the way. It's a slow, tedious process that never eases. Then, the jungle gives way to an open area about 100 yards across to my left. It's a barren spot riddled with craters caused by massive B-52 bombings. As we pass, I notice two people walking along the edge of the tree line on the other side. I know we are in a free-fire zone, so I quickly raise my rifle and squeeze off several rounds. As they dart into the jungle, I realize they're a woman and a boy. Dusty and Scott run forward and kneel beside me. "What are you shootin' at, man?" Scott asks.

"Looked like a couple of gooks over there in the trees," I say.

"Almost got your first gook, huh Drew?" Dusty has an eager smile on his face.

"Yeah, but I don't want to bag a woman and kid to get a notch on my rifle."

"Well, if Charles had any doubts about where we are, he doesn't anymore. Those two gooks made sure of that. You still don't understand. If they have slant eyes, they're the fuckin' enemy." Dusty sounds as if he's giving a lecture on the facts of life. "The quicker you learn that lesson, then the longer you'll stay alive. Let's get movin' back to the ville." Dusty points in the direction of the ville.

I head back into the tree line and continue working my way toward the ville. We have been away for about two hours. The trees are thinning out and I hear faded voices coming from the direction of the ville. I listen intently, deciding to move toward the sounds which grow louder and surprisingly grotesque. As I get closer to the ville, I can see a small group of women surrounding something on a bamboo cot. They are shrieking and raising their hands to the sky in grief. Suddenly, Dusty runs past me and pushes into the group of women. When I walk up, he lifts the straw cover from the cot, exposing what lay beneath. The women wail louder. I look down at the mat and see a man with no head. A severed neck-bone sticks out from his bare shoulders and blood oozes down onto a red-soaked mat. The man's head is perched upside-down resting between his left arm and ribs. It's the face of an old man with dark eyes that were stuck open at the moment of terror when his life abruptly ended. He is small and bony with wrinkled, olive-colored skin, and has an ear missing. It's the old man I had forced to walk point for me! The VC must have come in and beheaded him for helping us get through the mine field.

Dusty begins laughing uproariously and poking the body with his rifle. He gleefully exclaims, "This fuckin' papa-san lost his head! Come on, mama-san, put papa-san's head back on." He laughs and laughs. Fuller and Phillips are now standing next to him forcing some laughter. I am in shock at the carnage, thinking papa-san had just saved our lives. At times like this I pity the Vietnamese. Our tours of duty will last for 13 months, but the villagers' torturous existence will go on until the war is over. Attila the Hun would have felt proud to work alongside the VC . . . *or* the Americans. We have our awesome weaponry and ferocious self-righteousness. The VC have their terminal pride and belief in spreading Communism throughout the region. The losers are always the civilians.

The only other fighting force that sends more terror into the populace is our allies, the South Korean Marines. The Koreans have even less respect for the civilians because they view themselves as the superior Asian race. The fact that a Vietnamese civilian would ever support the VC means certain death. I quickly recall some memories of this from last week.

We had been on a company sweep through a hilly, forested region with small villes dotting the area. Our platoon was crossing over top of one of the hills when I heard an explosion in the distance. All of us dropped onto one knee and looked into the valley below where a platoon of South Korean Marines were on patrol. Evidently, their point man tripped a mine taking him and the duce-point out. The booby trap was located very close to the ville, which meant the civilians knew it was there. The Marines left a squad behind to aid the wounded and the others walked into the ville, torching the hooches and shooting anything that moved. Fortunately, some of the civilians escaped out the backside of the ville. The rest were silenced and torched along with everything else. The atrocity took only a few minutes and the civilians were once again punished for being caught up in a brutal war.

I am staring at the beheaded old man and thinking about the insanity of it all. Dusty is laughing and poking the body with his rifle. "Come on, let's get outta here, 'cause Charles has got to be nearby," I say.

Dusty counters, "Mama-san, where's the VC?"

A woman cries, "VC! VC!" She points in the direction we are heading. The VC have gone out ahead of us to possibly set up an ambush.

"Drew," Dusty blurts, "take Cars and Scott out ahead in a killer-team to search out the enemy. Wait for us at the big rice paddy we crossed earlier on the outskirts of no-man's-land."

"How far ahead do you want us to go?" I ask, nervously.

"We'll leave 15 minutes after you. If anything happens, we'll be close enough to come up and pound 'em. Get Cars and Scott and take off." Dusty's lips widen, almost grinning, as he looks the other way.

The rest of the unit of 23 guys is strung out like a centipede in the jungle behind me. I stoop down and drop back to tell Scott and Cars our fate. "That old man who walked point for us earlier was killed by Charlie. Dusty has decided to send us up ahead of the platoon as a point killer-team. There isn't much we can do about it, so let's go."

"Drew," Cars' voice is choppy. "Where's Charles?"

"Don't know, Cars. He's either just ahead in the bush, or he's waiting for us out in the rice paddy we crossed before we got into this stinkin' jungle. Either way, we're gonna get hit by Charles. Don't know why we can't do this as a platoon."

"Yeah," Cars says with a red face. "Dusty's an asshole! He's actin' like a fuckin' stormtrooper."

"Yeah, and we're his bait," I say. "Lets go." I wave Cars and Scott forward. The three of us move past the group of women and I take one last look at papa-san's head perched upside down between his arm and side. It's the blackhearted insanity that haunts me the most, and the fact that Charles is waiting for the right opportunity to do the same thing to me. I can't run, hide, or beg for mercy. Religion, civilization, and morals are all meaningless entities in the jungle. I have to remind myself—I am a grunt and point is my duty station.

I look back at Cars and Scott who are starring at papa-san. "Let's go!" I order. "Stay in my footsteps and be really quiet." We move quietly and steadfastly through the danger zone around the ville. We know booby traps are strung everywhere, so Scott and Cars step in my boot-prints, leaving an indentation for the others. A smart grunt never steps outside of his buddy's boot-print. I clutch my scapular and pray to get me past the booby traps. Each step is followed by a prayer of thanks.

I finally reach the fringe area of the jungle. Miraculously, I haven't encountered a booby trap or the VC. I kneel and study the terrain while waiting for Scott and Cars to catch up. Directly ahead is a 300-square-yard rice paddy with tall stems of rice poking out of foot-deep marshy water. It will be difficult to cross in full pack and gear. We are at the south end of the paddy where the jungle ends. The north end is guarded by thick brush and trees. To our east and west are other large rice paddies that are guarded by trees on their far sides. We have no choice but to cross the open expanse of the rice paddy.

Scott and Cars make it up beside me. "Drew," Scott says, while studying the situation, "can we talk Dusty into calling for choppers to haul us outta here?"

"Fat chance we got of that," Cars says, while throwing his M-16 down. "Dusty's gonna use us as guinea pigs to cross this paddy."

"Maybe we can get him to call in arty on the north side of this paddy before we cross," Scott states, sounding like he is pleading for sanity.

"That makes good sense to me too, Scott," I say. "I'll bet Charles is set up over on the north side waitin' for us to cross this paddy. Let's wait for the rest of the platoon. Cars, come on, pick your rifle up." Cars mumbles something and picks up his weapon, then we sit down and rest.

About 15 minutes later, Dusty arrives grinning from ear to ear. "Boy, we're havin' a good time today, aren't we, guys?" No one says anything. We continued peering out at the rice paddy. "Hate to break this party up but we got work to do. Drew, take your killer-team across to the other side of this paddy. When you're halfway across, I'll send the rest of the platoon over in line. All right, get movin'."

I feel it would be a waste of time to pursue options with Dusty. He seems determined to do this the hard way. We move forward into the marshy water with 70 pounds of gear drooping from our backs. I raise each knee waist high to keep the rice stems from tangling around my ankles and tripping me. The 105-degree temperature bakes the decaying vegetation while millions of mosquitoes hover over the smelly paddy.

"Goddamn mosquitoes taste like shit!" Cars mutters. "Scott, I thought you were gonna say something to Dusty about gettin' some arty to help us out?" he asks emphatically.

"No way! Drew's walkin' point. He's the one supposed to get it on with Dusty."

"Yeah, you think Dusty's gonna' listen to me? You're crazy. Dusty wants to see how fast you can run across this paddy," I quip. "I can't see anything on the north side, can you Scott?"

"Nope, haven't seen a thing. Charles might not want to mess with us. We're almost halfway, and I'm fuckin' tired. I gotta stop and catch my breath, so hold on."

We stop and I look back to see the rest of the platoon begin to cross the rice paddy. "You know that Charles isn't gonna hit us until the rest of the platoon is committed to crossing the paddy," I remark. Just as I complete my statement, a couple of distant thuds emanate from the northeast end of the paddy. We momentarily freeze, locking eyes on each other. Then, the unmistakable whistle of mortars descends on the tree line behind us. The Marines in our platoon scatter forward into the rice paddy just before the mortars explode in the trees. Boom! Boom! Then come three more quick thuds in succession. The remaining guys in the paddy near the tree line are struggling with ferocity in the knee-deep water to put some distance between themselves and the impending mortar explosions. The mortars explode at the water's edge, sending shock waves across the trees. No one appears to be hit.

Cars hollers, "It's a cluster fuck!" Suddenly, fierce gunfire erupts from the northeast side of the rice paddy. Zing! Zing! Pop! Pop! Pop! Bullets zip past my head and hit the water around us. Instinctively, the three of us start thrashing forward in the knee-deep water trying to make a beeline to the northwest side of the paddy. My worst fears are realized: being ambushed in the middle of a water-filled rice paddy like wingless ducks in a pond. Bullets whiz by my head and snap the water around my knees. Whenever I slow, the gunfire increases. Charlie is homing in on slow-moving targets. I'm gasping for hot air as rice stems wrap around my ankles and legs, causing me to stumble. The merciless sun has heated up the paddy like a furnace and my lungs feel like they are on fire. The harder I inhale, the more gnats and mosquitoes I swallow. I begin to feel sick to my stomach. I stop and put my hands on my legs to try and hold myself up. With all the gear on my back, I can hardly stay upright in the water. Then, I begin to puke my guts out. The VC open up with a tirade of bullets, spraying the water around me. I start running again, but trip and fall facedown in the water with the weight of my gear on top of me. In desperation, I push up, raising my head above the water, and struggle back to my feet. I'm gasping so hard it feels like my balls are being sucked into my chest. I become enraged and thrash forward like a maniac, firing blindly at the northeast end of the paddy. Cars and Scott are also struggling through the paddy and firing their weapons in a frenzy. As we get closer to the other side of the paddy, the incoming fire spreads over the breadth of the platoon.

Finally, I reach the other side of the paddy and have to make a quick decision. I can take the path of most resistance up a steep hill, which will lead me through some trees where counterfire can be set up, or I can take the path of least resistance up an old amtrac road to my right, which will also end up on the hilltop. I am exhausted, but know the easy way is usually booby-trapped and the whole platoon will eventually follow my lead. I decide to avoid the old amtrac road.

Cars and Scott have dropped behind from sheer exhaustion and a black guy named Jessie from Second Squad catches up with me. With Jessie close behind, I head up the hill digging my fingernails into the red earth and grabbing hold of anything that provides leverage. By the time I reach the top of the hill, I am a safe distance from the firing zone and can see the others still thrashing through the paddy below. I run toward a clearing about 30 yards away where we can begin a counterassault. Pow! A sharp blast throws me down onto my knees. "God, my foot!" Jessie screams. I turn and see Jessie cradling what is left of his bloody and mangled foot. His shoe is torn half-off and his foot dangles like it has been snapped at the ankle. "God, my foot, it's gone!" he cries out.

I jump up to help Jessie but see a gook running away from us. It dawns on me, Jessie hit a booby trap that could have been command-detonated by the fleeing gook. I holler, "Dung li! Dung li! Fuckin' dung li!" But, he runs faster.

I hear Jessie screaming, "My foot! God, it's gone!"

I have to do something quickly or the gook will get away. In confusion and rage, I raise my rifle and point at the man's head. I holler, "Dung li! You fucker! Dung li!" He continues running. I start to squeeze the trigger and everything goes into slow motion. I still hear Jessie screaming and the loud gunfire directed at the Marines still caught in the shooting gallery below us. I'm confused about no longer being in a free-fire zone since crossing the rice paddy and wonder if I can still shoot anything that moves. I start to squeeze the trigger again but hesitate. I have never shot anyone. He is no more than 40 yards away and I'm able to see his face. He's about 30, has a mustache, and is wearing a broad-rimmed coolie hat. He looks scared and for an instant I feel a commonality between us as human beings. I try once again to squeeze the trigger but the thought of killing him is too much. I lower the rifle, point at the man's legs, and start squeezing rounds off in rapid succession. His legs fly out from under him and he lands on his back. I still hear Jessie moaning.

I feel pumped with rage and run toward the man. "He did it! He detonated the booby trap! I'll kill him!" The man lies on his back, holding what is left of his right leg. His upper leg is blown away and only his femur is still attached to his lower knee. He is crying out, "Numbah-ten, Marine! Numbah-ten!"

"Shut up, you fucker!" I holler. "Shut the fuck up or I'll kill you! I promise, I'll kill you!" He continues wailing, so I raise the rifle and pound the stock into his face. "I'll show you, you fucker! I'll show you!" I hit him again.

"Drew! Stop, man!" You're killin' the bastard!" Cars hollers as he pulls me away. I finally catch a glimpse of sanity and realize what I'm doing. I look behind me and see the rest of the platoon coming over the top of the hill. Red is setting up his mortar team, and Cap is on the radio calling a medevac for Jessie. Dusty and Fuller have cleared the hill and come running toward me.

Dusty looks surprised. "Whadaya know, at last we got something to show for our troubles," he laughs, pointing down at the man. "Yeah, he's a dink for sure. Fuckin' A! Nice job, Drew!"

The thought occurs to me for the first time that he might not have been a VC. He could have been a civilian just trying to run away from the scene of battle. But why was he even around here and what about the booby trap? "Dusty, think he set the booby trap off?"

"Who gives a shit. He's a gook or a VC. Doesn't matter either way." Dusty looks down at the moaning man. "That fucker's leg's almost blown off. What happened, Drew? Couldn't waste him with a head shot?" He smiles and walks away.

Cars, Scott, and I move to the edge of a cliff where we are able to see the entire valley and dig a foxhole. Arty whizzes over top of our position like a freight train and explodes on the northeast end of the rice paddy. I sit on a small embankment with Scott and Cars and think about Dusty's comment. I am stunned that he knows my innermost thoughts. He's like a human bloodhound, focused on sniffing out fear and weakness and stamping it out. It was so easy in boot camp to point at those human-like targets and squeeze the rounds off without emotion. The whole Marine Corps training is designed to get us beyond the thinking element so we will react without hesitation. They never told me that I might actually *relate* to Charlie. Now, I understand the stories about soldiers who committed the cardinal sin of not squeezing the trigger on the enemy. For one split second they must have looked into a mirror and saw themselves. It occurs to me Dusty had also looked into that mirror but he had reached deep into the dark side of his soul which no man wants to know. This is the world of no return that I am being slowly drawn in to each day.

The medevac arrives and we help put Jessie and the wounded prisoner onboard. It quickly takes off and heads toward DaNang. I return to our foxhole and listen to the sounds of the chopper trailing off and consider the possibility of having stepped on the booby trap myself. Jessie will return to the States minus a foot, but at least he will return alive. I don't know what the future holds for me, so losing a foot might be worth it. Then, there is the gook I shot who is occupying a spot on the chopper. Someone else will have to deal with him now since I hadn't wasted him. Worse yet, what if I had shot an innocent civilian?

The confusing thoughts end as friendly fire continues to belt the tree line on the northeast end of the rice paddy. My senses are aroused by the awesome weaponry ripping through the tropical forest. The stench of gunpowder mixing with the aroma of floral gases creates a sweet stink in the moist atmosphere. The lush green jungle disintegrates with each bomb burst, rocking the region for miles around. I scoot down into a small crevice as debris falls from the sky like rain. It's an awesome spectacle of victory in Vietnam. If the guys back home could be with me now, they would definitely say, "Unbelievable!" For the moment, we can revel in our little victory, knowing Charles is on the run. Another artillery shell swoops down, exploding with a vengeance in the trees, leaving only a gaping crater in the aftermath. "Yeah, that'll teach 'em!" I shout.

"Get some!" Cars yells.

It's good to be alive because I have survived a patrol in the chamber of horrors. Not too many point men make it through no-man's-land unscathed. I also shot my first gook today, which will win respect within the platoon. This is as good as it gets in the Nam. Thank you, Lord, I am alive. We gathered our gear and Cap gives the order to return to Battalion. We have been in the field for about three weeks and I am looking forward to a shower and some badly needed sleep. I will also be able to eat some hot food, write letters home, and maybe see a movie. I just hope it's not a war flick. We form a staggered column and move slowly toward battalion headquarters. Once back at Battalion, we spend the day in our billets writing letters and cleaning gear. Guys stop by to congratulate me on shooting my first gook. The platoon tunnel rat, Killer, is especially happy for me. He says, "Drew, there's a certain pride that goes with gettin' your first gook. Mine happened to be a gook woman. It gets a lot easier after the first one." Killer smiles and shakes my hand.

Other Marines from the platoon drop by to congratulate me. It is a rite of passage in Vietnam for a grunt to get his first gook. I hear statements such as, "Nice shot, Drew!" "Drew, got a slant-eye?" "Gung ho, Girene!" "Hey, Drew, got some slop!?" I try to contain my shame and appear to have nothing but pride for what I had done.

Later in the evening, in a strange twist of events, I hear through friends I could have charges brought against me for shooting the dink. I am told he could have been a civilian instead of a VC. A few hours ago I was trying to feel like a hero. Now, I am trying not to feel like a damn criminal. I wonder if Dusty has something to do with this. He might be trying to get rid of me any way he can. During the next hour, I replay the chain of events leading up to the shooting over in my mind. I have nagging doubts about our location and if we had moved out of the free-fire zone. Even so, Jessie was screaming after he hit the booby trap and the gook was running from the scene. It would have been a dereliction of duty if I hadn't done something to stop him. I feel my actions were justified, but in this country, insanity prevails.

During the rest of the evening, I continue working on my gear and wonder about my fate. It's late when Fuller returns to the billet. He walks in saying, "Got some news for you. Cap says the dink was definitely running supplies for Charles. He fessed up about a lot of other things, too. There's boo-coo land mines booby-trapping that amtrac road near the rice paddy that we just missed taking. It was bad that we lost Jessie, but we all could have been blown away. So, Drew, you did the right thing. We're gonna go back out tomorrow with a mine-sweepin' team and clear the road. You guys wanna go over to the club and suck down a few cold ones?"

I breathe a sigh of relief knowing my perception of the event was correct. Cars and Scott are sitting next to me. Cars spouts, "Yeah, I'm getting really tired of this John Wayne shit. Just as long as they're not servin' that rotten tiger piss at the club. Gimme a blond bombshell and a bottle of booze and I'm outta here."

We all laugh and walk to the club for a well-earned rest. I remember my promise when I first arrived at Battalion not to get near the club again, but near misses don't seem so bad anymore. Scott starts hassling Cars. "Cars, I don't think you could handle a blond bombshell. You think the word hump means to carry shit on your back. If you ever got so lucky to pull your tube steak out, you'd kill her with laughter. What do you think, Drew?"

"Cars is a pogue, man. He just thinks he's a trained killer. Did you see him running across that rice paddy this morning? He looked like a damn jack rabbit."

"Yeah," Cars remarks. "Drew was so scared, he was serpentinin' like he was back in boot camp. Did you see when he fell down? I ain't ever seen one swingin' dick jump up so fast in all my life."

Scott joins in, "Yeah, Charlie opened up on him and you'd think that white boy had just seen a ghost. He was haulin' ass!"

We all laugh like we've done many times to break up the tension after battle. Fuller joins in by saying, "I didn't see you lifers laughin' this morning. It looked to me like all of you could have used a crapper." We pass by the CP when Fuller quickly changes the tone of the conversation. "Hey, you guys! Hear that incoming red phone? Listen up!"

We walk over to the CP so we can hear what is coming down. "This is One-three. Say again what your position is, Lima-two?" It sounds like Sergeant Tanner on the radio talking to second platoon of Lima Company. His voice is urgent. "Say again your position, Lima-two."

A panicky voice responds, "We're on an old amtrac road just outside the free-fire zone in no-man's-land. We need help! Only twelve of us left, over."

We can hear rifle fire, explosions, and screaming men in the background of the radio talk. Listening more intently, I hear the faint explosions and gunfire in the distance. It is where we had been this morning. Lima-two must have taken the old amtrac road—the road I decided not to take.

"Who's down, Lima-two?" Tanner questions. "Over."

"Oh God, please help!"

"Settle down, Marine!" Tanner orders. "Tell me what's goin' on out there, and I mean now! Over."

"Sir, we hit two mines on this road. Doc stepped outta Sarge's footprints and four guys got blown to hell. There's nothin' left of 'em. Just some boots and bent-up rifles." He starts to sob as the gunfire grows more intense.

"Where's the rest of the guys? Over."

"We're pinned down on this road and Charlie's tryin' to take the rest of us out." Just then, another explosion.

"What the fuck's goin' on?" Tanner yells.

"Someone just hit another mine. Please get us some help!" "Hang in there! Lima-three's in the area and we'll get them over there."

Making the decision to avoid the old amtrac road this morning was the difference between life and death for our platoon. Life in Vietnam is like a crapshoot. As long as lucky 7 or 11 keeps coming up, I will stay alive. One bad roll of the dice, and I'm history. I wonder how high the stakes will be tomorrow.

CHAPTER IV

The Black Magic Carpet

Late October 1967

It's shortly after shooting my first gook that I begin losing track of the days—only the months matter. I have ten months to go in Nam and I am already an experienced combat veteran. In two months since joining the platoon, we have lost Demarco, Matthews, Nichols, Carter, Layman, and Jessie. Nearly one-quarter of the platoon is gone, and most of my tour looms ahead of me. I smile very little now, usually only when I receive a letter from home.

A new replacement by the name of Bowman arrived a few days ago. He is a farmer's son from Iowa and had enlisted in the Marines just five months ago. Bowman has a boot haircut which makes him stand out like a new Cadillac among a bunch of old jalopies. He wears thick eyeglasses, has a large frame with muscular arms and legs, and is barrel-chested. His face is covered with red pockmarks, a sure sign drill instructors made him use a scrub brush on his pimpled face in boot camp. DIs always ridiculed guys who had pimples because it was a symbol of adolescence. They made them shower separately, and the DIs would sometimes take it upon themselves to scrub the faces of these recruits. Blood covered the shower floor on these occasions. I'm sure Bowman couldn't wait to get out of boot camp, even though it meant the DIs were going to send him directly to Vietnam because of those pimples. Anyone who appeared to have a weakness or inferiority was seen as expendable. Eight months ago, Bowman had won the regional championship for pole-vaulting in his state. Now he's humping ammo in our squad and learning all about being a grunt in the Nam.

It's late afternoon and we've been in the bush all day looking for Charles without any success. Dusty makes a change and designates me as point man for the platoon. I cross a rice paddy and enter jungle terrain that is difficult to traverse. I choose to walk on a beaten path against my better judgment because the bush has become so thick. I am taking a gamble that the path isn't booby-trapped, since the civilians need to use it for the same reason.

I reach a steep incline, overgrown by roots and vines, and pull myself up to where the path divides to the right and left. I look to the left and am startled to see a group of women and children standing in the middle of the trail about 20 yards in front of me. We lock eyes and freeze. Suddenly, two VC men shouldering rifles take off from behind the group of women and children. I quickly raise my rifle and point at the VC but can't get a clear shot since the civilians are in the way. I run down the jungle trail passing the civilians and open fire on the enemy. At that moment the VC leap over a dirt mound alongside the trail and disappear into the dense underbrush. I could have shot one of them, so I carefully move forward like a hunter on the trail of a wounded bear, not knowing if the angry prey might be hiding around the next tree. Within a few minutes, Dusty catches up with me and joins in the hunt. We alternately move forward using trees as cover but the thick foliage makes the going tough. After about ten minutes of the cat-and-mouse-game, there is still no sign of Charles. I surmise he disappeared into one of his caves. It isn't long before we have to give up our pursuit because of the dense underbrush.

I turn to see where Dusty is and, to my surprise, he's rushing toward me with a scowl on his face, one arm pumping, while the other hand clenches his M-16. He shouts, "You let them get away!" I am stunned by his accusation. It isn't my fault the VC got away. He stops inches from my face, "If you ever again hesitate with blowin' civilians away, I'll kill you! You hear me?"

I realize that Dusty had seen the civilians on the trail. Now I have no choice but to face off with him. "If I get outta here, whether I'm walkin' or in a body bag, I'm gonna have a clear conscience!" I clamor.

He snaps, "If this ever happens again, where you spare the civilians, or if you ever disobey one of my orders, I'll kill you!" Then, Dusty storms off.

Scott and Bowman are standing in the background and witness the confrontation. Scott and I have become close friends while sharing foxholes over the past months and we trust each other implicitly. He knows Dusty had been on my case ever since Tanner kicked the women off the cliff. Now, Dusty is threatening to kill me. Scott pulls me aside and tells me that some of the black guys in the platoon will help protect me from Dusty. Although the blacks hate civilians because of the booby traps that kill and maim Marines, they hate Dusty, too. Dusty is from the South and is a bone-chilling racist. He treats the blacks like dirt. They take it personally whenever he exposes them to unnecessary risks. This is an opportunity for them to help me and get even with Dusty. Having some of the black guys as allies is an unexpected break.

Later in the evening our platoon stops for a rest near a deserted ville. This provides a good opportunity for me to meet with the others. Scott quickly gathers some of his friends along with Cars and me. We secretly go into a hooch and sit in a circle around a small statue of Buddha. There is our machine gunner, Taylor; our ammo humper, Big Haus; a rifleman from Third Squad named Ray; Scott; Cars; and myself. Scott starts the meeting by sharply announcing, "Dusty threatened Drew!"

"He's a gungy son-of-a-bitch!" Taylor hisses. "He's from the South and you know how he hates our black asses."

"Dusty's out to get us all wasted," Cars, sneers. "He's always makin' us take risks we really don't have to take."

"I think we ought to frag him," Haus hammers.

We all start talking at once about things Dusty has done. "Okay, keep the noise down," Scott, whispers. "I just don't think we ought to let Dusty threaten us." Everybody shakes their heads in agreement. "If it can happen to Drew, then it can happen to any one of us."

"Yeah, I agree," Ray says, unequivocally. "He threatened me when I first got to this stinkin' hole."

"We just can't let Dusty get away with this," Scott pleads. "I say we all make a pact to kill Dusty if he tries to hurt any of us."

Everyone shakes their heads in agreement. Then Scott raises his hand saying, "Everyone put your hands on mine. Promise to live and die together." We all agree. "Just remember," Scott cautions. "Don't mess with Dusty unless he tries to waste one of us."

We leave the hooch and go back to our perimeter positions. I feel some sense of relief knowing I have support from others. I walk to my foxhole and can see Dusty sitting next to a hooch meeting with Fuller, Sergeant Tanner, and Cap. Dusty must have talked with them about what had happened up on the trail. I'm not really worried about what Tanner or Cap think. Cap stays to himself and lets Tanner run things.

Tanner is mostly concerned that we pull our duty stations. I have never refused to work any assigned position so Tanner should have no beef with me. Fuller is a different story. He is always sucking up to Dusty and reporting to him about anything Cars and I do. I don't trust him, and it's obvious he's using Dusty to avoid the high-risk positions in the platoon. However, I can't blame him, since he's just another 18 year-old kid trying to stay alive in the jungle. Nonetheless, I'll have to keep a close eye on him.

Much of what had taken place is quickly put behind us when word comes down that there is a large force of the North Vietnamese army in the area. Now, we all need to stick together to survive. We only have a few hours of daylight left to work the bush so Dusty now assigns Phillips' squad to walk point for the platoon. I breathe a sigh of relief. "We're headin' back into the boonies," Dusty orders. "We'll set up a perimeter tonight somewhere inside the jungle to get ready for those NVAs."

I follow Scott into the foliage and Bowman follows close behind me. Tension is high because we know there is enemy in the area. We slowly track through the jungle without a trace of the NVAs. Scott drops to one knee and I quickly follow his lead. The new guy, Bowman, creeps up beside me and also kneels on one knee. He clumsily gouges the stock of his M-16 rifle into the jungle compost. He leans forward on the rifle, panting hard, not used to the heat, humidity, and the weight of his gear. Bowman is still petrified of the jungle. Being scared is one thing, but FNGs seek comfort by trying to get physically close to someone. Not to be alone is his only aim and the closer he can get to someone, the better.

I am irritated. "Bowman, I've told you not to ride up on my ass like that. Damn it! If there's some action or if one of us hits a booby trap, there's gonna be two of us bitin' the dust instead of one. Now, back off!" Bowman crawls back to a position by himself like a hurt puppy.

I look forward at Scott who is crouched near a tree. He whispers, "Drew," and motions me up to his position. I slowly duck-walk forward feeling the weight of my gear. He looks worried, his eyes fixed on the jungle growth in front of us. "Tell that new guy, Bowman, to keep some distance 'cause he's gonna get us all blown away. The word just came back from point we're about to pack it in for the night, that is, as soon as we get out of the middle of this stinkin' jungle. There's a clearin' up ahead and we're supposed to set up a night-defensive perimeter there when the sun sets. Okay?"

"I don't like havin' to set up a perimeter so close to all this jungle cover. Those NVAs could be on top of us before we know it. I wonder who made this decision?" I ask.

"You know, gungy Dusty. No choice now, Drew, so move on back." Scott's eyes are still trained on the jungle. His helmet has a photograph of his girlfriend attached to it. I always feel a moment of relief whenever I look at her picture. She glows with energy through her smile. Her youthful face and sparkling eyes are soft and alive. She reminds me of a life I had in the oh-so-distant past.

I crawl back to my position and wave Bowman forward. He eagerly scampers up to me. I speak very clearly, looking directly into his terror-filled eyes. "We're gonna set in for the night up ahead. Keep your distance and everything will be okay," I say, reassuringly. Bowman remains silent. He's an accident waiting to happen and I hope he makes it through the next few weeks.

Scott slithers through thorny vines and around trees and bushes. I follow him, keeping the back of his jungle fatigues just in sight. That's the way to do it, moving forward only when you are about to lose sight of the guy in front of you. Today, that distance is only about two yards. After that, a man disappears into a mass of green. We carefully inch our way through the jungle until we reach the clearing. The sun is setting when Dusty gathers us. "All right, here's the scoop. Something big is brewing out here tonight. Don't know yet what it is, but Battalion is supposed to radio us by 1100 hours with the details. Now that it's almost dark, we'll crawl up that hill and dig foxholes for the night. We'll form a perimeter of ten foxholes with two guys in each hole. Scott, you and Drew take the position straight ahead. Bowman, get Cars and take the position next to them. Any questions?"

"Yeah," Bowman's voice is cracking. "What do you mean by something big?"

"You remember hearing about us losing those guys a few weeks ago, Bowman?" Dusty is smirking. He likes inflicting fear into FNGs. "Yeah, I remember." You can barely hear Bowman's voice.

"Well, tonight will make that seem like a piece of cake, if it's what I think it is." Dusty crawls off into the darkness toward another foxhole. Bowman stands still, groping for words.

"What do you make of that shit, Drew?" Scott is angry.

"I don't know. No tellin' with Dusty. You know how much he craves action. Maybe he's just itchin' for a good fight tonight."

"What do you mean by a good fight?" Bowman questions. "I mean, what does a good fight mean?"

"Let's just get up on that hill and dig our holes," I respond.

"Fuck that shit, man! I want to know what this means." Bowman's lips are quivering and his hands are shaking. "Does it mean sappers, machine guns, rockets, or what?"

"Look," I say sharply. "I really don't know. This could simply mean that Dusty wants a good fight or that he knows that we are in for a good fight. See?"

"Oh yeah, now I fuckin' see! That's great, you guys." Bowman's voice is high-pitched and his speech is rapid.

Scott throws his rifle down and grabs Bowman by the collar, pulling him forward. He speaks slowly drawing words out as if he were back in the ghetto. "Hey, w-h-i-t-i-e! Charlie's gonna get some tonight. He's gonna mess your ass up if you don't hold it together, boy." Scott's eyes are glazed and his teeth are shining in the darkness. He tosses Bowman onto his backside, then picks up his rifle.

Bowman's face is red and his glasses hang from one ear. He quickly straightens his glasses and turns his head toward the jungle like a wounded animal. He seems to have his wits again.

"Now, let's get up that hill." Scott orders.

Darkness has settled in as we use our elbows and knees to slowly crawl up the side of the small hill. It's a barren hill about 15 meters high with a 90-meter perimeter bordered by jungle. I have a bad feeling about being on the top of a hill in the middle of the jungle. It's always better to have the high ground but the NVAs can easily see our foxholes from the tree line and, having lost the element of surprise, they can overrun us in a matter of seconds. I dig my elbows and knees into the earth, cursing Dusty with each forward move. Once we reach our positions on the top of the hill, Bowman crawls off to look for Cars. Scott and I slip out of our gear and dig a 4-foot-deep foxhole. We put our gear in the bottom of the hole and etch out a dirt shelf for our grenades. Scott reaches inside his pack and pulls out three Claymore mines, which are fan-shaped anti-personnel mines that detonate hundreds of steel balls.

"Drew, you crawl out and place these Claymores at the edge of the jungle in case of an assault. I'll go over to Cars' hole and tell him that you're out there. Go for it!"

"Just make sure Bowman understands that it's me out there, okay?" I always hate going back outside the perimeter to set up Claymores. I run the risk of being mistaken for the enemy by an unwary Marine. I say a prayer and belly-crawl down the hill to the edge of the jungle. A half moon dimly lights the hillside, casting shadows off trees and bushes. I place the three Claymores 10 feet apart facing into the jungle in case of a frontal assault. I cautiously crawl back, unwinding the electrical cord to detonate the Claymores as I move along. Scott peers at me over the edge of the foxhole with the eyes of a black cat.

"Drew, give me the handsets to those Claymores and I'll put 'em on the ledge," Scott says, anxiously. I quickly give him the handsets and crawl into the foxhole. "Good, that'll make 'em easy to grab," he says.

I look to my right and see a crouched figure moving toward us from Cars' foxhole. As he gets closer, I see it's Dusty and he looks really tense. He jumps down into our hole and peers out toward the jungle. His voice is penetrating. "Well, we just got word from Battalion that it's the end of the world for us tonight! There's an estimated force of at least 2,000 NVAs heading toward DaNang. The only problem is, we're in their path and there's only 21 of us. Intelligence says they know our position and are planning to take us out. We have orders to hold this pod at all costs. I hope ya'll hear me. This is it for ya'll. Prepare to die!"

Dusty stoically moves toward another foxhole, carrying his message of death. Scott and I sit still for what seems like an eternity. Finally, Scott breaks the enduring silence. "Dusty really has a way of puttin' things. You know, it seems as if he enjoys this shit. He likes messin' with our heads and watchin' us die. He just doesn't give a shit, not even about himself."

"I know, that's the unreal part for me. Hell, he's already been wounded twice and I think he's gone completely dinky-dau. I've never heard him talk about home either. He says this is his home, and he means it! Scott, we're in a bad way tonight."

Scott's eyes widened. "Hey," he whispers. "Someone's crawlin' toward us."

A choppy voice emanates from the large, shadowy figure moving our way. "You guys, it's me, Fuller. Hold your fire. I'm coming into your hole." Fuller rolls into our foxhole. He brushes the mosquitoes and dirt from his face.

Scott's voice is alarming. "What's Dusty sayin' about those NVA units? How many are supposed to be out there, anyway?"

"Intelligence is estimating about 2,000 of Ho Chi Minh's finest," Fuller states. "They are supposed to attack at about 0200 or 0300 hours. This is no bullshit. We'll be real lucky to see the light of day again. Those NVAs are supposed to have orders to overrun us before they hit DaNang. Word is for everyone to hang on as long as you can. There's no hope to beat 'em, but we can sure as hell fight to the end. Helluva war, ain't it? I'll be back later with a starlight scope to check out the jungle on this side of the perimeter. See ya later, I hope."

Scott shakes his head saying, "I can't believe we got ourselves into this, Drew. I hadn't bargained on this kinda shit. Of all the places we could've ended up, it has to come down to dyin' tonight in this shit-hole. I wonder if anybody will ever know what happened to us? We'll probably just be another stat of Marines killed in action in the paper back home? I don't want to be remembered that way."

"I don't either," I say, feeling anger welling up. "I can tell ya this, though, if we put up one helluva fight, they'll hear about us. That's the only thing we have left. Our families will hear about our courage right up to the last man. If anything, we could do something so heroic that they'll have to write about us. You know, like Hill 881, where all those Marines got wasted holding the perimeter. We used to talk about it in boot camp."

Scott becomes indignant. "Yeah, we could make those NVAs pay up big for this one. Whadaya say, Drew? Let's get some tonight."

I begin feeling enraged and imagine us being in the news. "Yeah, I want my friends back home to remember me by the way I fight tonight. They'll know we just didn't lie down and die. I want them to know that we are the best that the Marines have. I'm gonna kill some gooks tonight! Lets prepare for a frontal assault, Scott."

Scott begins unhooking grenades from his shoulder harness. "Drew, bend the pins of the grenades back so we can pull 'em out real easy. I have 12 grenades. How many do you have?"

I go through my pack and check the shoulder straps of my clutch belt. "I have ten."

"Great!" Scott smiles for the first time in days. "Place each one of those mamas on the ledge." We carefully position the grenades side-by-side on the ledge in front of us. "Good!" Scott exclaims. "Now come at us, Charlie, and we'll show you some fun! You got any Willie Peter's, Drew?"

"Yeah, I got two in my pack. That white phosphorous will burn the shit out of 'em. I'll get 'em out and fix the cotter pins," I say eagerly.

"Yeah, fix 'em, 'cause we're gonna fry up some gooks tonight. All right, get your magazines out and then put your bayonet on your M-16."

"Okay, I have 14 magazines with 18 rounds apiece." I hold one up to show Scott.

"Great! Now here's the story: When they hit, they'll hit fast. There could be 2,000 of 'em comin' at us. They'll start with a mortar barrage to keep us down in our holes. We got to keep our eyes above the ground," Scott insists. "Then they'll come right at us in a human wave assault." Scott's jet black eyes are blinking intensely. "We'll blow the Claymores first, then we'll throw grenades as fast as we can." He hesitates for a moment in thought. "If a Chi-com grenade rolls in our pod, toss it back at 'em. Once we've thrown all our grenades, start firing your M-16. I'll toss the Willie Peters and fry the mothers." Scott is squeezing a grenade in one trembling hand while holding up a Willie Peter in the other. "Whadaya think, Drew?"

"It's time to kill some gooks, Scott," I say, with conviction. "I'm gonna take as many with me as I can." I have never felt such a strong urge to fight in spite of any consequences. Life has no other meaning but to leave a legacy of heroism about myself. "Victor Charlie is definitely messing with the wrong platoon tonight, my man. Mike Company, Third Platoon, will be in the headlines tomorrow and all our people back home will know it was us. We're gonna go down hard. Now, let's be quiet and wait."

I scoot down into the foxhole eye level with the ground. I look into the jungle for the least little movement and listen for any unusual sounds—the rustling of a bush, the snap of a twig, or even voices. It's a sinister, hot, and sticky night. Mosquitoes hover inches from my face, closing in as the repellent begins to fade. About every half hour, I dowse my face and hands with just enough sweet-stink to keep the bugs at bay. Nice stuff but it has its drawbacks because the gooks can smell us a mile away. We advertise our position like a neon sign in the jungle night rather than being chewed up by mosquitoes. The gooks never use it. They are at one with the bugs, flies, and mosquitoes. They grow up as hosts to all that slithers, hops, and flies. As I crouch in my foxhole, I vividly recall the awful scene a few days ago of an old Vietnamese woman in a godforsaken hooch.

*   *   *   *   *   *   *

We had just completed a standard sweep through a ville searching for VC when I came across what appeared to be an uninhabited hooch. I remember how I inched my way along the front of the hooch to the door, trying to sense anything unusual. Slowly, I opened the bamboo mat that covered the entrance and carefully walked in keeping my eyes focused on the floor for booby traps. I almost gagged from what smelled like something decomposing inside the hooch. I thought I was seeing things. The whole floor appeared unusually black and, at second glance, was literally vibrating. I stood still, peering down at the moving floor. Again, I thought my eyes were playing tricks on me. I concentrated on a smaller piece of the floor. It seemed that each small segment had its own creepy, crawly little glitter to it. Wings! They turned, twisted, fluttered, and gleamed. It covered the whole expanse of the dirt floor. It looked like a black magic carpet of filth. My eyes weren't playing tricks on me after all. I finally made out what I was actually seeing. It was thousands upon thousands of black, beady-eyed flies dancing in a circular motion with their own dirty little mission of devouring and regurgitating the wretched soup beneath. Slowly, purposefully, they each teetered and circled with upstretched silky black wings. Together, the swarm of thousands moved and swayed with a hideous hypnotic rhythm.

I scanned the surface for more horrible truth. The hooch was miserably hot and smelled putrid. I tried not to squint, fearing a moment's loss of concentration might be my last. The silky black carpet of flies seemed to rise in the center and then taper off. It looked like a mound rising from under the black carpet in the middle of the hooch. I observed the humped figure more closely and the reality of what I was seeing began to sink in. It was round and small at the top and it suddenly turned a little to the right. I wasn't sure if it really moved. I looked at the figure again. The large round middle rose and fell. It seemed to be breathing. There were two long lines that trailed from the middle of the figure ending a few feet from where I stood. Chills ran up my spine when the whole figure moved. The flies danced around, momentarily exposing parts of what lay beneath the magic carpet. I glimpsed a finger, an earlobe, a shriveled breast, and part of a leg. I looked again toward the head. She blinked her eyes and two black slits opened in the carpet of flies. Two human eyes peeked out of the depths of hell itself! An old woman lay on her back under the magic carpet from the underworld!

The old woman ever so slowly blinked again and the flies moved across her eyes. They were so thick they covered her eyelids. They were one with her and she was one with them. She moved her hand in a waving motion across her face. Hundreds of flies stirred and moved down onto the floor exposing more of the old woman's body. A finger dangled from one of her hands. Stubs and parts of fingers composed the other hand. Open sores covered her mid-section and flies sucked and danced on her wounds.

The stench within the small hooch intensified and I became aware of her plight. I couldn't mistake the horrid smell, because once you've smelled it, you never forget. I had first smelled it about a month ago outside the village of Nui Kim San. It was a colony of dying lepers. It was a safe haven for the VC since the Marines avoided the colony because of the fear of getting leprosy.

I looked down at the old leper woman with pity. No one should have to die like this—alone, with the only living thing that will accompany her—a carpet of flies. A moving suction cup that soothed her irritated wounds.

Two Marines walked in the hooch and immediately started laughing. I turned to see it was Taylor and Haus, who were still pissed about losing Jessie out of their squad. They had lost another friend to a booby trap just before I arrived. They hated the civilians almost as much as they hated the VC. To them, the only good gook was a dead gook. They looked down at the old woman and started jiving and chuckling like they were back in the streets of Camden, New Jersey. I smiled in recognition. It was a defensive smile, so not to show fear or sympathy or guilt or any of the other so-called normal emotional reactions to the horror. It was a good way to hide the part of me that still related to another human being, regardless of the color of their skin or beliefs. Smile, just keep smiling.

"Hey, you mama-san bitch," they snapped. "What you doin' livin' like a fuckin' druggie?" They gave each other "five." "You're a filthy mama-san bitch and you need to get your silly ass cleaned." They laughed more while unbuttoning their pants. Then, they held their genitals over the old leper woman and pissed all over her. She didn't move. The instant hum of hundreds of flies hovering a few inches from the floor mixed with the splashing urine that stirred the magic carpet.

I watched, not saying a word. Her eyes never left mine. She had large, penetrating black eyes that spoke to me through the filth and degradation. I felt her tugging at my soul, pulling me close to her.

Suddenly, the two Marines started beating her with the barrels of their M-16s. The old woman grunted but her eyes never flinched. She kept peering into the depths of my being. God, how I wanted to do something! Just say no! Please, no! I wanted to scream it, but I didn't say a word. Instead, I acted brash and arrogant, forcing a smile to hide my revulsion.

Finally, the beating stopped. We walked out of the hooch and the two Marines pulled their Zippo lighters out and lit them. My heart sank as I realized what they were about to do.

"Hey baby, let's torch this hooch for Jessie!" Taylor was no longer smiling.

"Yeah!" Haus yelled. "Jessie's foot for a hooch! We'll write him about our payback for the booby trap that got his black ass. He'll be real happy to hear this shit."

"Let's waste this whole mess!" Taylor said.

"Ma-ma-san's still in there," I said.

"That's her fuckin' problem," Haus snapped. They were in no mood to argue. "She can crawl her silly ass out, if she wants. Beat it, Drew!"

They ignited the dry straw of the hooch. Within a minute the entire outside of the dwelling was ablaze. I shuddered to think what was about to happen as the walls of the hooch began to crumble. In defense, I quietly turned and walked away. All those hideous flies swelling and bursting in the heat of the flames—it was music to my ears. I felt good about the destruction of the black magic carpet. Yeah, it was nothing more than a toxic waste dump that had to go. I won't think about the horror that lay inside the hooch. Easy enough, I will just put it out of my mind.

*   *   *   *   *   *   *

Now, still crouched in my foxhole, I stare into the jungle thinking about how the old woman and the flies were one with each other. This is how they live over here, outside in the jungle and rice paddies with the animals and insects.

The mosquitoes hover inches from my face. I pull the mosquito repellent from my helmet and dowse my face with the sweet-stink. The mosquitoes back off six inches and await their next assault.

Scott snickers, "Hey, Drew, quit messin' with those mosquitoes, man. They gotta eat, too."

"Well, let 'em try some dark meat instead of pickin' on me," I say. Like everyone, I hope to catch malaria and get a cheap ride back to the States. However, after tonight it isn't going to matter once the NVAs attack. This will be my last night on earth. The thought of dying sends waves of panic through me. That's when I keep remembering the old woman's eyes. I don't want to die like this—being haunted by those dark, penetrating eyes peeking out of the black magic carpet. I still see the slow blink of her eyelids that the flies had grown accustomed to. It must have been years that she had lived like that. Jesus, how could anyone live like that?

I know Taylor and Haus aren't haunted by her eyes. They laughed and said that she was a joke—a freak of nature that needed to be wiped off the planet, a human garbage dump for the flies and maggots that had to be destroyed. They had no second thoughts about burning the hooch. Just a simple flip of the Zippo and it was history. A good deed done, and one less gook to worry about.

God, I want to be like them—to make her eyes go away. Why can't I believe my rationalizations about her? The truth is, I hadn't done anything to help her. I stood by watching the carnage feeling like a detached bystander, something I was learning to do since my first experiences in the field. Now I was getting good at it. You could turn your back, close your eyes, or just walk away, but don't ever challenge the beating and killing of civilians or you're a marked man. What a hellhole this place is.

So, tonight I will leave a legacy of myself for others to read about. Something like the Alamo, Pork Chop Hill, Iwo Jima, or some other heroic place where men gave their lives for a good cause. It will be difficult writing a story so that people will see us as heroes. It will take a good military journalist to do that. I imagine the piece reading: "Early yesterday morning at 0400 hours, a handful of Marines gave their lives to hold a clearing in the thick jungle terrain outside DaNang, Vietnam. They heroically fought down to the last man before B-52 bombers were called in to destroy the embattled encampment. As a result of their efforts, the Communists were dealt a serious setback in their efforts to gain a foothold in the area."

Yeah, I hope they make it sound as if we died for a good cause. Not for the hooches and villes we destroy each day, nor for the civilians we waste like animals. Closer to the truth could be read in the Communist people's newspaper distributed in Ho Chi Mihn's Hanoi. The truth would read like this: "Two battalions of the Fourth Regiment, Fifth NVA Division, were involved in heavy hand-to-hand combat south of DaNang yesterday morning. The enemy was identified as elements of Mike Company, Third Battalion of the First Marine Division. The South Vietnamese people joined in celebration as a long and brutal rule was finally ended in the area. The People's Republic reported many civilian deaths over the years since the U.S. Marines infiltrated the area. The people that inhabit the villages in the area have suffered innumerable atrocities at the hands of this force of Marines. The NVA regiment went on to inflict heavy casualties on enemy forces closer to DaNang, causing great loss of life and territory. We the people are beginning to take our country back!"

That's the truth of it! We are not the people and we are not fighting for the people of this country. We are simply trying to save our asses—plain and simple. We all just want a ticket out of this bullshit hellhole, and they can have this bug-infested place forever.

Sweat drips from my forehead. I wipe my brow and brush away mosquitoes that got through the sweet-stink. I reach up and squeeze the cloth picture of St. Joseph that hangs around my neck. My mother had given me this scapular believing that if I were killed while wearing it, all my sins would be forgiven. She knows I believe in God and country. I am glad she will never know about the old woman that lay beneath the black magic carpet. She would say it was not like me to have turned my back like that. I was raised better and should have done the right thing. Well, she will never know what happened. No one else will either. This will go to the grave with me tonight.

"Drew," Scott snaps. "Hey, are you keepin' your eyes open or are you dreamin', man?"

"No, I'm awake and ready for whatever Victor Charlie wants to throw at us. Just thinkin' a little 'bout my girl."

"Yeah, well you know what thinkin' will do, so knock it off!"

I scoot down into my foxhole and scan the perimeter. The moon has slipped from the sky and in its place, thousands of galactic jewels light the jungle. The time passes quietly until 0300 hours. Then, I hear what sounds like small twigs snapping. "Scott, I hear something out in front of us in the trees." Scott leans forward and peers into the abyss. It's as if he has some kind of mental radar he developed over six months of combat. He strains his eyes and listens intently to the sounds in the jungle. "Yeah, they're out there."

"I hear someone coming at us from the right," I say.

"Get ready to blow those Claymores, Drew!" Scott whispers.

"Hey, it's me, Fuller. I got the starlight scope." He rolls over into our hole.

"Drew! Scott! They're all around us. Hundreds of 'em." Fuller's voice is shaking. "Here, look through the scope."

I grab the scope, not believing his words. The whole jungle takes on a neon-green haze as I look into the magical starlight scope. The trees and shrubs are dark objects cast in emerald green. The ground cover is a dark hunter green. Stars sparkle in the background as squiggly white lines. I hold the scope very steady now. Behind the trees are hundreds of small human figures that appear to be moving in a line in front of our position. I look harder into the scope and see they are men with rifles wearing helmets. Their green heads bob in the foliage like a pack of wolves anxiously awaiting the time to attack.

"God, Scott." I whisper. "This is incredible. Look at this!" I hand the scope to Scott.

He peers into it and says, "Isn't there any chance of getting reinforcements from Battalion, Fuller?"

"No dice. You know everyone's got to hold their ground in other areas. By the time reinforcements get here, it will be all over."

"Fuck that shit!" Scott pounds his fist into the ground. "What about B-52s helping us?"

"Scott, you know we're in too close for that shit. Anyway, Dusty wants to wait until they're all over us before he calls for air strikes, so you better keep them off us. Hey, give me the scope," Fuller demands. "I gotta get to the next hole so the rest of the guys can see." Fuller grabs the scope and crawls off to the next foxhole.

Scott keeps his eyes focused on the jungle as he speaks. "Yeah, right, keep them off us. Just who does Fuller think we are, super grunts or what? He's getting to sound more and more like that fuckin' Dusty."

"Scott, you can hear them much clearer now. What time is it?"

"It's 0400 hours, Drew."

"They're everywhere and they don't even care if we can hear them." For some unknown reason, they aren't attacking.

"Yeah, I just wish they would go ahead and get it over with," Scott says, impatiently.

We stay crouched in our foxhole peering at the tree line. I squeeze so hard on my rifle, my hands go numb. With each second, I feel the intensity of sitting in an electric chair wondering when the executioner will throw the switch. Then, to my surprise, the jungle sounds begin trailing off.

"I sure would like to know what's goin' on out there, Drew." Scott is bobbing his head up and down trying to get a clear view into the trees. "There hasn't been a sound for a good five minutes. Charlie's either losing his balls or he's in for bigger kill. Whadaya think?"

"Man, this is weird. Things aren't happenin' like they're supposed to. What time is it, Scott? I haven't heard anything for a while."

"Shit, it's 0500 hours. I wonder why they aren't attackin' us."

"I don't know, but it's gonna be light soon and they will have lost their advantage."

"Fine by me," Scott says.

There are no more sounds coming from the jungle. I am beginning to sense some hope for the first time since this horrible night began. My adrenaline rush ends and my body begins to relax. I see the morning dawn slowly forming over the jungle. Scott's face becomes more visible.

"Hey, Scott. It looks like you're turning colors on me."

"Yeah, that's because I was close to bein' scared to death. What the hell happened? Where did all the NVAs go?"

"I don't know, but it's nearly light now, and they're nowhere around." I see clearly into the jungle and hear the stirring of Marines. "Here comes Dusty!"

"You grunts eat your mornin' C-rats. We're outta here in 30 minutes," Dusty says, as he walks by our foxhole wiping his bayonet on his jungle fatigues.

Scott asks, "What happened to all those NVAs out there, Dusty?" "Don't know. Cap said they decided against assaultin' us at the last minute. Says they figured we'd slow 'em down too much, then they'd miss their main objective—DaNang. They had that right, for sure. Well, just another uneventful night in the Nam, fellas." Dusty laughs and walks away.

We eat our C-rats, pack up our gear, and slowly maneuver our way back into the jungle.

CHAPTER V

The Devil

Early November 1967

After surviving the "uneventful night" in the Nam, we were in the bush for another week searching for Charles and avoiding booby traps. Some days went by with no action at all, while at other times we were engaged in small firefights with Charlie all day long. Reports keep rolling in that NVA units and the VC are hiding in villes and ambushing Marine patrols as they approach. Most platoons have taken casualties over the past couple of weeks and I sense it's just a matter of time before we begin calling for medevacs.

Today, Dusty assigns me to first squad to help walk point and look for booby traps. We are uptight from recent sniper attacks as we approach a VC-controlled ville located on the far side of some rice paddies about five miles from our battalion area. Suddenly, loud cracks from what sounds like two AK-47s come from the general direction of the ville. I squat onto my haunches and hear bullets hitting the tree limbs around me. At this point, I'm not too alarmed, just getting more angry with each near miss. Then Cap passes the word for us to get on line and assault the ville. We move forward, alternating one squad at a time, shooting at suspect enemy positions as we move along. By the time we get to the ville, the enemy fire has stopped and there is no sign of Charlie. Dusty comes forward looking pissed and starts rounding up the civilians. He pushes them around and begins hitting them on their heads with the flash suppresser of his rifle. The older women and the kids start crying, so Dusty makes them sit down in a circle poking them with his rifle if they don't shut up. He calls us together and assigns us to small groups of civilians. He clamors, "Okay, Drew—you, Killer, Caldwell, and Taylor take these mama-sans and kids and check out their hooch for signs of Charlie. He grabs two old women, two boys of about 9 or 10, and a young girl of about 17 out of the group. He tosses them at us one at a time like he is handling ragdolls.

They hold their hands out in prayer, wailing and pleading for mercy. "Oh no! Please, Murine. Me, mama-san! No hurt mama-san!" they beg.

It has been a long, hot, anxious day of avoiding booby traps and it's now topped off by taking fire from this ville. Killer smacks the two old women upside the head saying, "You fuckin' bitches, shut the fuck up!" Killer isn't much bigger than any of them but he is meaner than a cornered rat. He chuckles while grabbing one of them by the arm and pulling her around in a circle. He keeps yanking her arm causing her to jump and jitter like a marionette. Taylor joins in by hitting the old women on her head with the flash-suppresser of his M-16 whenever she stops jitterbugging. After the fun and games are over, Killer pushes the two old women ahead of him toward a couple of hooches that are tucked next to some bamboo trees. I grab the two kids by the arms and pull them along behind the others. Caldwell grabs the young girl by her hair and is laughing as he drags her alongside me.

I keep my eyes on Killer as we approach the hooch, since his reputation is built around being a tunnel-rat and a callous killing machine. He's only about 5'5" and can wiggle through the narrow openings of caves made by the VC. Killer will confront danger almost anywhere but especially underground. Once I was told to go underwater to find the entrance of a VC cave hidden somewhere along the banks of a river. I was absolutely petrified, but Killer jumped at the opportunity, saving me the embarrassment of trying to beg out of the job. He built his reputation by killing VC women with a knife, without emotion. He speaks very little to anyone, keeping to himself, and seems to enjoy the Nam.

"Tie these bitches up!" Taylor shouts. "Let's check the hooches out for Charlie. Yeah, if we find that Charlie's been in the hooch, let's get some slant-eye pussy!" he says excitedly.

I take the kids away from the hooch and make them sit on the ground facing a rice paddy. I stand by watching Killer tie the three women up and face them belly-down on the ground. Caldwell and Taylor are inside the hooch yelling and throwing things around. Caldwell's a tall, skinny redneck who's slow on the uptake, and enjoys spitting tobacco on the civilians. He doesn't have any limits and will participate in anything.

"Oh, boy! Look what I found." Taylor is smiling as he walks out of the hooch, holding up some old boots and a small rucksack. "Check those kids out for pack marks, Drew. I'll bet those gook kids are humpin' supplies for Charlie." Taylor throws the feeble evidence to the ground next to the three women. I stand the kids up and pull their shirts down off their shoulders exposing their backs. "Yeah, look here," Taylor says. "See those pack marks!" Taylor points just below the shoulder blades of one of the kids. I look hard at the kid's back but can't see anything. "Yeah! These kids are truckin' for Charlie," he says. "See those marks, Drew?" I move to within a few inches of the boy's skin and study his pigmentation.

"Yeah, I think I see it!" I am beginning to see something, but as I back away, it disappears.

"Yeah, all these gooks are working for Charlie," Taylor snarls. "I want some pun-tang for my troubles. Whadaya say guys? I'll go first!" Caldwell yanks the young girl he's been in charge of by the hair and pulls her into one of the hooches. Taylor grabs one of the two older women and drags her into another hooch leaving the mat open to the inside. I watch him pick her up and lay her down on a small crude bamboo table. She doesn't make a sound or try to resist him in any way. It's as if she has been through this many times before. Then I hear the young girl crying loudly from the other hooch.

"Come on, bitch, suck on it and all is forgiven!" Caldwell bellows. "That's it baby. Suck!"

Killer's eyes are as big as saucers as he says, "Hey, Drew, I'm next. Then, it's your turn." He looks as if he can hardly contain himself.

"Hey, I don't know about this, Killer," I say with trepidation. "This isn't what I call fun. Killer, this is bullshit." I hardly muster up enough will to talk and begin to feel sick to my stomach. I look back toward the other hooch where Taylor is openly raping the older woman. His pants are down around his ankles and the woman's legs are sticking up and around his back. Taylor is pumping away as if there is no tomorrow. I see other Marines in the background routinely searching out the remaining hooches. Some look on, but with little or no concern. Caldwell walks out of the hooch, saying, "Okay, Killer, she's all yours. She has some good lips on her." Caldwell high-steps toward Killer and gives him "five." The girl is still crying as Killer parts the stray mat with a smile and walks into the hooch. I can't look toward the other hooch where Taylor is raping the old woman. I sit next to the kids and stare out at the rice paddy.

I'm really feeling the pressure to become one of the hardcore members of the platoon. Getting my first gook is one thing, but I am expected to move on to more insidious, evil acts. Becoming an animal in the eyes of others is the next step. Now, I will be evaluated on how well I rape or kill in cold blood. It seems I am constantly being pressed to walk the fine line between bravery and blackhearted insanity.

The young girl is crying and I hear Killer laughing and taunting her. He has been in there awhile and it will soon be my turn. The word will get back to Dusty on how I handle myself today. Will I be seen as a coward or part of his killing machine?

"Hey, watch the kids for a minute," I say to Caldwell. "I gotta take a leak. I'll be right back." I walk over to the other side of the ville between two hooches where there are some trees. I turn to walk behind the hooches and stop dead in my tracks. Ten yards to my right front, four Marines have a woman stretched out in midair like they are dusting a blanket. Each of the guys has hold of an arm or a leg and is swaying her high into the air and smashing her down onto the ground. There is a loud thud when she collides to the ground, followed by a hissing sound as the air is forced out of her dying lungs. She is unconscious and the guys go about their task without emotion or concern. I look at the stone cold faces of the four Marines and remain paralyzed, trying to comprehend the rationale of this brutality. I shared foxholes with all of them at one time or another and I thought I knew them as well as I know myself. They are putting a lot of effort into each slam as if to end it quickly. There is no reasonable answer to this senseless act; only rage and the belief that to kill a gook is a good thing. I am still resisting the hard reality that life in Vietnam is nothing more than a training ground for the American killing machine.

"Thud!" Her body smashes to the ground again. Then, "swish" as the air squeezes from her lungs. There doesn't appear to be any life left in her pancaked body. In defense, I turn and walk away from the carnage, hoping it will stop before she is dead. Yeah, they will stop and she will be okay. She didn't seem to be hitting the ground that hard anyway. She could have been just faking being unconscious, thinking that the Marines will soon let up. Yeah, they'll stop in a minute. I'll just stroll back over to the other hooch and forget all of this.

When I get back to the hooch, I wonder if I had really seen what I thought I had seen. I know these guys, and they would never do anything like that. They all have families, friends, and girlfriends back home they care about. This is just a figment of my imagination. I am probably overreacting and the woman will be all right. Easy enough, just put it out of my mind.

Killer exits the hooch saying, "Hey, Drew, it's your turn, baby. Don't pay any attention to the whiney bitch. Yeah, buddy, Drew's gonna get some now!" Caldwell joins in by clapping and laughing.

I can't believe I am becoming part of this horrendous act. I am feeling enormous pressure to do something or be labeled a coward by the hardcore members of the platoon. If I'm labeled a coward, I will be fragged or wasted in a firefight. I slowly get up and walk into the hooch. The young girl holds her finger out shaking it at me, while she huddles in a corner crying out, "You devil-Murine. You devil!"

"Come on, Drew, get some!" They holler from outside the hooch.

"Yeah, get some of those big lips, Drew."

I hesitantly walk toward the young girl. She cries out, "You devil-Murine! You devil-Murine!" I unbutton my pants feeling sick to my stomach. She raises herself while crying, and leans forward toward my midsection. She knows what is expected of her. Her wailing racks my insides. She reaches up and grabs hold of me and starts pulling while she cries and sobs saying, "Devil! Devil! Devil!" Her words pound away at my insides and echo in my head—Devil!—the true spirit of evil—the ruler of the great underworld. My Catholic upbringing taught me well about this evil spirit from Hell. Now, I'm his angel. In self-disgust, I push her away from me and button my pants back up. She puts her hands over her eyes and falls back into the corner of the hooch, sobbing.

"Damn it!" I shout, while walking out of the hooch. "You can't even give a good blow job. Shit, I can't get hard with her cryin' like that."

Caldwell and Killer are laughing. "Drew, you just don't know when you're hard or soft, man," Killer says. I force a laugh and then turn and walk over to where the kids are sitting. Inwardly, I feel disgusted with myself. Some of the others must feel the same way but it's the kind of thing that no one talks about. There are too many firefights, booby traps, and ambushes caused by civilians to take the risk of sticking one's neck out to help them. I wonder how much longer I'll get away with living on the edge of this insane world.

Later, we torch the ville while the civilians stand at the edge of the jungle watching their homes go up in flames. We form a staggered column and move toward distant rice paddies that are closer to the battalion area. I look back and see a cloud of dark smoke rising high into the blue sky above the burning hooches. This is the Vietnam War I had never envisioned. I had always believed that American fighting men were brave and honorable like John Wayne and Audie Murphy. This war, however, is nothing like the movies. I feel empty, betrayed, and alone in a world of chaos. Nothing makes sense any more.

After marching for several hours, we set in at the end of the day forming a perimeter around a friendly ville consisting of five hooches. It's been a hot, grueling afternoon and we welcome the opportunity to rest and put the earlier events behind us. Forgetting and going onto something else is always the hardest part for me. I sit on a straw mat next to a tree, thinking about the woman who had been unmercifully slammed to the ground. Maybe she was faking being unconscious, perhaps believing the guys would stop. Maybe they did stop and she's all right. That ville had it coming anyway since there have been so many Marine casualties in the area surrounding the ville.

As I ponder what happened today, I see some Vietnamese children in the distance chasing each other in a game of tag. They seem oblivious to the war, momentarily escaping into a world of make-believe. Watching the children takes me back to my childhood when a time of innocence and freedom was suddenly interrupted by confusion and uncertainty. I wish I could turn the clock back and change the course of events which led me to Vietnam. I had no idea what was awaiting me over here. I sink deeper into myself as I watch the children play, and recall the fateful events that led me to this far-away Asian land.

*   *   *   *   *   *   *

I was born in New Orleans, Louisiana, following the roar of victory and celebration after World War II ended. My father had been in the Navy and was seriously wounded while onboard an aircraft carrier during the battle of Tarawa. He was sent to Columbus, Ohio, to recover from his wounds and to recruit for the military. During his stint in Columbus, he met Mom, a pretty 16-year-old high school student looking for the right guy in uniform. After a few blissful months of courting, they were married and quickly moved back to Dad's hometown of New Orleans where I was born nine months later on July 11, 1946. Mom and Dad were Catholic and practiced the rhythm method of birth control. My brother Hank was born a year later, followed by Bradley, Mark, and Cynthia.

We lived in New Orleans, not far from the French Quarter where the sound of ragtime and jazz drifted through the night air like sweet perfume. Our house was an old, white two-story with chipped and blistered paint from years of baking in the bright Louisiana sun. My playhouse was a backyard shed full of the most valuable junk on earth. The shed was also a hideout for an old tomcat who stalked mice and cockroaches through the rubble. He purred proudly whenever he brought a trophy to the back door for Mom to see. Mom usually grimaced and hollered at the old tom and shooed him away. When he ran away, he never jumped the fence to the house next door. It was believed to be haunted and inhabited by strange creatures. The grass was nearly 7-feet high and draped over our fence like the wispy hands of a ghost. My grandfather told us the overgrown yard was home to several large alligators who were known to dine on small animals and children. No one ever ventured into the yard or the vacant house, not even the old tomcat. When I turned 4, while chasing dragonflies in the back yard, I fell on a bottle cap and split open my kneecap. Blood was everywhere and I could almost hear the alligators stirring in the yard next door. The old tomcat sat on the roof of the shed, his head tilted slightly downward, stoically watching me. Oh, how I wanted to change places with him. Before long, Mom and Dad ran out of the house screaming louder than fire engines. That's when I broke down and cried. Dad carried me to our car and we rushed to the hospital. A doctor wearing a mask and white coat used a needle and thread to stitch my knee. Mom embraced my head so tightly, I could see only the doctor's hand as he raised the needle after each stitch. Afterwards, Mom told everyone that I was a good boy because I didn't cry during the procedure. I wanted to be strong, like the old tomcat, and never again break down and cry.

When I was almost 5, one of Dad's friends offered him a traveling sales job in Columbus, Ohio. Dad jumped at the opportunity to make more money, and Mom was glad to move back home where her sister and friends lived. We left the old tomcat with grandma and traveled north in a 1949 Studebaker equipped with running boards and a silver horse on the hood. We all rubbed the hood ornament for good luck whenever we got into the car. The trip took three days of traveling on winding roads, past fields of tobacco and cotton, and through towering mountains and woodlands. The whole country changed before my eyes. One night, Indians wearing warpaint checked us into a motel cottage made in the shape of a teepee. During the evening, they played drums and danced around a bonfire. They looked just like the Indians on "The Lone Ranger" and it was the most exciting thing I had ever seen. The rest of the trip was uneventful, other than the stifling air circulating through the car and the fact there was never a bathroom when we needed one.

Once we arrived in Columbus, we settled into a small apartment located on a brick alleyway close to downtown near the railroad depot. Around the corner from our apartment was a bar called the Seven Eleven Club. Country music blared from the early afternoon through the wee hours of the morning. One night, curiosity about the lively place got the best of my brother Hank and me. We sneaked out of the house and made our way to the open doorway of the bar and looked inside. I saw three band members dressed in glittery cowboy suits strumming guitars and singing foot-stomping music. Colorful lights flashed while men and women spun around in a frenzy, unlike anything I had ever seen. People at the bar were drinking beer and smoking cigarettes while they sang along with the band. Smoke flowed out the door like the mist from a genie's lamp. They seemed to be having such a great time, I hoped that someday I would be able to dance with the girls at the Seven Eleven Club.

The people in the bar were a stark contrast to the men with straggly hair and long beards who hung around our apartment. They sat in the alleyway with their heads down, leaning against the walls of buildings, occasionally raising up to drink wine out of paper bags. During the day, they would come to our door wearing dirty bib overalls and beg for money. Mom gave them sandwiches, explaining to us that they were alcoholics and would use the money only to buy booze. Some nights they would force open an outside entrance to our basement and go downstairs to sleep. I could hear them stumbling across the cement floor in clodhoppers as they prepared to bed down in the musty, rat-infested basement. I lay awake listening to their every move and wondered how they got into this horrible condition. Late one night when Dad was away on business, I heard two of the old bums walk up the wooden steps from the basement and onto the sidewalk in front of my window. One of them stuck a screwdriver under my window trying to pry it open. I pulled the covers over my head and curled into a little ball. They were talking and hitting the wooden window pain with their fists to jar it loose. My heart was beating with such a frenzy, I literally froze with fear and was unable to move. Fortunately, Uncle Jack lived in the apartment above us and heard the commotion. He dropped a vase on the sidewalk next to where the intruders were standing and scared them off. The police arrived a few minutes later with sirens blaring and lights flashing. After taking their report, the police assured Mom they would make regular checks by driving by our apartment at night, since Dad was on the road a lot during the week. I was always scared of the guys who walked the alleyways near our apartment, and grew up believing all alcoholics were skid row bums.

Mom had her hands full raising five kids who produced enough dirty dishes and muddy clothes to equal a small platoon. She was always there to tend to our needs and nurse our wounds. My fondest memories are of Mom's Sunday dinners when the smell of macaroni and cheese and homemade rolls permeated the house. I always took a nap in the afternoon and would usually awaken to the sound of chicken crackling in the frying pan. Mom would ask us to set the table and there was a frantic rush to the kitchen to help out. Once dinner was on the table, we fought for a seat closest to the platter of chicken. Dad started the dinner with the sign of the cross followed by the blessing. I bowed my head in reverence and gibbered along with the family, feeling guilty because the only thing on my mind was food. When the blessing was over, everybody grabbed for their favorite piece of chicken, like a group of heathens who hadn't eaten in days. Ten minutes later, dinner was over and no one volunteered to do the dishes.

Because of his sales job, Dad was rarely around during the week. I didn't see much of him on weekends either, because he was usually out with friends at bars. Dad could really hold his booze and, like his father, he was proud that drinking never interfered with his ability to bring home a paycheck. I once waited all week to tell him about how I wanted to become a football player. Dad finally stumbled into the house, reeking of booze. He walked into the kitchen and leaned against the stove. I eagerly began telling him about my aspirations when his head fell to his chest and he started snoring. I was mystified and puzzled by the way he could fall asleep while standing up.

One Christmas Eve when Dad was sitting on the sofa drinking beer, I asked him what time Santa Claus was coming to our house. He said Santa had a long trip from the North Pole and would arrive sometime after my brother Hank and I went to bed. Then, he walked over to the cabinet and pulled a fifth of whiskey down from the shelf, saying Santa would like to have something to nourish his tired body when he arrived. He told us to arrange shot glasses of whiskey on the kitchen counter for Santa to drink. We thought alcohol was the best Christmas gift we could give Santa. Consuming alcohol was as common in our household as drinking water. Mom and Dad sentenced all of us to Catholic school for 12 years. My second grade teacher, Mrs. Deach, had striking white hair and wore colorful hats and pretty dresses to school each day. She was a very caring teacher, who had a special fondness for me and depended on me to set a good example for the rest of the class. I passed second grade and felt very proud of getting A's in all of my subjects. I have a picture of my class in 1954, standing in front of Sacred Heart Church on a sunny spring day with blossoming flowers, budding trees, and bright green grass all around. Mrs. Deach had her arm around me and I felt supported and loved. That was the last time I remember feeling that way.

My problems started when Dad built us a new home on the west side of town during the summer of 1954. The move to the west side put us in the Diocese of St. Mary Magdalene where Franciscan nuns ran the school with corporal punishment. My third grade nun, Sister Gertrude, was a crusty old bag on the verge of retirement or death, and I didn't care which came first. She was stubby like a fire hydrant and had a round, wrinkled face. During the first week in her class, she caught me talking to another student while she was teaching. Sister Gertrude ordered me to the front of the room while the rest of the class sat at attention. "You children pay heed at why this new whippersnapper is being punished," she scolded. "Hold your hands out in front of you! What's your name? Oh, yes, Mr. Martensen." I cringed as I extended my palms out in front of Sister Gertrude. "Not like that, dummy!" She growled, grabbing my wrists in a vise grip and flipping my hands over. "Now hold them out straight like a man." She exhaled a smelly fish odor into my face and I almost gagged. She picked up a ruler from her desk, slapped her hand with it and said, "Three with the sharp end and three with the flat side for talking out of turn." Sister Gertrude smacked my knuckles six times as the class watched in horror. "Now put your hands down and go back to your seat," she ordered.

"Mr. Barr," she hollered. I turned to walk back to my seat and saw Ray Barr laughing. Ray was the most notorious third grader in the school. "What do you think is so funny? Has the cat got your tongue, Mr. Raymond Barr?" Ray looked up from his desk with cow eyes. "No, sister! Mr. Martensen was so stiff it looked weird, Sister."

"Oh, it did! I think you need to be taught another lesson, Mr. Barr. The rest of the class didn't think it was funny. Now was it, class?" The class chimed, "No, Sister Gertrude."

"Mr. Barr, step out of this classroom. Now!" Gertrude grabbed Ray's ear as he passed her and pulled him out the door. The classroom was dead silent, punctuated by sharp thuds on the outside wall. Sister Gertrude was scolding Ray as she pounded his head repeatedly onto the concrete wall. "Now, is that funny Mr. Barr?" she tooted.

You could hear Ray yelling, "No, Sister! No, Sister!" Eventually, Ray walked back into the classroom holding his head down. The class remained quiet but nervous the rest of the day. I felt guilty and stunned by the whole incident.

Throughout the year all the boys in the class were engulfed in a constant battle with Sister Gertrude. I failed third grade as the final punishment imposed upon me. I never saw her again and surmise that our school principal, Father Bouchard, probably got sick and tired of hearing her confessions and forced her retirement. When Mom and Dad learned that I failed third grade, they asked if there was anything I wanted to say about it. Part of me wanted to break down and cry and have them hold me. Nevertheless, I told them everything was okay and I could handle things. I thought Dad would be impressed by my courage.

The elementary years crawled by with numerous battles with the nuns and a multitude of confessions for boyhood sins. My grades in most subjects were low or failing and I absolutely dreaded going to school.

Fortunately, a man came into my life who gave me a sense of learning and accomplishment. He also provided me with the knowledge of weaponry, a skill his family had passed down from generation to generation. This was my next door neighbor, Paul.

Paul was a hulk of a man from the hills of southern Ohio. He was a welder by trade and loved the outdoors. He hunted on weekends and during the weekday evenings, he worked on guns in his basement. I was absolutely fascinated with learning about real guns and ammunition. I had grown up playing cowboys and Indians with neighborhood kids and watching television movies that depicted American men with guns fighting victoriously over the Indians. This was an opportunity for me to learn about the most powerful tool a man could own—a gun.

My early experiences with Paul began in fifth grade. I eagerly went to his house after school and watched him load shotgun shells, and listened to tales of hunting wild game. I learned about gun safety and how to handle weapons. He stressed to always check the chamber of a shotgun to make sure it wasn't loaded, and to never point the barrel at someone unless I was prepared to squeeze the trigger. He taught me how to put my thumb on the safety and my index finger on the trigger while cradling the upper portion of the stock over my left arm so the barrel pointed at the ground. "A good hunter never forgets where the barrel of his gun is pointing," he stressed again and again.

Eventually, the day came in the winter of seventh grade when Paul took me to a field for target practice. I shot at paint cans he placed about 20 yards in front of me. After each shot, we examined the extent of the damage to the cans and compared it to hitting a live target. I was in awe of the sheer power of the gun and even more fascinated by the thought of killing wild game. Paul promised to take me hunting when I got a little older and after I gained more confidence with handling a shotgun. In the meantime, he taught me how to trap muskrat and raccoon at the creek near my house. By eighth grade, I had 24 traps and knew how to string lines for two miles along the Frank Road Creek. I got up before school at 4 a.m. and walked miles checking traps, hoping to get just one precious pelt to show Paul. I was lucky if I caught one muskrat a month. On Thanksgiving morning, I trapped two muskrats and one raccoon, which I cleaned in the basement. I can't tell you how mad Mom was to wake up to the foul smell of coon guts instead of roasting turkey.

Later that year, Paul fulfilled his promise and took me rabbit hunting in southern Ohio. We went with three other experienced hunters and their beagles. We walked on line about ten yards apart with the beagles in front, happily sniffing for rabbits. The dogs yelped and howled whenever they jumped a rabbit, and the hunters shouted weird calls at the dogs to bring the rabbits full circle. Suddenly, a rabbit popped out of the bush and everyone unloaded on the poor thing so hard, there wasn't anything left to bring home. We gathered around laughing about the overkill and tried to decide who shot it first. By the end of the day, we had hit 14 rabbits but only 10 were good enough to take home. Paul gave one of the rabbits to me, claiming I had shot it. I accepted it in spite of the fact that I was well off-target all day.

When I reached high school, my relationship with Paul continued, but I also got involved with track and field and playing football. By my sophomore year, I pole-vaulted 13 feet 3 inches, just 7 inches shy of the state record. In the summer of 1963, it seemed I had a promising future in track ahead of me, but a fortuitous event occurred which changed everything. In 1963, the Beatles took America by storm and music groups sprang up across the land. I had always wanted to play guitar, so I saved my money and purchased a classical guitar from a local pawn shop. I spent countless hours after school and on weekends teaching myself how to play guitar with the aid of a cord book. Eventually, I joined a rock-and-roll band with some guys from my high school and we began playing around the state, making a name for ourselves and some extra cash to boot.

One Saturday morning in August, I was driving the band members to practice down a side street while talking about the latest hit songs. Our lead singer, Bobby Saint, was arguing that he wanted us to sing more of the old black music. Bobby loved to sing songs like "Tears on My Pillow," "Glory of Love," "What's your Name?" and so on. One of the other singers in our group, Chris Masse, liked folk music, and our base singer, Barry, was into contemporary music. It was always an accomplishment to get the three of them to agree on anything. As we drove along chattering, all of a sudden, a young boy ran from behind a bush and into the street in front of my car. I slammed on the brakes, but Mom's big Buick kept moving forward like a runaway freight train. There was nothing I could do to stop the forward velocity of the car. I caught a glimpse of the boy's blond hair as the car's hood smashed into him. He shot forward from the impact, hitting the pavement, then bounced into the air. I stomped on the brake pedal, trying to push it through the floorboard. Stop! Stop! I kept pleading. The boy fell onto the street in front of us like a ragdoll. The car kept skidding forward and I lost sight of him. Then, I heard the boy tumbling and hitting the frame beneath us. The merciless plummeting moved from the front of the car to the rear. Finally, the car came to a stop and the boy tumbled from the rear of the car onto the street. Everyone sat speechless for an eternal second.

My first thought was to stomp on the gas pedal and speed away and pretend it never happened. I looked in the rearview mirror and saw the twisted image of a small body lying in the street. Instinctively, I jumped out of the car and ran toward him. The boy's father must have heard the accident because he bolted out of a nearby house. We both reached him at the same time. The father picked up his dying son and cradled him in his arms. The boy was about 5 or 6 and he was bleeding profusely from his ears, nose, and mouth. He was unconscious, with a blue face, and his body was twisted and bent. Before long, the boy's mother darted out of the house screaming, "Jesus God! Jesus God!" All the commotion brought the neighbors out of their homes. The mother and father cradled their young son in their arms and cried out, "No! Oh my God! No!" In the distance, I heard the emergency squad's siren closing in on us. After what seemed like an eternity, the squad arrived and the medics worked feverishly on the boy to revive him. They quickly put him into the back of the squad and whisked him and his parents off to the hospital.

The siren trailed off and the scene became quiet and surreal. For a moment, I wondered if the accident had really happened. A large blood spot on the street reminded me that it had. The neighbors stood around in small groups whispering and pointing at me as the driver of the automobile. I heard more sirens in the distance approaching us. Several police cruisers pulled up and some officers jumped out of their cars. They coldly took statements from all of us. As they mapped out the accident scene and measured the skid marks, I overheard one of the policemen say that the boy probably wouldn't make it. He also said that it didn't appear I was speeding and probably couldn't have seen the boy. They took pictures of the large bush from where he had darted. I realized the bush prevented me from seeing him until he hit the hood of the car. My only thought was a burning desire to turn the clock back and make it all go away. Eventually, the police sent me home and no charges were filed.

That night, our parish priest accompanied my parents and me to the hospital to meet with the mother and father of the critically injured boy. His parents cried most of the time and told us they didn't blame me for what had happened. I was so upset, I could hardly speak. My parents rendered our deepest apologies and sympathy. Our parish priest prayed and blessed all of us. The boy teetered on the edge of life and death during the 24 hours following the accident. He eventually pulled through but suffered brain damage which required extensive rehabilitation. Our parish priest suggested we not see the family again because of the deep hurt they were experiencing.

After the accident, I stayed at home in my room thinking endlessly about the horrific event. I shared my feelings with no one, because I believed that men were supposed to be strong and handle adversity without complaining. My coaches and teachers were aware of the accident but they never said anything to me about it. I guess everyone thought the problem was being taken care of by someone else. The only way I had to deal with pent-up emotions was through sports. Unfortunately, a few months after the accident, I was cut from the football team because I was running poorly due to my deteriorating emotional state.

At that point, I was vulnerable to almost anything that would ease the pain. During the fall and winter, I started drinking alcohol on weekends with some of my friends who were old enough to buy beer. Alcohol quickly eased the mental anguish, and drinking seemed very natural, since I had grown up around it.

Dad had told me many odd and braggadocio stories about the "good life" pertaining to our relatives in New Orleans who had died of heavy drinking. My dad's father was the head of the sewer and sanitation department of New Orleans in 1925. He was also a gambler, owned a bar in the French Quarter, and prided himself on drinking a fifth of bourbon a day. At age 54 he had an esophageal hemorrhage brought on by his drinking, which killed him in a matter of minutes. My mom's mother died of sugar diabetes exacerbated by drinking alcohol. She had both legs amputated due to circulation problems from the diabetes and, when she died, a fifth of booze was at her bedside. My aunt Connie was a daily closet drinker who committed suicide after experiencing another of her long bouts of depression. Then there was Uncle Sam who died of esophageal cancer two years after retirement. He was a daily beer drinker and ran sales routes up and down the Gulf Coast all his life. He believed he couldn't be an alcoholic because he just drank beer. Alcohol had always been a common part of our family history but I didn't believe that any of these bad things would ever happen to me.

I continued playing in the band but started using our shows as an opportunity to party more often. When spring rolled around, I had failed geometry, making me ineligible for track and field. Eventually, I lost interest in pole-vaulting, which could have been my ticket to a successful track career. My drinking then increased from three to five nights a week. During the summer prior to my senior year, I was charged with a DWI. Alcohol had subtly become the dominant influence in my life. My senior year was one long alcohol binge. There were many days I was either coming off a drunk or going on another one. Outwardly, I appeared to be having fun but my innermost thoughts told me my drinking wasn't normal. There was lots of guilt and remorse following each drinking episode. I was in a fog the entire year and barely graduated from high school in 1965.

Vietnam had escalated dramatically during my last year of high school. "The Evening News with Walter Cronkite" carried live coverage about troops in combat with an elusive foe known as the VC. It had little meaning to me other than being a police action that was drafting young men into the military who didn't have deferments. Following graduation, many of my friends entered college or got married to avoid the draft. I decided to go to an electronics school in Louisville, Kentucky, which had limited academic requirements, but could still keep me out of the military. I teamed up with a couple of guys from high school and we moved into an apartment-style dormitory on the school's campus. It was my first time away from home and it proved to be a real fiasco.

I attended classes in the morning and worked at a local department store in the afternoon. Most of my evenings were spent drinking with friends and some of the evening parties became absolutely hazardous. One night I went to a party on the second floor of an apartment complex where about 25 people crammed into a one-bedroom flat to have a rendezvous with loud music, dancing, and heavy drinking. Sometime around midnight, I had to use the bathroom, so I walked out onto the balcony of the apartment and began to take a leak over the rail of the porch. However, someone in a nearby apartment had called the police, because the party had become so noisy. Two policemen who responded to the call walked under the balcony as I relieved myself over the rail. Unfortunately, they looked up and took a direct hit of pee in the face. They jumped back, pulled their guns out, and darted toward the steps leading up to the apartment. Even in my drunken state, I realized I was in big trouble. I stepped over the rail of the balcony and leaped to the ground. I landed on my feet and precariously tumbled down a small embankment. I jumped up and bolted into a cornfield next to the apartment and into the adjoining woods. I continued running for 15 or 20 minutes until I felt somewhat certain the police weren't following me. I became so tired I lay down under a tree and went to sleep.

The next morning, I walked back to my dormitory where a few of my friends were waiting for me. They stated I was fortunate the police hadn't found me. The police roughed up some of the guys at the party trying to find out my identity. The cops broke up the party and promised they would continue looking for me. By the end of the week I gathered enough courage to venture outside the school grounds, but was constantly looking over my shoulder for those two cops.

The heavy drinking and late hours began taking a toll on my school work. By the time Christmas rolled around, I was hopelessly behind in most of my subjects. Just before the holiday break, I decided to drop out of school rather than flunk out, so I returned home to live with my parents in Columbus. In January, I received my draft notice and was given two weeks to make a decision about which branch of service to enter. Both the Navy and the Air Force had a six-year waiting list before I could even begin my enlistment. The Army and Marines were the only branches I could immediately begin serving. The only other branch of service was the National Guard, and it had a billion-year waiting list.

One evening I was watching the movie To Hell and Back with Audie Murphy while consuming a 12-pack of beer. At some point during the movie, killing enemy soldiers and winning medals seemed very appealing. I also thought this might be a way to make Dad proud of me. The next morning, hungover and wanting to be a man, I enlisted in the Marine Corps for three years. The recruiter persuaded me to enlist for the additional year so I could be assigned to a battalion as a tank mechanic, which would keep me out of the infantry. Now that I was half-sober, killing enemy soldiers was beginning to seem somewhat frightening. I entered boot camp in San Diego in July of 1966 and immediately found myself marching endlessly on a parade deck while sadistic DIs yelled, kicked, and beat me into submission. It was nothing like the movies made it out to be and I realized I had made a huge mistake.

*   *   *   *   *   *   *

As I sit on the straw mat watching the Vietnamese children play, I want to turn the clock back and change the course of events that led me to this godforsaken land. Now I am living on the edge of life and death where guns are a part of my everyday existence, unlike anything I could have imagined while hunting small game with my neighbor, Paul, back in a distant Ohio countryside. Survival seems to hinge on becoming an animal like many of the others in my platoon. I think about that old tomcat perched on top of the shed in our yard in Louisiana when I was a boy. It sure would be nice to change places with him now. Of course, he would look at me indifferently as if to say, "Glad it ain't my problem, kid."

CHAPTER VI

The Riviera

Mid-November 1967

Our platoon has been assigned to a firebase along the South China Sea known as the Riviera. It's a narrow strip of beach and hedgerows just south of DaNang, as striking as the French Riviera. The only problem is, it's infested with booby traps and ambush site, making walking on this lovely beach a living nightmare.

We've been in the area for two weeks and are waiting for another platoon to reinforce our position and help defend the firebase. The word is, it will take Second Platoon about three days to get to us, so Cap orders us to reinforce the bunkers with sandbags and to dig extra foxholes to improve our defenses. Charles has been hitting us every day with mortars and machine gun fire. Just when we start to get a little peace, Charlie abruptly appears and messes up our day. The Riviera has been a lively place but everything has become unusually quiet since last night. We haven't seen hide nor tail of Charles and it seems he just vanished. Cap says that Charles has left the area and we are in for a skate. It couldn't have come at a better time, since we're all dead tired from the constant harassment.

The Riviera firebase is on a barren hill about 400 yards from the sea, surrounded on three sides by jungle. The jungle has been cut back about 100 yards beyond the perimeter and layers of concertina wire surround the entire camp. There are five wooden bunkers reinforced by sandbags around the perimeter where we stand guard day and night. Between the bunkers are small foxholes to accommodate fire teams. The jungle forms an ominous horseshoe around us with the sea at the open end. This is the problem area, because Charles crosses from north and south along the sea without being seen, then surrounds the firebase in the jungle. If we position a listening post on the sand dunes close to the beach, it could prevent Charles from surrounding us and wreaking havoc on our lines.

Cars tells me that Cap has decided to position an LP on the beach. Dusty gathers four of us together to work out the details of the LP. He points out at the sea with his bayonet as he speaks. "Set your LP up on the beach straight across from us. Scott, you're in charge, so keep these assholes in line. We think Charles has left the area, so this should be a skate for y'all. Cars, Drew, Bowman, take all your fuckin' gear, 'cause y'all will be out there for three to five days. Y'all be out there far enough we can't get to ya quickly, so don't be fallin' asleep. Any gooks walkin' along the beach during the day ain't supposed to be there, so card 'em and give us a call on what we want y'all to do with 'em. Any movement at night, blow 'em the fuck away. Just remember, we need ya to stay out there until relieved, so dig in and keep on your toes, y'all hear?" Dusty turns abruptly and walks back to the CP where Sergeant Tanner and Cap are sitting.

Scott gets nervous whenever he is put in charge of us. He speaks loudly as he begins briefing us on our assignment. "Okay, you guys know what's comin' down with the LP, so make sure we got enough ammo out there in case the shit hits the fan."

Cars is grinning at Scott. "Come on, Scott, ya know old Charlie's done hightailed his ass to monkey mountain by now. Whadaya say we relax and hang out on the LP for a while. Anyway, Dusty ain't gonna be coming' out to the LP. He'll be rolled up in that CP for the next couple of days. All we have to do is keep callin' in every four hours, so what's the big deal?"

"Ain't no big deal, Cars', just want to make sure that old Dusty thinks you're on your toes. He knows I got my shit together."

Cars chuckles, "That's not why he put you out here with us, pogue! Dusty knows we're in for a skate. That's why he put you in charge."

I put in my two cents' worth, "You guys better hope this is a skate, 'cause if it isn't, we're gonna be in some deep shit out in those dunes by ourselves." Bowman's eyes widen.

Scott points to the sea saying, "All right, let's get our gear out there before Dusty comes back and starts messin' with us." We gather our gear and slowly depart the perimeter in single-file toward the South China Sea. It's a sunny, hot day tempered by a warm breeze blowing in from the sea. The fringe of the jungle is a 100 yards to our right and left flanks as we walk toward the beach. I feel at ease knowing that Charlie has probably flown the coop, but still keep a cautious eye on the foliage around us. I notice a bush under a bamboo tree begin to vibrate and bend. My heart races and I release the safety switch on my M-16 and tighten my finger around the trigger. I keep walking forward, peering at the bush and then feel a gust of wind blow into my face. The bush suddenly bends and I realize it's just the wind blowing it around. I switch the safety on and relax the grip on the rifle. It's just another false alarm that ages you a little each day.

We cross over the top of the sand dunes and see a roar of white water smashing onto the beachhead. The surf fans out onto the beach and vanishes into the sand. The sweet aroma of an ancient sea blows into my face. Clamshells, driftwood, and dead kelp mark the tide line. It's a stark contrast to the jungle I had become accustomed to. I look into the vast open dimension of the sea and hastily shrug off my gear. The others begin to stack their gear next to mine. We all strip out of our clothes and run into the surf, yelling and beating our chests in a spontaneous release of emotion. The saltwater stings my parched lips and caresses my aching muscles. Scott jumps onto my back and throws me under the water. I try to chase him, but am knocked off my feet by a towering wave. We all laugh and play water games like a bunch of kids on vacation at the beach. It feels good to be happy, but we are on the Riviera, the place that kills.

"Better get back to our gear," Scott cautions.

"Yeah, can't believe we left our rifles on the dunes," I reply. The reality that we had put our lives at risk for a moment of freedom begins to sink in. Reluctantly, we walk from the sea and don our gear in silence and despair. "Scott, that freakin' jungle's too close for comfort." I speak with concern while shouldering my clutch belt.

Bowman takes a deep breath and says, "I'd rather be back in the perimeter than on this beachhead." He nervously scans the jungle.

"It's so close, you can see into it, but at least it will make it easy if there's some kind of movement tonight," I shrug.

Cars lights a cigarette and says, "Come on, guys! I say we take it easy for once. I mean, Charlie's gone out to get some pussy and it's time for us to have some R&R. Let's just give Dusty a call every few hours and the rest is a skate."

"Yeah," Scott says, scratching his head. "Let's dig our holes and assign watches for the night and then get some sleep."

We finally agree to take it easy and set in for the night. We begin digging foxholes in the sand but it's like digging in quicksand. After several unsuccessful attempts, we decide to use the natural ruts along the sand dunes as our cover. The sand dunes form horseshoe-shaped walls all along the beachhead which can provide adequate cover from sniper fire. Beyond the grassy dunes are weeds and shrubs that give way to the jungle. We pick a large, well-camouflaged rut in the sand dune to set up camp. I stick my head up and peek over the edge of the dune and can easily see the jungle to my right and left front. Directly in front of us, some 400 meters away, is the Riviera firebase. It seems we are in a good defensive position to observe any movement around us, but there is one possible loophole: If Charlie is able to slip down from the jungle's edge unnoticed, he could easily use the maze of sand dunes as cover to make his way toward us. In that event, we're all dead meat. However, this is unlikely, because Charles is on vacation.

Scott assigns two-hour watches starting at 2300 hours through 0700 hours. We decide to keep the same watch while on the LP until Second Platoon relieves us, which could be in a few days. Scott has the first watch, followed by me, Cars, and then Bowman. Not bad—I will net close to six hours of sleep per night—two or three more hours than usual. I relax my tired muscles and curl against a rut in the sand dune. Within a few minutes, I drift into a deep, peaceful sleep.

I dream of swimming in the Frank Road creek back home. My girlfriend, Gayle, is standing behind a tree watching me. Her blond hair blows in the wind, glistening like gold. She yells that she hasn't seen me for a long time and wants me to come to her. I grab a vine and swing over the creek dropping into the deep clear water. I begin swimming to the shore where she smiles and waves to me. I want to be with her but there is a current pushing me away. I swim harder but rapids beat against my flailing arms and legs. With great effort, I force open my eyes to find Scott kneeling above me. "Drew!" Scott barks. "Wake up! I'm gettin' tired of you actin' like a maniac every time I wake you up." I lie at the bottom of the sand dune looking up at him trying to get my bearings. Over the months in Vietnam, I developed a violent, startled response whenever awakened from sleep thinking the VC are attacking us. I sleep with "one eye open" most of the time, so this is one of the few pleasant dreams I will have to remember.

"What time is it?" I ask, shaking my head.

"It's midnight. Time for your watch. You gonna be okay?" he asks with concern.

"Yeah, I'm awake now. I'll take over. Go ahead and get some sleep." Scott crawls next to a bush growing out of the side of the sand dune, pulls a poncho over his head, and goes to sleep. I belly-crawl to the top of the dune and peer over the edge, parting the weeds to see the jungle. I stay motionless for a while, trying to get my bearings. I slowly become aware of the magnificent powers that are erupting around me. The moon illuminates the sand dunes, casting long shadows over the beachhead. The surf spirals forward onto the sand, shooting white caps into the night sky. The roar of the surf is tempered by periods of quiet harmony when the water retreats into the sea. Looming above me, on both sides, is the colossal dark jungle canopy. The jungle growth is visible only when streaks of moonlight race across the beach and onto the trees. In the distance, Puff The Magic Dragon silently spits hellfire at the ground. A free-fire zone where anything that moves is being pulverized as Puff moves across the sky. A distant thud erupts from the firebase as a four-duce mortar fires an illumination round. The object pops and a brilliant phosphorous flare ignites under a parachute, which drifts across the black sky, hissing and swaying as it glides along. An unearthly orange glow illuminates the landscape as eerie foreign objects. It just as easily could be a dream.

My watch passes quickly and at 0230 hours, I awake Cars to take over. Then, I lie comfortably into the sand and drift off to sleep. I sleep long and deep, unlike anything I have ever experienced in the bush. I wake up at 0730 to the roar of surf rolling onto the beach. The hypnotic sound caresses my mind as if I had taken a drug. It's a cloudy morning and a cool breeze blows in from the sea. This is not the Vietnam I have come to know and fear. The Riviera is too beautiful and divine to harbor evil. I am being lulled into a trance-like state and unable to resist the forces of nature. The others also look relaxed and at peace with themselves, a feeling all of us have missed. "Just another day in the Nam," says Cars.

"Yeah, I can stand this for a while," replies Bowman. "You know what this reminds me of? Those days I spent down at the river on our farm. Those were days when I could hike around the farm with my dog until evening. Then I would go home and have a great dinner, ya know?"

"Yeah, boy!" Scott interrupts. "I loved my mom's Sunday fried chicken dinners." Scott licks his lips. "Man, did you see Drew trying to cook that gook chicken the other day?" Everyone starts laughing. "Yeah, that bird left somethin' to be desired. Drew tried to sell me on just how good it tasted. Man, you white boys don't know good chicken. When we get outta here, Drew, you come up to Buffalo, and I'll treat you to some real down-home fried chicken."

Just when I'm ready to tell Scott I'll take him up on his offer, I look to my right just below an adjoining sand dune and am stunned to see three Vietnamese children about 10 to 12 years of age standing together watching us. "What do we have here?" I holler. "Where did these kids come from?" I can't believe how the kids suddenly appeared out of nowhere.

We inquisitively walk toward them. The three kids toot, "You numbah-one Murine. Murine, I your numbah-one son. Take us ta U.S. of A., Murine. We no want ta live here. Take us ta U.S., Murine. Ho Chi Mihn, VC, bad! We go with you." They beg and hold out their hands to us. "We bring you good stuff, Murine. You want tiger piss? I get you my sistah, too. You want good sistah, Murine? She give you good blow job, then you take us back with you. What say, Murine?"

Cars questions, "You got beer for Marine?"

"Yeah, Murine, we get you tiger piss. You want my sistah, too?"

"Hey, Cars, let's not be messin' around with any girls," I say.

"Let's find out what his sister's like. Maybe I want her." Cars is grinning as he speaks.

The kids blabber, "You want my sistah, Murine? Come on, Murine, I get you my sistah." I start thinking about the rape scene in the ville last week. I still hear her cries and the mournful tone in her voice when she cried out, "You devil-Murine." The words send a piercing sensation of self-hatred and shame through me. I look straight at the kids and bellow, "No! No want your sister, boy. Go get us some tiger piss." Cars, Scott, and Bowman all hiss at me. The three kids run back across the sand dunes and into the jungle.

I sit on a ridge in a sand dune and wonder how the kids were able to walk up to our position unnoticed. If they had been VC, they could have easily blown us away. There is something very suspicious about the whole thing. I share my feelings with the others but no one seems concerned, so I dismiss it, thinking they are just kids and my imagination is probably getting the best of me.

Later in the afternoon, at about 1500 hours, the two girls and the boy return with four bottles of beer. "We brought Murine good tiger piss," they say with smiles. I am excited about drinking some beer because we rarely have a chance to drink while in the field.

Cars is skeptical. "Drew, hold that gook beer up to the sun and check for glass." I grab the bottles of beer and hold each one up to the sun. It's a common procedure to check for ground glass before drinking Vietnamese beer, just like it is to check for razor blades hidden in the vagina of a

Vietnamese whore, and to wear a rubber to prevent the dreaded black siff, a venereal disease for which there is no known cure. There are many myths which we live and die by in Vietnam. "Looks good to me," Cars says, looking up at the bottle of beer. "No ground glass in this batch of tiger piss." We pop the caps on the bottles and lie back into the sand enjoying one of the few pleasures one can find in the Nam. The kids laugh and play on the beach while we enjoy our tiger piss. It's hard to believe that I am still in Vietnam.

The rest of the day and night pass uneventfully. We haven't heard a shot fired for nearly four days, a record in our platoon. The lull in the fighting and the tranquillity of the sea leave us in a state of relaxation and peace that is welcomed by all. The next afternoon the kids reappear again, playing along the beach, assuring me that my original fears are in fact unfounded. Then, at 3 or 4 o'clock, we are sitting on the side of a sand dune watching the kids play, when a fire-team led by Fuller unexpectedly ventures out from the perimeter to check on our position. When he sees us lounging in the sand with empty beer bottles strewn around and the kids playing on the beach, he goes nuts.

"You dumb fucks!" Fuller hollers. "What do you think you're doing? Get those gook kids the hell out of here!" Fuller runs onto the beach and chases the kids into the jungle. Then he walks toward us with haunched shoulders and raised eyebrows. "What the hell are you guys up to out here? Dusty's not gonna be pleased to hear about those kids hangin' around out here. He'll definitely give you a good ass-chewin' when I tell him what the fuck's been goin' on at your beach party. Dusty'll send all of ya out on a night patrol, you fucks! I came out here to let you know we have Second Platoon arriving in a little while to reinforce the perimeter. Word is that Charles is in the area again and might be planning something. Lucky that you guys weren't on his hit list. We're outta here so you better get your shit together and I mean now!"

Fuller's fire-team gets on line and walks back to the perimeter. Scott looks worried saying, "Dusty's gonna' be pissed when he hears about this shit. Here we been on vacation and Charlie's still in the area. Shit, we're lucky we didn't get our asses in a sling out here. Drew, you and Cars get up on that dune and keep an eye on the jungle. Bowman and I will stay down here and keep an eye on the beach area. Okay, let's get with it."

We maneuver into our positions with a flash of intensity that had been missing over the past three days. The hypnotic rhythm of the surf is replaced by a sixth sense that hints of danger lurking at the edge of the jungle. It's a familiar feeling that grabs and twists my gut reminding me I'm back in the Nam. It's already 1800 hours and there's only about three hours of daylight left. I remain crouched within the dune, keeping an intense fix on the terrain in front of me.

It's about 2030, just as the sun is setting, when I notice a column of four Marines moving toward us from the firebase. Scott grabs the radio and calls into the CP and relays the information to us. "Got some relief comin'. Second Platoon has arrived to reinforce the perimeter and one of their fire-teams is coming out to relieve us." New faces are always an oddity in the field. I look them over as they move closer to our position. They are all white guys with very tan skin, except for one, who is white as flour and is clinging to the others like there is no tomorrow. His high-tech jungle boots are still polished and stand out from the worn, frayed boots of the others. It's obvious he's a cherry from the States; the new meat that hasn't been seared by the sun or aged by the terror. He will be worth his salt after he walks-the-walk in the boonies. Eventually, he will fade into the platoon or he'll be wasted.

The four Marines laboriously tramp onto the dunes and the point man waves his hand at us in recognition. Scott motions him forward to our position. The transition is quick and without much talk. There are some cautious words about the areas of concern around us. The sound of rucksacks dropping onto the sand are followed by sighs of relief. "Where you guys from in the States?" I ask, while donning my gear.

"I'm from Frankfort, Indiana," the cherry says with a gleam in his eye. Won't be long before he loses that gleam.

"Mansfield, Ohio," the point man comments.

"Hey, I'm from Columbus!" I respond.

Some quick hellos and good-byes are all that's necessary. There is no name-sharing since we all share the collective name of grunt. Darkness envelops the area when we leave the LP.

Scott leads us back into the perimeter and I see Dusty walking toward us from the CP. He doesn't waste any time chewing us out about our escapades on the LP. Then, he assigns the four of us along with Fuller, Roberto, and Killer to a bunker near the CP. There will be eight of us standing watch for the night. All of us will get a full night's sleep and I'm not scheduled for watch until 0600 hours. I reach into my rucksack and pull out a crumpled rubber lady which I've never had the opportunity to use since being in Vietnam. I blow the air-mattress up and place it in a long trench that I had dug next to the bunker. I lie down on the mattress and look up at the stars thinking that the Nam really isn't such a bad place after all. I close my eyes and begin drifting off to sleep.

Without warning, explosions and gunfire erupt from the general direction of the LP! I automatically spring up to a sitting position and focus on the awful battle sounds that are coming from the sand dunes. "My God, it's a sapper assault on the LP!"

The explosions continue simultaneously with brilliant flashes of light that illuminate the whole area. I see VC swarming over the dunes, firing rifles and throwing Chicom grenades into the air. I jump to my knees and peer out at the LP, mesmerized by the intense flashes of light that expose profiles of men frozen in combat. It's like watching a stage play at a distance illuminated by the constant flicker of a strobe light. I see two dark figures attacking the LP, holding rifles with bayonets above them pointing down. There's another flash and the bayonets jab at a man on the ground. Faint, ghastly screams rise amidst the explosions of satchel charges, grenades, and automatic weapons. For one grisly moment, I think about the cherry that had just arrived from the States. The horror for him is much worse than for the others. Then comes the voice of Cap frantically calling out to the LP over the radio. "LP-one, LP-one, do you read me? Over!"

"This is LP-one." A surprisingly calm voice responds over the radio. "Hit us with everything you got. We're bein' overrun. I repeat, this is LP-1, not much time left, hit us with everything you got, over."

"LP-one, how many are left?" "Click." "LP-one, I repeat, how many of you are left?" "Click." There is no response coming from the radio. I barely hear Cap discussing the options with Dusty. "What do you think? Should we hit 'em or what?"

"No, might be live Marines out there. Let's get out there and take the position back." In the darkness I now hear men scurrying about. The explosions continue to rip the LP apart. Then, as if I had witnessed an apparition, a deathly silence settles onto the LP. At that moment, I realize what happened. The kids were all part of a plot to set up the LP for the sapper attack. They had been sent by the VC to pinpoint our exact daily position and to lower our guard. Ironically, the Marines who relieved us on the LP became the sacrificial lambs. We had unknowingly participated in the demise of the LP. God, I hope someone is still alive out there.

Dusty runs to our bunker shouting, "Get your bayonets out and fix 'em. We're gonna assault the LP. Say your prayers, fuckers!"

My heart is racing so fast it could jump out of my chest. I hurriedly pull out the bayonet that hangs from my utility belt. My hands are trembling so hard I have difficulty snapping it on the end of my rifle. Get ready, it's time to be wasted.

Dusty grabs my arm, waves at the others to follow, and pulls me forward toward an opening in the concertina wire. It's clear he wants me as point man in leading the assault. We reach the gateway in the concertina wire, which leads to the LP a few hundred yards away and Dusty gives us our final orders. "Drew, you and I are gonna lead the assault." I glance back at Scott and Bowman. Their eyes are filled with terror. "The rest of you form a V and keep pace with us as we move forward. We're gonna rush the hill and use rifles only. No grenades, you hear me? No grenades—some of our guys might still be alive. Put your selectors on full automatic and I wanna hear some mean fuckin' yells when we go over that hill. Ya'll hear me?" There are some high-pitched responses from the others. I look out into the abyss and can see the sand dunes in the moonlight. A shadow streaks across one of the dunes.

"Dusty, did you see Charles?" I clamor.

"Fuck it, man! Let's go!" Dusty pushes me through the opening in the concertina wire. Once clear of the wire, we start running toward the beach as the rest of the guys form a V around us. I am panic-stricken as we close in on the LP. Dusty starts yelling and then shouts, "Kill! Kill!" We all lose control, screaming and howling while running full speed at the sand dune in front of us. I run up the dune first and cross over the top firing my M-16 on full automatic. I expect to see VC dug in on the beach ready to counterassault. The others clear the dune behind me, firing their weapons and yelling. There's so much noise and confusion I can't tell what's really going on. I dive onto my stomach and quickly shove a new magazine into my rifle. By then, Sergeant Tanner has cleared the dune and starts hollering, "Cease fire! Cease fire!" Everyone's so scared and excited the firing continues for a few more seconds. I said, "Hold your fire! Fuck-heads, stop firing!" Then, like being in the eye of a hurricane, a quiet storm settles over the LP.

The VC must have already escaped into the jungle. I quickly look around for the guys who are manning the LP. There's a naked body at the edge of the sea. "Look there," says Scott. Several of us jump up and run down to the water's edge. The body of the Marine is lily white with streaks of red oozing from many wounds into the moonlit sand. He's lying on his side with his eyes and mouth wide open as though he died during a frightful scream. "He's the cherry from the States," Scott says, in a low voice. "Fuckin' Charles!"

"No shit," responds Fuller. "He tried to run out to the sea. Musta not known how to stand his ground."

Scott's voice is sorrowful. "What a way to go."

"Look! They bayoneted the shit outta him," I say.

"You guys pull that body up here, didi mau!" Sergeant Tanner demands, in a deep voice. "Fuller, Killer, Cars, get your asses up on that dune and keep watch for Charlie. Dusty, the rest of you guys, start crawlin' through the brush and feelin' for bodies. There's three more guys out here, so let's find 'em."

We fan out into the underbrush looking for the rest of the guys who were on the LP. My hand reaches blindly through the grime and weeds feeling for flesh. Voices whisper around me. "Yo! Got one here." "Fuck, that's only a leg!"

"Hey, here's a guy's head! They chopped his head clean off!" "Here's a guy over here!" The grisly talk emanates from the dark dunes like the dialog from a hideous nightmare.

I crawl next to Sergeant Yokley from Second Platoon who is giving mouth-to-mouth to the Marine from Mansfield, Ohio. He tries desperately to blow air into his lungs. Sergeant Yokley abruptly turns his head and spits out red vomit as the Marine throws-up C-rats in his last gasp for life. "Come on man, breathe!" Yokley pleads.

"Hey, he's gone. Let him go," says Dusty. "This place is a mess. Nobody's left alive. Fuckin' Charlie's gonna pay for this shit. So's that gook ville where those kids came from. They're gonna pay, too."

Dusty gets on the radio. "CP-one, this is Mike-three! Over."

Cap replies, "We read you, Mike-three. What you got out there?"

"Fuck the dust-off, Cap. Ain't much left to even send back, over."

"Get 'em tagged and bagged and bring 'em on in, Dusty."

"Okay, you guys get those body parts in bags and let's get the fuck outta here!" Dusty orders.

The cherry's lily-white skin seeps blood and sags from the bone as we bag what's left of him. He had the right idea. Almost made it out to the sea. Charlie would never have gone after him out there. Yeah, that's where I would have gone, too, for the sea. Shit, it should have been me out there anyway. A frightening rage settles within me as if a swarm of killer bees have made their home in my gut. I'm gonna waste those fuckin' kids if I see 'em. Cherry, I'll get some payback for you, I promise.

CHAPTER VII

Sugar Report

Thanksgiving 1967

It's been two days since the LP was wiped out by a squad of VC. We're still smarting from the attack and hesitant to move freely within the perimeter of the Riviera firebase. Everyone knows Charles is nearby and suspects he's waiting for the right time to attack us. We split bunker assignments with the platoon that lost the four guys on the LP and await orders for the day. Dusty, Cap, and our platoon hillbilly, Caldwell, huddle near the CP talking to the battalion about how we're going to get some payback for the guys who were killed. Eventually, Fuller is sent around to each bunker to pass on the word for the day.

"All right, guys. Got some good news." Fuller kneels and stares into the jungle as he speaks. He has a twinge of authority in his voice, almost as if he's trying to imitate Dusty. "Cap says Battalion is gonna drop us some air mail in a few 'cause it's Thanksgiving."

"Thanksgiving?" I interrupt. "Hell, where's the bird?"

"They gonna drop some boom-boom girls on us, Fuller?" Cars grins. "Cars, you dipstick," Fuller snorts. "It's been so long since you had any, we'd have to give you instructions on how to use it." He cautiously glances away from the trees. "Anyway, Battalion's gonna drop us some beer, letters from home, extra C-rats, and ammo. As far as I'm concerned, that's your Thanksgiving." Then, Fuller raises his eyebrows and haunches his shoulders, trying to act like Dusty. "Enjoy it, 'cause we're going after Charlie this afternoon at 1400 hours. You boonie rats be ready to get some payback for those four Marines that got busted the other night. Happy Thanksgiving, guys." Fuller makes his way around to the other bunkers, spreading the word.

Within 30 minutes a small cargo plane scarfs the firebase and drops a load of bennies, which breaks open in the center of the perimeter. I carelessly leave my rifle in the bunker and run up the perimeter hill scraping up everything in sight except for the beer, which unfortunately exploded upon impact. Fuller snatches the mailbag and passes out letters from home to everyone. He hands me a pink envelope, and I immediately know it's from my girlfriend, Gayle. I stay on the top of the perimeter to quietly read my mail and to chow down on C-rats.

"Sugar report time!" I shout. A letter from your girlfriend is like receiving a pot of gold. I sit for a moment studying her handwriting to make sure that it's real. I raise the envelope to my nose and inhale the remnants of her touch. I carefully open the envelope and read, "Here's a kiss for my Marine," written on the flap inside a heart. I hurriedly unfold the letter. Printed boldly above "Dear Drew" is, "I miss you a whole bunch!" Her blond hair and blue eyes seem very close to me now. "You have been on my mind a lot," she writes. My heart throbs. "I don't know what to do about it. I can't come and see you but if I could, I would give you one big kiss." I recall how hard she would kiss me. "Remember when we talked about getting married? I still think about that and hope we still can someday." Now, I regret not going ahead and marrying her when I had the chance. "I stopped over at your house last weekend to say hello to your parents. Pig, Stumpy, and your brother, Hank, were all there talking to your dad. I watched the news with them and got really scared for you. I want you to come home to me so we can be together."

I am lost in her words when the VC cut loose with a tirade of carbines and AK-47s on our positions. The hideous sounds rip through me like a hot iron. I see Charlie in the jungle to our right flank firing mercilessly into our lines. For one eternal second, all strength leaves me, and I just want to give up. Intuitively, I reach for my rifle and feel only dirt and sand. I grossly erred by leaving my rifle down in the perimeter foxhole. A DI's voice comes back to me. "Never part from your rifle! Your rifle is more important than your girl, your wife, or your mother! Sleep with your rifle by your side!" I feel stupid, naked, and alone. Then a thud from the tree line is followed by a loud whistle of a descending mortar. I automatically flatten onto the ground, covering my head while holding Gayle's letter. The mortar explodes not more than 20 feet away. I clutch my gut, dropping her letter, which spins to the ground. I reach to grab it but bursts of gunfire pelt the earth around me, forcing me to pull my hand back. Rat-ta-tat! Pop! Crack, crack, crack! The sickening, unmistakable sound of VC carbines pop and crack in my ears. I plead with God to spare my life.

I see my bunker at the bottom of the hill about 40 yards away where we're taking most of the fire. In a desperate move, I claw down the hill, my head bobbing from near misses, and dive into the bunker. Scott and Cars are taking turns springing up over the edge of the bunker, returning fire. Bowman huddles in a corner clutching his M-16 like a baby holding onto its mother. Cars tosses my rifle to me and I roll over next to him. I vow never to get separated from my rifle again. Suddenly, an outburst of automatic fire descends on our bunker. Little missiles of death pop through the bunker's outer shell of tin, lodging inches away from us in sandbags. I feel the impact of the bullets ripping through the tin shell. We bunch together and lean forward against the sandbags to wait out the fusillade.

Then I hear, "You fucking gun bunnies!" I turn to see Dusty walking down the hill with his rifle at his side like he's taking a walk in the park. He stops short of our bunker and puts one hand on his hip, looking at us pathetically as bullets pepper the hillside around him. "Get your fucking asses outta that bunker—now!" I can't believe Dusty is so oblivious to the enemy fire. "I said to get your asses up here, and I mean *now!*" He calmly looks out at the tree line surveying the points of fire. Bullets ricochet off trees and pop in the dirt around him. Dusty never flinches, steadily peering into the jungle the whole time.

We dart out of the bunker and begin serpentining up the hill, dodging bullets, and diving to the ground in sheer panic, while Dusty walks calmly up the hill ahead of us, still holding his rifle at his side, talking to himself. By the time we reach the top of the hill, the enemy fire stops and our mortar team cuts loose with a series of 60mm mortar rounds into the tree line.

Dusty stands with his hands on his hips and with piercing blue eyes and furled brow, blurts, "What the fuck y'all afraid of? Y'all afraid of dyin'? Did any of those bullets have your name on 'em? Huh? See, all that worrying for nothin'. Just 'cause y'all wantin' to get outta here alive. Got a surprise for ya. Ain't none of y'all gettin' back to the real world. Your job is to take as many gooks with ya as ya can. Death! It don't mean nuthin'. Now get your gear 'cause we're goin' out to bait Charlie into attackin' us. Charlie thinks we're gonna stay here in the perimeter and hide out, but we're gonna walk along that tree line and beg him to hit us. Drew, you're walkin' point."

Dusty turns and walks toward the CP. Bowman is leaning on his M-16, shaking. My heart is pounding.

"Dusty's gone completely dinky dau!" Cars blurts. "He's out to get us all blown away. I think we should waste him before we're all dead. Whadaya say?"

Watching Dusty walk away, Scott retorts, "Sure! We're just gonna up and waste Dusty with all his cronies around. You ever think what'll happen if ya miss? He'll make you die slow. Did you ever see the picture of that gook Dusty wasted before you got here?" Cars shakes his head no. Scott duck-walks down to the bunker and returns with a picture that he hands to Cars. Bowman and I move in close to have a look. It's a picture of a VC with a rope around his neck hanging from a tree. His body had been blown in half and organs hung down from his chest.

Scott speaks sharply, "Dusty was pissed 'cause Thompson hit a booby trap. A dink started running away but made the mistake of givin' up. They tied the dink's hands behind his back and put a rope around his neck. He pulled him along until he found a nice hangin' tree. He threw the rope over a limb and pulled the dink up on his tiptoes. Then, he tied a block of C-4 around his mid-section and set it on a five-minute fuse. He walked back to a safe distance away and sat down on the ground to watch. He looked real happy sitting there. He even took his bayonet out and picked his teeth clean. Yeah, Dusty kept looking at the gook and laughin'. Finally, there was a muffled explosion and body parts flew everywhere, leaving a pink mist in the air. Then, Dusty walked over to what was left of the swaying torso and put his arm around the shoulders of the gook. That's when Fuller took this picture. I've never seen Dusty in a better mood." Scott is wide-eyed as he tells the story. "I'm trying to get my ass outta here alive. Unless Dusty tries to waste one of us, I say we don't mess with this dinky-dau motherfucker." "Yeah, I'm with Scott on this one, Cars," I reaffirm.

"What are you guys talking about? Bowman quips. "I mean, what's this about Dusty wanting to kill us?" Bowman is still trying to make real-world sense out of the Nam. He's been in country about three weeks and he knows what's happening. Scott has little patience for Bowman when he plays dumb.

"Bowman, get your head out of your ass!" Scott snaps. "Dusty ain't your fucking dad and this ain't a cornfield. You better stop jackin' off in my foxhole at night, too, 'cause if we get hit and your pounding your pud, I'm gonna cut it the fuck off." Scott pauses in a huff. Bowman stops shaking but his eyes are blinking and his face is as red as a beet.

"Here comes Dusty with Killer, Calahan, and Fuller. Keep it down!" Cars peeps.

Dusty walks toward us wearing a cartridge belt, shoulder straps strung with grenades, jungle T-shirt, and hat. Fuller carries an M-79 grenade launcher and a 45. Killer is hauling the radio with a fully extended antenna that looks as big as him. Calahan carries a Browning automatic rifle over his shoulder.

"Oh shit! Looks like Dusty's out for payback," Cars whispers. Bowman starts shaking again. My heart starts racing.

"All right, Drew, take us straight across the tree line where Charlie's been firing from. If we get hit, start moving at them one guy at a time. Let's go!"

We all get on line and move slowly forward. I traverse through an opening in the concertina wire and begin walking between the tree line and our perimeter. It's a long, slow walk where I decide to accept my fate and play hardball with Dusty. I figure there is no sense in trying to resist any longer, especially since Dusty has us backed into a corner. My mood begins to change from fear and trepidation to fierce anger. It could be from all the firefights, LPs, night patrols, lack of sleep, or a hundred other reasons. Then there's the LP that got wiped out the other night. The VC are due some major payback. Now, I just want to kill a gook.

Everyone follows in a staggered column and we eventually clear the right flank of the jungle terrain without anything happening. Dusty comes up to give me further orders and he seems to be having fun as he speaks. "There's a small ville about a click-and-a-half away, beyond the end of the clearin', hidden inside the jungle." He points at the middle of a horseshoe clearing surrounded by trees. The ville's somewhere to the right after y'all enter the trees. Charlie's definitely hangin' out around the ville. Get movin' toward that ville, Drew."

It's obvious that Dusty isn't going to settle for anything less than some cold bodies. I head across the clearing in a slow, tedious walk that fully exposes us to the enemy. About halfway across, I spot some movement on the fringe of the tree line to our left front. I decide to move directly toward the enemy in a bold attempt to put them on the defensive. I push my selector to rock-and-roll, quicken my pace, and walk directly toward the enemy position. I point the spot out to the others and motion them forward. Charlie gets nervous and opens up on us with carbines way too soon. Bullets zip over our heads and everyone hits the dirt, except Bowman, who begins running in circles like a chicken with his head cut off. Roberto tackles him and the rest of us open up on the enemy positions. Then, the firing stops. I get up and move forward using trees and bushes as cover. It takes about ten minutes to get into the tree line where the firing had come from, and Dusty moves forward again to give further orders.

"Nice move, Drew," Dusty says, with a smirk. "Now, take us along this path to the ville where Charlie's been hangin' out. We're gonna get some meat real soon." Dusty drops back but first positions Bowman at duce-point behind me. I wonder if he's preparing Bowman to take my place if something happens to me.

I vigilantly move forward, then realize Bowman is following too close. "Back off, Bowman!" I snap. "If I hit a booby trap, your ass is gonna get greased, too." Bowman drops back a few feet, only to move forward again, blindly bumping against my backside. "I said back the fuck up!" Just then, my right foot slides downward as a large section of earth collapses in front of me. In desperation, I grab Bowman's arm, holding on for dear life. I am hanging precariously on the edge of a deep hole, with my left foot on solid ground, and the rest of me dangling over the edge. I look down and see sharp tips of punji stakes dripping with feces sticking out of the ground. Bowman pulls my arm and I kick my way up the side of the pit until I am on solid ground again. The pit is at least 5-feet deep with a 4-foot circumference. I envision myself falling onto the stakes and realize I wouldn't have stood a chance of surviving.

Dusty moves forward and looks at me with that mean grin. "Looks like Charlie almost reamed you a new one, Drew." He looks into the pit. "The ville's only a hundred yards up this path. Those hooch gooks know this pit is here. I'll bet those stakes are booby-trapped." Dusty pulls out a block of C4 and throws it into the pit. We step back and watch it explode.

"Drew," Dusty shouts. "Move on down this path and find out where Mr. Charles has gone. Those gooks will tell us or somebody's gonna pay." I feel things are about to get ugly.

I hold my rifle at the ready and move slowly down the path toward the ville. It's very hot and humid, which adds to the killing fever. I feel Dusty pushing me toward becoming the animal he so wants me to be. He once said all grunts are born to kill and predestined to fight in a war. I hate what he said because it hints of something evil inside of me that I don't want to consider. But, why am I here when so many other young men aren't? Is my purpose to be a warrior and die in the Nam?

I turn a corner and see a hooch tucked in along the jungle path. I cautiously study the situation before moving forward. There's a fire burning and rice is cooking in a crock. Mama-san is mending a hole in the hooch door with strands of bamboo. I hear a baby crying and women blabbering in Vietnamese. The musty odor of old fabrics and ancient collectibles permeates the air. They are either having an ordinary day or faking really well.

I vigilantly move forward, keeping my eyes peeled for Charles. As I approach the women, they start talking frantically and pointing at me. If they're faking, they're doing a good job of it. I wave my rifle at them, pointing to an assembly point near the front of the hooch. "Didi mau!" I order. I then open the mat that hangs from the hooch door and look inside. It's empty.

I hear Dusty's voice. "Get on your knees, bitches!" He orders, pushing all the women down onto their knees. One young girl of about 15 is holding a baby. She looks too young and pretty to be in this place. Her teeth are still shining, not yet discolored by years of chewing beetle-nut. Dusty points to her saying, "This one's Charlie's girl. Fuckin' bitch done hatched a VC. Where's your old man, bitch?" Dusty starts smacking all the women on their head with the flash suppresser of his M-16 to show he means business. They scream and cry. He fixates on the pretty one. "Where's your old man holding out, bitch? Where's Charlie? I said, where's the VC?" Dusty swings his rifle in different directions, encouraging her to point somewhere. The women continue crying and holding their faces in the palms of their hands. "I'll fix 'em," he says. He grabs the baby out of the pretty girl's arms. She starts pleading with her hands extended out, begging for her baby. Dusty holds the baby out at her, then retracts the infant when she reaches for it, saying, "Where's the VC, bitch?" The girl cries, hysterically. He then walks over and hands me the baby.

"What do you want me to do with this kid, Dusty?" I ask, hesitantly.

"Take the bitch's kid and hold it over the fire. If she doesn't tell us where the VC are, drop the gook kid in the fire."

The rest of the guys are standing around the hooch looking at me. I hear Killer's voice. "Yeah, Drew's gonna' fry some gook. Get some, Drew." Dusty starts laughing.

"Okay, bitch," Dusty yells. "Where's the VC hiding out? Talk, or the kid dies!" He points at me ordering, "Hold that kid over the fire, and I mean now!"

I see the others looking on with blank stares. I'm confused and still frazzled from nearly falling in the punji pit. I walk over to the fire and hold the baby above the flames. The kid is squealing and squirming in my hands. It's only about a foot long and weighs only 12 to 15 pounds. My body is tense and my mind is twisted with crazy thoughts. If I don't drop the baby, Dusty will kill me before the day is over. The kid deserves to die anyway. Mama-san knew there was a punji pit on that trail. It would have been my life had Bowman not grabbed me in the nick of time.

Dusty screams in an uncontrolled rage, "Where's the VC, bitch? Okay, Drew, get ready. Where's the VC, bitch? Drop that fucking kid, Drew! Drop that kid, now!"

The young girl cries, hysterically. "No! No! Numbah-ten, Murine!" Dusty looks on in anticipation.

Calahan's voice rattles through me. "Go ahead! Fry the baby gook! Do it, Drew. Do it!"

I reach a point of no return. I begin parting my hands to drop the baby in the fire. Then, the young mother screams and points to the tree line where the VC are hiding.

"Fuckin' bitch, I knew she'd talk!" Dusty smirks.

I give the child back to the young girl and wonder if I really would have done it. I came so close, it makes me sick to think about it. With each passing day, I am being consumed by more evil. Dusty now has me in the palms of his hands.

"All right, let's move out!" Dusty orders. I take the squad onto a path that will lead us to the VC. We follow the path up hill for 200 yards before it flattens out on top of a ridge. Carefully I walk across the ridge looking down at the valley, which is surrounded by forested hills on three sides. In the center of the valley, I spot a group of farmers carrying hoes, casually walking across a large rice paddy. They stop periodically to work the land. Dusty moves up to survey the situation, taking a few minutes to formulate a game plan. He points across the valley where the farmers are headed and says, "That's the tree line where the bitch said the VC are holding up. Drew, keep moving across this ridge until you begin a descent onto Charlie's position. We'll get on line and assault him. No. Wait a minute. There's something weird about those farmers out there. Weren't they over this way a little while ago?"

"Yeah," I respond. "They were about half a click this side of the ridge where Charles is supposed to be hidin' out. Now they're almost at the bottom of the ridge. Looks like they're moving in a staggered column, doesn't it?"

"Yeah, how many farmers move in a staggered column?" Dusty turns and calls out to the guys behind us, "Killer, get your butt up here with the radio." He raises an eyebrow and says, "Only NVA know how to move in formation like that. Could be part of the group that wiped out the LP last night, or part of those two battalions that has been messin' with India Company the last few weeks? Either way, I got a big surprise for 'em." Dusty grabs the handset of the radio. "Charlie-four, this is Mike-three requesting HE on enemy position, over."

"This is Charlie-four, what's your coordinate and where do you want the HE placed? Over."

"Ah, Charlie-four, Mike-three's coordinates are 289036. Enemy position is located at the base of the ridge to our left front, over."

"Ah, roger, Mike-three. Got ya pinpointed. Heat's on its way. Get your heads down, Mike-three, over."

"They better not be that far off," I remark. "I don't even want to see some short arty comin' our way."

The NVA farmers enter the tree line at the base of the far ridge. The faint sound of a cannon explodes miles away; then the squealing projectile tears into the trees where the NVA had disappeared. Ca-boom!

"Yeah, get some," Dusty whispers. Five more cannon shots from Battalion send missiles streaking across the valley onto enemy positions. Suddenly, Dusty jerks my arm and points to a man running across the valley floor. "Would you look at that?" he mutters. "Drew, let's see how good a shot you are. That gook's probably about a mile away. Damn hard shot but see if ya can nail his ass."

Fuller and Roberto move forward to our position and view the gook through binoculars. I take aim, raising my rifle sight above the gook, and squeeze the trigger. He slumps but continues running toward the tree line. "Did I hit Charles?" I ask, my heart pounding.

Roberto is still looking through the binoculars. "I could see the bullet hit on the other side of him, so it either went through him or just missed. Good shot," he says.

It's getting as simple as shooting rabbits. There's no remorse, just a hard, long, adrenaline rush.

"Okay, you bonnie rats! Saddle up, we're headin' back to the firebase," Dusty orders. He looks contented for the moment, since the artillery was well placed and certainly did a number on those NVAs. "Fuller, you take point. Drew, take tail end."

We work our way back to the outskirts of the firebase without further incident. It has been a rough afternoon and I can't wait to get some badly needed rest. Once we enter the firebase, Dusty assigns Cars, Fuller, Roberto,

Bowman, Scott, and me to one bunker. It's the most forward post and the one most likely to be assaulted at night because of its close proximity to the jungle. We have about three hours of daylight left, so we chow down in the bunker and clean our weapons. We talk "grunt talk" and try to make sense of it all, but there's an eerie perception of impending doom in our words.

Scott takes a deep breath and says, "Two nights ago was a bummer 'cause of losin' those guys on the LP, and today wasn't much better. I just hope tonight's a lick."

"I haven't slept in two days," Roberto sighs. "With all five of us in one bunker, maybe we can catch some shut-eye." Roberto usually doesn't complain.

Cars retorts, "We're out here in bumfuck Egypt where Charlie likes to use bunker busters, so I say we don't sleep tonight. I don't want to end up gettin' rat-fucked like those guys the other night. Some of us have to stay out in the foxhole next to the bunker. All of us can't stay in here tonight."

"Roberto, Bowman, and I will do the foxhole," Fuller responds, like he's shooting cannon balls out of his mouth.

"It's a lick," I say. "We'll do the bunker, so long as it ain't rocket city over here tonight. Sure would like Cap to call in palm or get Puff to do some kill-fire around us. I could stand a little outgoing mail tonight."

"You're dreamin'," Cars answers. "Cap's as gungy as Dusty. Shit, they ain't happy unless were out here playin' John Wayne."

"I don't think they'll have us doin' anything stupid tonight, Cars," Fuller raises his voice. He doesn't seem to be defending Dusty, just more concerned with making sense of it all. I detect an underlying hint of fear in him, which I had never noticed before.

"I think we just need to stay really alert tonight," Roberto says, with a lack of confidence. "If we stay on our toes, then we'll be okay."

"What if they come at us with rockets?" Bowman stutters. "What are we supposed to do then? This bunker's sittin' up here as big as a barn! Shit, they'd have to be blind to miss us."

"That's right, Bowman," Scott growls. "That's why you're in the foxhole, asshole—'cause you get to throw some smoke on 'em, and I don't even want to hear any AMF from your silly ass tonight."

Bowman's eyes start blinking while he glances around at the rest of us. I look up at the sky saying, "It's gettin' time to button down. Another half hour and Charlie's on the prowl. I can't see any shit happenin' yet."

Night once again envelops the firebase in its usual hellish manner. All the daylight clinks and clanks begin to subside. A twilight aura descends on the perimeter and everyone shifts into a heightened state of awareness. It's a time when all of us are truly forced into believing in God, the devil, good and evil spirits, and how to get on our knees and pray. Superstition, religion, and even magic are never ridiculed in the Nam. I grab my scapular and pray the *Our Father* like I've done every night since I got here. Roberto makes the sign of the cross while holding a medallion of Saint Joseph that hangs around his neck. Fuller raises his head above the foxhole and peers over the edge to test his night vision. Bowman tucks into a corner of the foxhole, holding a grenade in his trembling hand, mumbling to himself. Scott takes the picture of his girl from his helmet and stares at it long and hard. Cars is in the other corner of the bunker rubbing the handset of a Claymore mine for good luck.

It's night. There's no moon, but thousands of galactic jewels light the blackness. The monstrous jungle is a dark shadow encircling the perimeter blocking out most of the sky. It's so humid, the dirt on my hands and face have turned to mud. Mosquitoes hover around our bunker and the smell of sweet-stink permeates the air. It's very still, like it gets every night before the kill. I peer into the darkness, straining to see anything unusual. I have to try and relax so my peripheral vision will take over, allowing me to see more out of the corners of my eyes than the front. Night vision is always limited and that's why an experienced grunt develops a sixth sense to survive. I have learned to extend my consciousness beyond my immediate physical area, a skill that comes from months of trying to see the unseen. It's something most grunts take for granted, because the unnatural becomes common when one is forced to survive like an animal. This technique is similar to what Indian shamans have used through the ages to extend their consciousness, by traveling in the body of another living creature. I thought it was funny when I read about it in school but now I know it's real. I prepare by peering into the darkness, trying to extend my thoughts into the jungle to find Mr. Charles. I spend 10 minutes in total quiet preparing myself for the journey. Now I'm relaxed and totally in tune with my inner-self. I extend my consciousness like a ship floating on a calm sea. I look beyond the perimeter, past the burnt landscape and into the jungle. I imagine myself crawling into the foliage and looking through the trees for the presence of another human. I slowly move to my right, floating effortlessly above the ground in search of the enemy. An emerald-green light mysteriously illuminates the jungle. I progress to the right of the perimeter, circling the trees, stopping only to examine hiding places. I faintly hear human voices deep within the jungle. I crawl up a hill and carefully ease over the top, looking down onto a small gully. My heart races when I think I see an enemy mortar team setting up a base of operation.

I enter my "real" mind again and say, "Scott, I think Charles is to our right over the hill!"

Scott's already looking in that direction. "Yeah, I sense he's over there, too. Go tell Fuller where they are."

I crawl out the side of the bunker and slip into Fuller's foxhole. "Charlie's over there to our right, so keep on your toes," I caution.

Roberto, Bowman, and Fuller are focused on the trees to our left. None of them look at me. Roberto whispers, "Got 'em over here to our left, too."

"Any idea how many?" I grimace.

"Can't say, but there's lots of movement," Roberto responds.

"I'll go back and tell Scott." I slither back to our bunker. "They're all around us!" I exclaim.

"This is gonna be another great night," Cars spits his words. There's a pop above us, followed by a brilliant burst of white light from a flare that slowly parachutes across the night sky.

"Check the jungle out," Scott whispers.

Dark figures dart among the trees and shrubs. It's as if the jungle suddenly becomes alive with spooks.

"Wait 'em out," Scott orders. "They'll decide the time and place." The glow from the flare fades as it hisses across the sky and then it goes out, leaving us once again in a black hole.

"Can't see shit now," Cars complains. Then, comes the sickening thud of a mortar shooting out of an enemy tube over the hill. The mortar whistles in a torturously slow fall to earth and explodes behind us to the right of the CP. Pow! The bunker behind us and to our right open up in a burst of kill-fire, saturating suspected enemy positions in front of them. Our mortar team cuts loose with three quick rounds into the jungle over the hill. Boom! Boom! Boom! It looks like good hits.

Scott points into the jungle to our right front saying, "I see a whole bunch of movement in there. I'll open up with tracers and you guys fire at will." Scott aims his M-16 and shoots tracers into the jungle. We all open up on that position until our magazines are empty. "Hurry up and reload!" Scott hammers. We lean against the bunker and wait for their next move. "Think they'll back off now?" Scott tries to sound hopeful.

There's a fusillade of enemy fire from isolated spots around the perimeter. Our lines once again respond with machine gun and rifle fire. I grab a handset to a Claymore mine and squeeze. Bam! Hundreds of pellets explode into the trees, inflicting misery on anybody in the line of fire. "We got four more Claymores out there, so let 'em come on," I clamor in excitement.

"Good," Scott says. "Let's just wait for 'em to make the next move." The jungle projects an eerie silence. None of us say anything. We just wait, peer into the abyss, and wait. At times like this, I do a whole lot of thinking about life and death. I wish my friends back home could be with me to experience this just once—to know what it's like to be on the verge of life and death, so they could better understand what it means to be alive and free. Now, in the arena of Old Man Death, I only cherish memories and hope that someday, freedom will be mine again. The chatter in my head stops as I become aware of something evil outside the perimeter.

Crack, crack, crack! A sniper peppers our bunker with a tirade of bullets. Cars squeezes another handset, hollering, "Fuck you!" The pellets rip through the jungle foliage with a vengeance and it becomes instantly quiet again for a few long minutes. "Murines die!" Then an outburst of enemy fire on the left side of our perimeter. A return burst of fire blasts into the jungle. Tension within the perimeter is fierce. The hit-and-miss game goes on for about 15 minutes, ending with another outbreak of fire on the right side of the perimeter. It's certain the enemy has surrounded us and is out to harass us throughout the night. It's unclear how many there are and if they will risk an all-out attack on a well-defended perimeter. The sapper assault on the LP was fast and furious but was carried out on an isolated position. We aren't the LP. A hush falls onto the perimeter and we begin waiting. Half an hour elapses and it's odd that Charlie hasn't tried anything. I look at the green dial of my watch. It glows 0200 hours.

Cars shakes my arm. "Here comes Dusty from the CP." Dusty grabs Fuller and points at Roberto and Bowman in the foxhole to come into our bunker. Cars, Scott, and I form a tight circle around Dusty, anxiously awaiting the word.

Dusty's eyebrows furl, his chest swells, and his teeth clench. "Charlie's been havin' his way too much around here," he says, looking each of us in the eye one at a time. "Wouldn't you say?" His voice agitated. We shake our heads in agreement. "Cap's decided that ya'll are to do a perimeter patrol around the firebase."

Fuller blurts, "What? There's boo-coo VC out there tonight. This is fuckin' dinky dau shit." I've never seen Fuller so upset about having to carry out a mission.

"This is suicide, Dusty," Roberto growls. "We can't go dillyboppin' around this perimeter without gettin' rat-fucked at some point."

"Sorry 'bout that guys, but I don't need a ration of shit either. I say you save it for Charlie, 'cause we're leavin' in a few. Get your gear ready. I'll go around the perimeter and alert the lines that we'll be out there." Dusty crouches and leaves the bunker.

I look around at the others. They are all leaning on the bunker walls looking into the jungle. "Think we should just not go?" Cars asks.

"It's an order, so we gotta do it," Roberto responds.

"It's a doomed mission," Cars growls.

"Man, they're all over out there," Scott whispers. "Shit, we'll be lucky to make it half-way 'round this number-ten perimeter before gettin' blown to hell. I'm with Cars. I say we don't go."

I speak in a steady voice, "I say we try talking to Dusty and changing his mind. I don't think he'll really do it. I think he might just go out part way and return."

"Fat chance we got of that!" Cars blurts.

"There's Dusty, he's coming back around. Get ready," Scott warns.

Dusty jumps into the bunker saying, "Okay. The lines are alerted that we'll be doin' a 360 startin' over there." Dusty pauses and points to our right rear near the South China Sea where the LP had been wiped out. "We'll move into the jungle there and do a circle around the perimeter until we end up on the other side by the South China Sea. Any questions?"

"Yeah," Cars speaks tersely. "Who the fuck came up with this idea and who the fuck thinks were gonna make it around this perimeter without gettin' our asses blown to smithereens?"

"That's why each warm body here gets a number." Dusty counters with an even voice. "After we get hit, I'm gonna call out numbers and I want you to say your number back to me. Scott, you're number one. Bowman, two. I'm three. Cars, you're number four and you get to hump the radio. Good luck."

"Great!" Cars bellows.

"Fuller, you're number five. Roberto, six. Drew, you're tail end and lucky seven. Let's do it!"

I sense Dusty knows we'll get hit and the numbers are his way of making things more suspenseful. However, this isn't a John Wayne movie and we aren't extras on the set. Death will definitely be paying us a visit tonight and Dusty doesn't seem to care in the least.

There's little hesitation as we accept our fate. Scott leads us out of the bunker toward an opening in the concertina wire at the far end of the perimeter. Once outside the wire, we make our way toward the area where the South China Sea meets the jungle. The closer we get, the more vivid the memories become of those ghastly screams from the other night when the LP was overrun. "Hit us with everything you got," the last Marine alive on the LP said. He decided to have us kill him and take as many NVAs with him as he could. I hope I will be so brave if death comes knocking at my door. Scott pauses at the bottom of the sand dunes and the rest of us drop to one knee. I watch Dusty and Scott crawl over a rim on the sand dune to check out the area at the sea. They slide back down, and signal that things are okay. Then, Scott leads us into the jungle.

The night turns darker as we move under the jungle canopy. It's so quiet that every step is amplified a thousand times, like eggshells cracking under our boots. I step lightly through the underbrush following Roberto's silhouette. We work our way along a shallow ridge using the trees and shrubs to camouflage our movement. It's a slow process filled with deception and terror. Every shadow prompts me to aim my M-16 and squeeze the trigger to the point of firing. Night stalkers have to develop nerves of steel to hold back from firing weapons. One shot will alert Charlie to an exact position. Throw a grenade, use a bayonet, but don't squeeze the trigger unless you have to. Immense bushes and trees extend branches like spooks in a fun house. I hear something. Is it real or did I imagine it? I turn and face the rear, squat onto my haunches, and clutch a grenade that hangs from my shoulder strap. I listen intently for more sounds, ready to toss the handheld bomb. Seconds elapse but there's only a pitch-black void radiating heat and evil at me. It must have been my imagination. I turn and walk briskly into the maze of vegetation, trying to find Roberto. He disappeared! I rush forward in a panic and run into him. He signals to back off. Feeling stupid, I slow and feel my heart racing and adrenaline pumping. We creep past the area to the right of our bunker where I had imagined the enemy mortar team was set up. Are they still waiting in ambush for us? They had to have seen us leave the perimeter. We stalk forward but nothing happens. I mentally rehearse how they might hit us. The tail end would be the most logical position for them to attack. It would be easy for Charlie to lie in ambush waiting for us to pass, and then jump out and slice me to pieces while the others walk obliviously forward. I will do everything in my power to not let this happen. I concentrate on each shrub, bush, and tree, examining each one as a possible hiding place. It's difficult to not become totally confused. I am obsessed with using every ounce of mental energy to stay alive. I creep and crawl with the others around the perimeter. We finally reach the halfway point in the jungle ahead of our bunker, and we stop to reassess the situation. We gather in a circle. "All right," Dusty whispers. "We made it this far, so the rest is a lick."

"I can't believe they haven't hit us," Fuller's voice is high-pitched.

"I'll bet Charlie moved over to the other side of the firebase when he saw us leaving the perimeter," Scott counters.

"He's still here." Roberto has a dead certainty in his voice.

"Okay, no more fuckin' talkin'!" Dusty orders. "Scott, take the lead and get movin'!"

Once again we begin our slow death march around the perimeter. The air smells of gunpowder from earlier skirmishes. The trees begin to thin out as we stalk along the left ridge line outside the firebase. Starlight now illuminates our pathway and I see the outline of the concertina wire surrounding the perimeter. We are now three-quarters of the way around the firebase and I am hopeful we will make it. The smell of the salt air from the South China Sea drifts into our path. It's a miracle. Charlie must have moved on, thinking he had harassed us enough. What luck!

Suddenly, I hear a pop from the point position. It's a muffled sound that I hadn't heard before. It is followed by a flicker of light and an intermittent hissing sound. I freeze. The spark of light suddenly erupts into a blinding white glare, illuminating the entire hillside. There is an eternal second of stunned silence when I realize what's happening. Scott accidentally tripped one of our flares that had been rigged for Charlie. We all drop to our knees, pointing weapons in every direction. Each of us is a brilliant candlestick in the night. Then, hell unleashes its avenging spirit on us.

VC to our right, who had been waiting in ambush, open up on us. There is a furious outburst of kill-fire on our position. We dive onto our stomachs as bullets snap bushes and tree limbs around us. Caught in a nightmare that continues to grow more grotesque, our firebase lines unleash their fire power on us. We are now caught in the middle of a merciless crossfire with green tracer bullets streaking inches above my head. I point my rifle up the hill in the general direction of the VC, bury my face into the dirt, and squeeze off rounds. My gut contorts from near misses and I pray for the firing to stop. Finally, the explosion of bullets abruptly ends.

Panicky voices emanate from the darkness. "Hit a jack-off flare!"

"Fuckin' lines are killin' us!"

All hell breaks loose again.

Bullets rip the ground around me. We can do nothing but pray and return spotty fire at a phantom enemy. We are totally at the mercy of Old Man Death and he will callously decide whose time is up. The glow of the trip flare finally fades and a raging darkness settles upon us. Flashes of gunfire jet out from above and behind our position, crisscrossing kill-fire above our heads. As quickly as it started, the shooting stops.

I hear Dusty's voice. "Hit the jack-off flare, Cars!" Cars jams the back of the flare onto his thigh, firing a green, hissing ball into the sky. For a split second our position lights up in an ghostly green fog from so many smoking guns. Then, I hear movement from above our position where the VC had been firing down on us. They blabber some words in Vietnamese and steal away into the night. "Reload! Reload!" Dusty growls. The sound of metal magazines slicing into empty chambers echoes through the night. Dusty bellows, "Gimme a count! Who's one?"

"One," Scott stammers.

"Two. Whose got two?" Dusty questions.

"Me, Bowman."

I listen intently to the death roll. "Five, number five," Dusty raises his voice. He had skipped Cars and himself.

"Five!" responds Fuller.

"Six!" Dusty hollers. "I said SIX! Where's seven?"

"Seven, seven!" I answer.

"SIX goddammit!" Dusty hammers. "Drew! Fuller! Where's Roberto?"

I feel blindly to my left where I thought Roberto had been. I feel a boot above my head. I look up and have just enough vision to see Fuller putting his hand on Roberto's head. "Here he is!" Fuller hollers. Roberto has his right hand clenched around his medal of Saint Joseph. Blood is streaming out of his mouth and neck. "My God, he's been shot in the neck! "Fuller screams. Fuller wraps his arms around Roberto's head and draws him into his bosom. "He's dying! He's fuckin' dying!" Fuller begins crying while holding Roberto in his arms. A gurgling sound comes from his throat as Roberto tries to catch his breath. Fuller rocks him in his arms crying out, "No God! Please no!" Roberto's body goes limp and the beautiful spirit of an 18-year-old boy sails into the heavens. Fuller sobs while holding Roberto's lifeless body.

Dusty grabs the handset of the radio. "We got a Zulu, one down and in desperate need of a dust-off, over."

"Get him in here, Dusty, over." It's Cap's voice on the radio.

"Drew, guard the rear!" Dusty orders. He and Fuller grab Roberto's shirt collar and pull him toward the perimeter. The rest of the squad follows while I stay in the trees guarding our rear. Once they pull Roberto through the concertina wire, I also make a beeline into the perimeter. We anxiously gather around Roberto while waiting for the dust-off. Fuller is still sobbing as he holds Roberto in his arms. I am still clinging to the hope that he is still alive when Dusty suddenly blurts, "He's dead!" It's as if he is reading all of our minds. Fuller slowly lays Roberto's body onto the ground. In frustration, he pounds the ground with his fist. As I watch him, the realization hits me that I will never see Roberto again, and neither will his family. His short life on earth will be marked only by a simple epitaph on a flat gravestone.

Dusty reaches down and slowly unwraps each of Roberto's fingers that are still clinging to the medallion of Saint Joseph. Lines of anger deepen in Dusty's face as he opens a body bag and rolls Roberto into it. Fuller takes a deep breath, as if to say it's over, and walks toward a foxhole to be alone. The torturous night finally ends when the dust-off lands and whisks Roberto's body off to Graves Registration.

It's 0530 hours and the sky begins to glow over the South China Sea. I have sad thoughts about our fallen comrade but I know Fuller feels worse than any of us. He was close to Roberto and will always miss him. I sit in the bunker looking out at the distant sea as the sun rises over the horizon. A mysterious spiritual hush descends over the firebase. It's as if Roberto's spirit is joined by the others that were killed the other night and they are making a final pass over the perimeter. I sense them whispering words of encouragement, "We are now your guardian angels. We will watch over you as best we can. Don't be afraid of what lies ahead for death is not such a hard way."

Suddenly, Dusty storms toward us from the CP. "We're gonna' blow this place to pieces, then we're movin' out. Battalion says we can't afford any more losses here."

"Where we headin', Dusty?" I ask.

"Cap says we're headin' up to the Dead Marine Zone. He says we're goin' afloat as a special landing force. That means we're goin' to the Widowmaker, guys."

"Oh, fuck!" Cars says, dropping his head.

"Aw, quit your belly-achin'," Dusty responds.

"Why did you call it Widowmaker?" Bowman asks.

"Bowman, you're one sorry fucker, I swear," Scott interjects.

"Anyway, get your C-4 out and start blowin' these bunkers," Dusty orders. "Cap doesn't want anything left for Charlie."

It takes us about an hour to level the Riviera firebase. The place that had been our salvation and our hell is now gone. I stand at the base of the perimeter where our bunker had once been and look out at the jungle. It's hard to tell who won or lost this lousy battle, but I clearly see there will never be victory in Vietnam. We will continue fighting and dying for useless pieces of real estate and then give it back to Charlie as a gift. This is a war for its own sake—each battle to be forgotten as quickly as it's fought.

We gear up, get on line, and make our way across the top of the perimeter toward the South China Sea. As I cross the top of the hill, something on the ground catches my eye. A small piece of pink paper is sticking out of the barren dirt. I reach down, pull it from the ground, and dust it off. It's a pink envelope, which I quickly open. On the inside of the flap is written, "Here's a kiss for my Marine," encircled by a heart. Below, it's signed, "Love, Gayle."

CHAPTER VIII

The Dead Marine Zone

December 5-24, 1967

In early December our battalion is transported by ship to the Philippines for training to do beach landings, and to get some badly needed R&R. After completing a grueling week of exercises, Scott, Cars, and I go on furlough in Olongapo, a port-of-call for the Navy. We're in a nightclub drinking beer and readjusting to the sights and sounds of the real world, when some Philippino girls ease over to our side of the bar. One of the girls places her arm around me, saying, "Would you like some boom-boom, Murine? Only ten dollas."

I spit a mouthful of beer onto the bar and everyone breaks out laughing. I look at Cars and he's shaking his head—yes! The money seems pointless and I begin to feel very excited about feeling the touch of a woman. I hand her twenty dollars instead of ten and she looks into my eyes and smiles. She grabs my hand and leads me up a narrow staircase and into a small, dimly lit room that has a toilet, sink, dresser, and bed. It's the closest thing to home I've seen in a long time. I look everything over again to make sure it's real. The girl boldly puts her arms around my neck and kisses me softly. She turns and looks in the mirror while slowly unbuttoning her red blouse. "What's your name, Murine?" she asks, softly.

"My name is Drew. You're really beautiful."

"Take your clothes off, Drew," she giggles.

I unbutton my shirt while watching her undress. "Unhook my bra," she smiles and turns her back to me. My hands are trembling as I release the hook on her bra. She turns toward me and teasingly holds the bra up to cover her breasts. She looks into my eyes, sheepishly grins, and drops the bra to the floor. She has large breasts with big dark nipples and her skin is soft and luscious. With the finesse of a striptease dancer, she slowly drops her skirt to the floor and turns a full circle making sure I see her entire body clad only in red panties. I start breathing hard and rush to get out of my clothes. She slips out of her red panties and lies down on the bed naked. She is the most beautiful of all the girls in the club. Her olive skin, jet-black hair, and brown eyes, are stunning against the white sheets. I nervously lie down next to her on the bed. The fresh scent of her body mixes with the fragrance of an exotic perfume, a wild contrast from the jungle stench to which I had become accustomed. "Let's talk first," she says. "Where do you come from in United States, Drew?"

"A place called Columbus, Ohio," I respond in a shaking voice. "It gets really cold there and snows a lot this time of year."

"I've never seen snow, Drew. Would you take me there sometime?" She asks sincerely while stroking my chest.

"Well," I hesitate, feeling stunned by the proposition. Then, I consider the impossible. "You would really want me to take you to Columbus, Ohio?"

"Oh, yes, I would love to play with you in the snow, Drew," she purrs. My heart begins throbbing.

"I would take you this moment, but I really can't."

"Why not?" she pleads, with pitiful eyes.

"Well, I'm heading back to Vietnam to finish my tour of duty. I could come back after that, if I'm still alive."

"What!? You, Murine! You will live! I feel it in my heart," she says, with conviction. "Then, will you come back for me?"

I look into her eyes. "If I live, I will return and bring you to America with me."

She giggles. "How many girls have you had, Drew?"

"You'll be my first."

"What!? You, Murine, never had girl before?"

"Well, I've come really close, but never really gone all the way."

She put both hands over her mouth giggling. "You baby-san." Then she stops giggling. "You sure I'm your first?" she whispers, inquisitively.

"I swear! You'll be my first."

She puts her arms around my neck and looks deeply into my eyes saying, "Promise you will come back for me?"

"I swear, when I get out of Nam, I'll be back for you."

She slips her tongue into my mouth and kisses me deeply. I gently rub her back and slide my lips slowly down to her breasts. I softly suck on her nipples. She giggles and begins stroking me. I grow hard as she sensually moves down my body, kissing, and licking my hungry skin. Finally, she slides her mouth around my penis and sucks until I reach a state of ecstasy. "I want you in me now, Drew," she whispers. My heart races as I get on top of her. I slowly push into her wetness. She moans and I freeze. "No! No! Don't stop," she pleads. I push in and out, feeling a woman's love for the first time. It feels better than I had ever imagined. I can't hold back any longer and I release a powerful orgasm into her. I lay on top of her soft skin trembling from head to toe. We hold each other and kiss for what seems like an eternity. I cherish every tender moment like it's my last night on earth.

We stay together until past midnight, which is beyond military curfew. I don't want to leave but she convinces me to go back to base before the MPs arrest me. We leave the club and ride on a rickshaw to the outskirts of the naval base. She kisses me one last time with the depth of a departing lover. Then she says that she will wait for me to return from the Nam. I reassure her we will be together again but an uncanny feeling of impending doom quickly replaces my fantasy. We wave to one another as I walk through the battalion gates and into the stark reality of, "Where's your fucking pass, Marine?!"

A few days later we hit the beach in Quang Tri Province, about ten miles south of the Demilitarized Zone that divides the two Vietnams. There are 800 mostly combat-hardened grunts in the battalion, ready to take on the best NVAs that Ho Chi Minh has to offer. Of the 44 provinces in South Vietnam, Cap tells us Quang Tri is the most valuable, because it's close to the Ho Chi Minh Trail where huge amounts of troops and equipment are constantly being transported from the North. The province has the largest number of battle fatalities and a bad reputation that goes back to French occupation when they called the only road through there The Street Without Joy. The Marines simply call the entire area The Dead Marine Zone.

The Marines have several large outposts in the area called Leatherneck Square: Con Thien, Go Linh, Dong Ha, and Cam Lo. To the north and further inland is The Rockpile and Khe Sanh. Activity in the area has picked up over the last few months and Cap says most of the outposts are under siege. It's our job as the only special landing force for the Marines to aggressively search out and destroy the enemy. While onboard ship, some of the guys in our battalion choose to get thrown in jail and risk getting a dishonorable discharge rather than hit the beach with us. There's something spooky about their conviction not to go north.

We are each loaded with 70 to 80 pounds of gear as we hit the beach. Our company moves inland about a mile and then tediously works northward. India Company stays closer to the beach on our right flank and they also move northward. The other two companies, Kilo and Delta, do the same kind of maneuver but moving southward. We are reduced to eating only two C-rats a day instead of the usual three, amounting to only 1600 calories. We all begin losing weight and feeling chronically tired. The humid heat sucks what little energy we have left as we hump extra gear and ammo. An occasional five-minute break eases the pain of the added weight. We sweat until there is no sweat left to ooze from the pores of our dry skin. We endlessly pop salt tablets to replenish our electrolytes, which colors our skin a chalky white.

Water is so scarce we use halozone tablets to kill bacteria before drinking from polluted streams. The water has a sickening taste and smells like it has come from a sewer. We usually set in for the night when guys begin passing out from heat exhaustion. The nights are threatening and punctuated by distant sounds of rolling thunder from B-52 carpet bombings. I frequently have nightmares of getting killed in combat. I awaken at times sweating, realizing my reality is far worse than the dream. None of us get more than three or four hours of sleep a night, further sapping our energy. I have welts all over my face and neck from the mosquitoes that find their way through the sweet-stink. My feet and toes are cracked and raw from jungle rot. They itch so much, whenever we stop for more than five minutes, I remove my boots and scratch my toes until they bleed. They are in such bad shape, I will probably be taken out of the field before long. We all have scratches from the many wait-a-minute bushes we brush against each day. My backbone feels like it's splitting from carrying 70 to 80 pounds of gear throughout the long day. I sometimes find myself praying for the million-dollar wound, while other times, I fantasize about being on a date with my girl. We hump through the boonies for two weeks with only sporadic action, but on December 23, 1967, I find out why they call the area The Dead Marine Zone.

It's 0730. I am eating C-rats with the other grunts who are scattered in foxholes or in old bomb craters. We smoke cigarettes, talk about home, and speak of what a lick this trip north is. There's still no hint of real danger and everyone is beginning to get used to the lull in the action. Then, out toward the South China Sea, a few distant gunshots catch our attention. "Whadaya you make of those caps bustin' out there, Cars?" I ask.

"Ah, just some scattered shit. Ain't nothin' to write home about," Cars says, confidently.

The popping sounds continue as grunts around me lift their heads like alert animals sensing danger. "Looks like Cap's on the horn talking to Battalion. Gettin' kind of noisy out by the sea," I say, nervously.

"Yeah, sounds like the shit's startin' to hit the fan," Cars says, with concern. The faint pops increase to a steady stream of gunfire. I wait for a few seconds, hoping the gunfire will stop, but it increases. Explosions begin going off within the zone of fire. Five minutes pass and a familiar terror settles over me. It's time to fight.

Cap gets off the horn and personally comes around to pass on the word. "Get your gear ready, grunts! We got a company of NVAs that want to become believers. Guess we can help 'em with that, huh? Point platoon from India Company has run head-on into an ambush." I wonder about casualties but Cap looks excited about the opportunity to fight. We start gearing up when a loud whistle erupts above our heads, signaling an incoming mortar. "Okay, find a hole and get in it!" Cap shouts. He smiles at me and I find myself smiling back. I almost feel him saying that this is what we have trained for and now is our time to show our stuff. I am lying along the side of a huge bomb crater and decide there is no sense in moving. Let it just happen. The mortar explodes about 30 yards away on the other side of the crater. I hear shrapnel whizzing over my head. Cap looks back at me, smiling again. My heart pounds with excitement and I wonder for a moment why I am feeling this way. I don't move as three more mortars streak down and explode nearby. The earth shakes as dirt and sand spew into the air. If any of those explosions had been more to the right or left, I would have been history. I sense that my danger zone is changing since I no longer flinch with terror from the close stuff. Dusty must have passed this way some time ago.

With the precision of a well-oiled machine, our platoon gets on line and heads toward the combat zone. Scott and Cars march alongside me, each of us holding our rifles at the ready. Every minute or so, a mortar whistles down on our position spraying shrapnel everywhere. Some guys dive to the ground, burying their faces in the dirt, while others drop to one knee. A few of us who are still feeling really lucky walk brazenly forward as the mortars drop around us. No one really cares much about how each handles it, except for the cherries who are crawling around and watching us like scared kids. As we grow closer to the action, I see figures darting around on the wooded hills leading to the sand dunes of the South China Sea. The salt air blows into our faces carrying with it the smell of gunpowder. Bullets begin whizzing by and snapping around us. Our pace slows as we adjust to entering the combat zone. Then we stop for a moment to survey the situation.

Three Cobra gunships hover above the battlefield in an awesome display of thunder and air ballets. The big skyships bow their noses at enemy positions firing rockets that explode, incinerating the ground below them. I watch intently as the middle chopper turns, facing its midsection toward an enemy position. It hovers for a moment and then a door-gunner points a machine gun down and cuts loose on the target below. A sudden barrage of return fire hits the gunship. The chopper quivers and retreats across the sea. The other two Cobras move higher into the sky, backing away somewhat, but continue their assault. A low-flying dust-off races across the sea approaching the rear area of the battle.

Below the air battle, Marines carry their fallen comrades toward the LZ. Moving to the front of the battle zone is a large M-103 flame-throwing tank, flanked on both sides by M-48 tanks. The two M-48 tanks have their cannons turned away from the enemy with tank gunners sitting outside the turrets firing M-50 machine guns at enemy bunkers. The rumble of the tanks' diesel engines vibrate in my chest. Trees surrounding the bunkers are blown into the air by the intense machine gun fire. Grunts on foot huddle behind the tanks using them as cover to move forward. The large 103 flame-throwing tank is busy incinerating points of fire in front of it. Three-man rocket teams are heavily engaged in firing on suspected enemy positions. Everywhere I look, grunts huddle in holes, firing M-16s at the enemy. The feverish pitch of the battle creates a steady stream of misery.

Dusty moves forward shouting orders. "All right, we're goin' into hell. India Company has already taken 12 dead and 17 wounded. Shit, we can't ask for more than that!" I wonder for a moment if Dusty has gone totally nuts. "We're gonna move to the left flank of the M-48 tank that is closest to us and give them support. Get ready, guys. This ain't the small stuff any more." Dusty is grinning from ear to ear. "Cars, get your ass over here and relieve Killer on the horn."

"Great! Dusty's bound and determined to get my ass blown away!" Cars complains to Scott and me.

"It ain't gonna matter whose carrying what, Cars. We're in some really deep shit now, so start saying your prayers." Scott speaks sharply as he peers ahead at the battle scene. Cars runs toward Killer to take over as RTO. Scott stares at me saying, "Look, Drew, things are about to get ugly. I want you to know that I'll take care of ya. You know, in case anything happens, I'll be there for you." It's the first time I'm aware that Scott must see me as a brother for whom he cares deeply. When death comes stalking, it's an act of valor to commit your life for the love of another. Scott's display of courage gives me the fortitude to face the evil that awaits us.

"Okay, move 'em out!" Dusty shouts. We move cautiously toward the tank near us as gunshots whiz and crack nearby. I spot a two-foot dike near the tank that can provide some protection. Many of us run for the dike as the machine gunner on top of the tank gives us covering fire. Most of the enemy fire is coming from a large camouflaged bunker within a cluster of trees to our right front. I see NVAs moving around inside the bunker with red stars on their helmets. They are focusing most of their fire toward the tank. Once we're in position, we open up on the bunker. The tank rolls slowly forward while the machine gunner hoses the bunker down. The tank halts about 30 yards from the bunker and we stop firing. The idle rumble of the diesel engine vibrates the ground as we wait to see if there will be any return fire. A few seconds later, NVAs inside the bunker unleash semi and automatic weapons on us. The bullets crack around us and we fire back in a ferocious assault. At the same time, the tank cuts loose again with a 50-caliber machine gun that shoots five-inch bullets at the target, blowing debris into the air like a bomb. Again, we stop and wait for their response to determine if anyone is still alive in the bunker. The answer comes quickly when the NVAs return fire. Once again, we open up on them in a hail of kill-fire. The tank also blows metal fury into the NVAs' position and smoke engulfs the entire complex. We continue firing for about a minute. I can't believe the NVAs could live through the barrage of fire power. We stop firing and there is an instant lull in the battle. The machine gunner on the tank raises himself up to get a better view of the bunker. Unbelievably, a sudden fusillade of fire erupts from inside the battered bunker. The machine gunner on the tank slumps and falls into the turret. Then, a crew member reaches up and closes the hatch on top of the tank. We all cut loose again on the bunker while the tank gunner slowly traverses the turret around and points the cannon down at the enemy complex. We stop firing just long enough to watch the spectacle. There's a moment of frozen anticipation, then the tank gunner fires his cannon.

The gigantic metal frame of the tank recoils on its rear road wheels. The bunker complex explodes into the air. The tank rocks a few times and the diesel engine roars as the tank races forward to run over the bunker and crush it. The tank gets to within 10 yards of the demolished bunker and, unbelievably, three NVA soldiers jump out of the ground with one of them firing an armor-piercing round point-blank at the tank. There's a sickening metallic thud as the round burns through 11 inches of the hardest metal on earth, followed by a muffled explosion as shrapnel ricochets within the tank, instantly killing all the crew members onboard. For a split second, there is stunned silence as we try to comprehend the turn of events. Then we unleash our hatred on the fleeing enemy with another blast of kill-fire. I fire quickly, popping rounds off at all three of the moving targets since they are so close together. The three NVAs' bodies simultaneously twist and contort in the air from the heavy hit of our bullets, and slam to the ground. A Cobra gunship circling above the fight, points its nose down on the NVAs and fires a rocket, blasting them all to the other side of hell. Our moment of payback is swift and certain.

"Move toward the beach," Cap orders. There is little time to process the quick and brutal chain of events that had just occurred. Without hesitation, Scott and I start serpentining toward the beach. Marines on top of the M-48 tank pull out the bodies of the dead crew members. They slide the lifeless bodies down the side of the turret into the arms of their buddies, leaving streaks of red on the tank. The papers will report it as just another body count. Maybe someone will tell their parents how bravely they fought. We pass in front of the M-103 flame-throwing tank and I feel the heat still radiating from its gun. The other M-48 tank is idling on the sand dunes of the South China Sea. When we reach the sand dunes, I clearly see the scope of the carnage.

Many NVA bodies lie clustered in groups where they had chosen to die, defending their space. The body bags of dead Marines who had been killed from the point platoon of India Company are strewn everywhere. Their boots, helmets, packs, and flak jackets dot the landscape. As I look closer, I see heads, arms, and legs sticking out of the gear. No one really cares about the scope of the bloodshed, because too much of the battle is yet to be fought. Soon it will be our turn to walk point.

Scott and I pick out a spot in the trough of a sand dune to rest. I lie back on my pack, listening and watching grunts prepare for more action. I see Cap, Dusty, and Tanner huddling around Cars and talking to the CP. The Cobra gunships hovering above us begin to head back to the aircraft carrier to refuel. Another tank rolls forward from the rear to take the place of the one that had been knocked out. Our mortar teams begin pelting suspected enemy positions about 1,000 meters to our front. Mechanical fury seems to be everywhere and there is never much lull in the action. Then a bright-eyed guy with a camera kneels beside me. He has the real-world look still in his eyes, indicating that he hasn't seen much action. "Where's the rear area?" he asks.

"Do you want to take some pictures?" I ask.

"Ah, yeah. I'm a photographer from the States. Where's the rear?" "It's back where the wounded are lying. A dust-off came in there a little while ago."

"I'm supposed to be taking pictures at the rear area!"

"Well, this is going to be the rear area in just a few, because we're going to be moving forward. Take a load off, and wait it out." The reporter reluctantly sits on the edge of the dune and begins checking his camera. It's always a novelty to see a real-world person in the bush because they just don't fit. He still has a gleam in his eyes, doesn't carry much gear, and has the notion that his safe zone is a God-given right. He sits nervously watching us as Dusty comes by to give further orders.

"Who the fuck are you?" Dusty snaps.

"I'm a combat reporter from the States," he says with pride.

Dusty laughs. "Ya ever killed a gook with that camera, boy?"

"No, I don't believe in killing. That's why I'm here, to let people know what this war's all about."

"Sorry 'bout that, cherry, but you're lower than an E nothin' around here. You rear-echelon motherfuckers got some real dinky-dau ideas that don't mean diddley-shit out here. Killin', it ain't nothin'," Dusty says, shaking his head in disbelief. He looks at the rest of us saying, "All right, fix bayonets. Now that we got Charlie on the run, we're going to assault him. You want to come along, Camera Killer?"

The reporter doesn't make eye contact with Dusty. "No thanks," he says, while fidgeting with his camera.

Dusty's words echo in my head: "Fix bayonets!" I nervously try to pull my bayonet from the sheath. The idea of a frontal assault, and possible hand-to-hand combat, makes me remember the counterassault we did on the LP when it got wiped out. A bullet might be quick, but a bayonet is painfully slow. Sometimes I guess you have to say it doesn't matter anymore and just go for it.

"Get those bayonets on those rifles!" Dusty orders. I look out over the sea as I connect the bayonet to the end of my rifle. The South China

Sea looks beautiful and serene. For a moment, I yearn to have a feeling of peace. Just to lie on the beach and feel the sand beneath my skin seems like a reasonable request, yet it's so impossible.

"All right, guys, let's move it out!" Dusty shouts, while waving his hand forward.

We leave the reporter sitting at the edge of the dune still in charge of his safe zone. We start walking along the left side of the M-48 tank with rifles at the ready. We look ahead for bunker complexes and one-man spider holes which are usually covered with a bush and extremely difficult to see. If you miss one, there is a hail of bullets followed by who knows what? That's the difficult part—knowing you are so close to finding out about the afterlife. The tank is about 30 meters away, rumbling along with the machine gunner sticking out of the turret. Suddenly, there's a crippling explosion beneath the left track of the tank. A shock wave jolts me down to one knee and a tank road wheel rockets by my head, hitting a tree and cutting it in half. A Marine near the tree drops to the ground from being hit by flying shrapnel. A corpsman runs over to give him aid. I kneel on one knee, wait for further orders, and think about how close I just came to a date with the Almighty.

The tank crew is outside the tank, assessing the damage the land mine had done. Then, mortars fall from the sky and explosions start ripping holes in the earth, spraying shrapnel everywhere. The enemy's about 200 yards in front of us from the sounds of the mortar tube thuds. The barrage is fast and furious. "All right, grunts," Dusty yells, "Let's get 'em before they have a chance to pull back again."

We start running forward to overtake the enemy positions as mortars continue exploding around us. The scene reminds me of the movie *Iwo Jima,* when Marines were trying to move inland from the beach and violent explosions sprayed plumes of gray matter into the air. The thought hits me that I am nothing more than a grain of sand in this universe awaiting disintegration. My life has no more importance or meaning than any inanimate object. My human dignity becomes unglued for a callous second. The piercing reality sends a shock wave of deep terror through me unlike anything I have ever felt. For one brief moment, I feel totally insignificant. Then, my eyes open wide when I hear the whistle of an incoming mortar sounding like it's about to hit me directly on my head. This is it! I dive to the ground a split second before the mortar explodes. The impact of the explosion jars my body and showers me with mud. I shake my head.

I panic, feeling my legs to see if they are still there, then rubbing my arms and chest for wounds. I'm still in one piece.

I look to my right where other mortar rounds had fallen and see Sergeant Yokley from Second Platoon cradling a Marine in his arms. The young Marine's face is speckled with small pieces of shrapnel and his eyes are glazed over. One leg has been blown off and the other is grotesquely bent and bloodied. Yokley talks to him in a desperate attempt to keep him from succumbing to shock.

"Drew! Are you Okay?" Scott dives next to me, frantically checking my body for shrapnel wounds. "Have you been hit?" he cries out.

"I don't think so. I think I'm okay but we gotta keep goin'." Scott helps me back on my feet and we blindly run forward. Then, the mortar barrage stops but a sudden burst of enemy fire pelts the trees and ground around us. We dive to the ground and see enemy soldiers about a 100 yards away peeking around the trees, bushes, and sand dunes. "Scott! Whadaya think is going on?"

"It looks like a squad of NVAs might have been left behind to slow us up. Cap's over there on the horn, probably calling in arty," Scott says, while scanning the perimeter.

The rest of our platoon positions themselves for return fire. Once we're all on line, we open up on several NVAs, but some of them take off running along the beach. Then, I hear what sounds like a freight train swooping overhead and realize it's a projectile from a nearby firebase. It explodes on the enemy positions along the sea. Five more rounds hurl over our heads pounding the NVAs. Suddenly, a Cobra gunship storms over us at treetop level firing rockets at the fleeing enemy. Tanks rumble forward about 50 yards to our rear firing 90mm cannons. Organized chaos is everywhere. We again try to start running but barely drag ourselves forward as best as we can. As I pass the bodies of the enemy, I shoot rounds in them for good measure. Out of nowhere, I stumble on a camouflaged bunker dug into the side of a sand dune. I'm only about 20 feet from it and am totally amazed by how oblivious I was to spotting the bunker. I cautiously crawl to the side of it and look inside. Three NVA soldiers are lying on their backs with boy-like faces peering out into space. I fire at them to make sure they're really dead.

I rejoin the platoon and we move on, finally reaching the last hill, which marks the northern-most point before actually crossing the DMZ. The area looks like the landscape of the moon with hundreds of bomb craters stretching as far as the eye can see. The NVAs are somewhere out there hiding in caves beneath the craters. Our platoon is on top of the hill looking for bunkers and caves where enemy ammo is stored. Dusty gathers a few of us together to survey the situation. "See that finger of land sticking out at sea," he says. "That's the DMZ. Sure would like to keep going north and fight our way to Hanoi. Whadaya say, guys?" We all agree that to go north into NVA country would be our only chance to win the war. Nowhere have I ever heard of fighting a war in the way we have been struggling through this conflict, capturing enemy territory then giving it back to them the next day.

Cap and Tanner walk over and start talking to Dusty. All of them look concerned. I hear Cap say, "Charlie has lured us all the way up to the Z. Problem is, the rest of our battalion is a good five miles south of here. We got orders to blow the ammo and then to hightail it south as fast as we can. It's already 1530 hours, so we don't have a lot of daylight left."

"What's the rush, Cap?" I ask.

"The rush is that a reconnaissance plane spotted a large contingent of NVAs scattered in those craters ready to make a counterassault." I look out at the coastline and see the small single-engine plane making passes overhead. "They sucked us into a trap and there's only a handful of us up here. India Company's back a few miles where the first encounter took place and they're already heading south. If we don't get movin' and keep ahead of Charlie, we're gonna be history. The tanks will guard the rear along with us. The rest of Mike Company has already started moving south."

I look behind us and can see lines of Marines moving southward. We're now the tail end, the ones at the fringe of the herd and most vulnerable to attack. Our speed will be our only ally. I turn, look north, and can see enemy heads bobbing above the crater rims. Some of them start moving cautiously toward us. "Blow these ammo holes!" Dusty shouts. We feverishly rush to get the job done before it's too late. The three tanks start moving slowly in reverse, firing cannons at the craters which now bulge with NVAs. It takes us only a few minutes to blow the ammo and we break into a jog heading south with 70 to 80 pounds of gear on our backs in a desperate attempt to link up with India Company. I look back at the NVAs who are now galloping toward us with their mortar teams ahead of them. I feel like a gazelle running for my life. We have to keep moving quickly or their point mortar teams will get within range of us. I try desperately to keep up with the tank next to me. It seems I take my eyes off the tank for only a moment, and look up again to find it a good 50 meters ahead.

I keep glancing over my shoulder feeling the presence of the hungry ones, but my legs are just too tired to run any faster. The stressful miles of battle have taken a toll on my body and mind. I am the weak prey on the fringe of the herd, falling helplessly behind into the kill zone. I'm breathing hard and try again to run but my legs just won't go. Suddenly, mortar tube thuds erupt from behind me, exploding near the tanks. The platoon hits the dirt during the mortar barrage and I am able to catch up before they move out again. Once the mortar barrage ends, we take off as the point mortar teams of the NVAs pack up and chase after us. The rest of the NVA infantry units are well behind the mortar teams, which gives me the impression they are biding time and have other plans.

We're now caught in a deadly game of leapfrog with the NVAs. Every time they catch up with us, they cut loose with a mortar barrage on our position. We throw casualties on the sides of the tanks and keep moving through the mortar barrages.

At one point, Scott and I run in the open along the beach when there's a particularly vicious mortar attack. "Drew!" he screams. "Dig a hole so we can get in it!" For an instant, I realize Roberto's instincts are still with us. Scott has his E-tool out digging a foxhole into the sand like a man possessed by a demon. I start digging along with him while mortars explode around us. Every time a mortar explodes nearby, we dig faster. I glance up at Scott and the whole scene looks like a *Keystone Cops* movie running in fast motion. He's chopping at the ground with such ferocity, he looks to be on the verge of panic. It all seems so ridiculous, I break out laughing. Scott's voice is high-pitched and rapid. "Drew! You crazy bastard. Dig! Dig!" Every time he says dig, he digs faster and I laugh harder. I curl up on my side in the sand laughing uncontrollably while mortars explode around us. My laughing scares him even more and he continues digging like a fiend. He must think I have lost my mind. Finally, the mortar barrage ends and Scott quietly gathers his gear and heads south. I catch up with him and apologize for scaring him half to death. He accepts my apology by smiling and calling me a crazy son of a bitch.

The enemy mortar teams fall behind and eventually stop chasing us. We slow to a walk with our shoulders drooping from the weight of our gear. As I pass the battle area where we had fought earlier, I jealously recall the combat reporter's safe zone. Everywhere I look, body parts litter the battlefield. I stumble on a decapitated body, tearing off the foot, which tumbles in front of me. No safe zone here. I absentmindedly begin kicking the foot as I walk across the scene of carnage.

Then, almost as if transported back in time, I recall my alley back home in Columbus when I was a boy. I can almost hear Mom calling me for dinner. "I'll be there in a minute, Mom!" I yell. I'm having too much fun kicking a tin can and yanking roaches out of the sewer with my friends to worry about dinner. I point a flashlight down on the wiggly whiskers of the roaches sticking out of the sewer lid and yank one of them out, throwing it into the air. We chase the roach and smash it to pieces.

The corpses on the battlefield remind me of the roaches and the smell of the sewer when I was a kid. I continue kicking the tin can as I walk, trying to make sense of it all. An overwhelming stench of body parts, gas, gunpowder, and burned earth permeate the air. I reach the far end of the field of battle and look back at the bloodbath. Old Man Death made a good showing today and the night is still to come. I glance down and realize I've been kicking a foot, not a tin can. It's the bloody foot that tore loose from the decapitated body I stumbled on earlier. I stand motionless for a few seconds and wonder what I'm becoming in this wretched place. I move forward in a daze.

"Whadaya think, Drew?" Scott sounds depressed.

"I don't know, man. It isn't gonna get any better tonight. Those NVAs are gonna be out for some major payback. They know we're on the run, so they'll wait till dark to make their move. Charlie likes the night." "Yeah, now that we ain't had a lick of sleep for God knows how long, they'll probably hit us in the middle of the night. I just need some shut eye." Scott's voice is really tired.

The sun is beginning to set over the mountains to our right when we make a quick move inland to link back up with India Company. Cars is still humping the horn as he drops back to pass the word on to us. "Cap's been jawin' with a couple of platoons from India Company." Cars keeps looking ahead as he speaks. "They're a few miles away in a clearin' waiting for us. We're supposed to link up with them and set up a double perimeter tonight. Guess the bummer's goin' to be who gets the outer perimeter. That's gonna be a definite number-ten position with Charles on the prowl. Just hope it isn't us. See you in a few." Cars mechanically walks ahead to catch up with Cap.

We walk inland for an hour through thick, forested hills and reach a clearing where India Company is waiting for us. The setting sun over the mountainous jungle to our right casts an ominous shadow over our position. The realization that we have penetrated deep into enemy territory settles into me. The air is very still and sound seems to carry a long way. We are on a barren spot, probably cleared as a firebase at some time in the past. I wonder how many Marines might have given their lives for this piece of wasteland. The clearing is a 200-square-yard position flanked by small hills to our left and the mountains and jungle to our right. Three tanks have gone ahead of us and are in the center of the perimeter where the CP has been set up. Two platoons from India Company are spread out in a circle forming the outer perimeter. It had already been decided—they will be the first line of defense against Charlie. I am relieved, yet disturbed that a fellow Marine will take my place in hell tonight.

Once inside the perimeter, Dusty starts shouting orders. "Scott, Drew, Bowman! You guys dig a hole here and hold it at all costs." Dusty's pointing down at a spot on the ground as he walks by. He continues making his way around the perimeter pointing out positions to the rest of the platoon. It's clear, we are in for a frightful night. There's been too much going on all day to think that Charlie will lie low tonight. Marines may run the day but Charlie always owns the night.

We dig deep holes as night imprisons us on the ground. Four foxholes of India Company are about 50 yards in front of our hole. They'll be the sacrificial lambs if Charlie decides to take us on. I hope that Charlie is half as tired as we are. Scott whispers, "Okay, I'll do the first watch until 0100 hours. Drew, you take second. Bowman, you're third. This is a bummer of a night, so sleep with an eye open."

"Scott," I say. "I'm having trouble staying awake." I haven't ever been this tired. My eyes are beginning to close at times, and only with great effort am I able to keep them open.

I look at Bowman as he speaks, "I'm really tired, too. I can't even think about rollin' out tonight."

I hear Bowman's voice but his image is blurred. I am straining to stay awake. "I think I'll get some shut-eye," I say. I lay my head down on the side of the foxhole and immediately fall asleep.

It seems that no time has elapsed and I feel Scott shaking my shoulder. "Drew, wake up," he whispers. "I can't stay awake any longer," he says. Scott curls into a ball and starts snoring almost at once. Bowman's head is cocked back with his mouth wide open. I look out at the foxholes in front of us but can barely see them. A mortar tube thud erupts behind me and an illumination flare ignites the sky above us. The landscape turns an eerie orange and I see Marines in front of me peering over the rims of their foxholes. Is this real or am I dreaming? The orange glow slowly fades and my eyes close. I snap awake again with great effort as another illumination flare pops above me. I barely make out human images in the trees in front of the perimeter. I see Charlie! Then, everything goes black.

I awake to flashes of light and silent explosions all over the perimeter directly in front of me. Dirt and bodies rocket into the air. Men are fighting with bayonets on the ends of their rifles. They are chasing and stabbing one another. I hear ghastly screams and explosions. I feel nothing. Then, I pass out again.

I open my eyes and raise my head. NVAs are swarming over the foxholes in front of us. A lone NVA holds a Claymore mine over his head. A split-second later, it detonates. There is a furious flash of light and bodies fly apart. There are NVAs everywhere! My eyes close and I pass out once more.

A loud noise wakes me—an enormous screeching whistle. I open my eyes wide and see the enemy running wildly over the outer-perimeter foxholes. The enormous screech grows with intensity until my insides feel like they're shaking apart. It sounds like the whole world is getting ready to explode and I'm totally confused. I hear another weird hissing sound following the screech in the blackness over my head. Suddenly, the whole perimeter explodes into a blinding firestorm. The brilliant flash of light burns my face and hands and a shock wave knocks me against the back of the foxhole. I pass out again.

It seems like a lifetime slips by. The long night passes and I awake to the unmistakable smell of napalm and burned flesh. I open my eyes and see Bowman and Scott unconscious next to me in the foxhole. I recall my last thoughts of the huge firestorm and the sound of what I now know was a Phantom swooping overhead. I try clearing my head by shaking it back and forth. I sit up and look over the edge of our foxhole. Boot soles! All I see are boot soles. I raise my head higher to see over the boot soles. Dark green ponchos are draped over the bodies of about eight believers—dead Marines, 18 and 19 years old. The reality begins to sink in. I sit down in our foxhole and stare at their boot soles. Flies twirl through the air attracted to the stench of the dead. It's overcast and about to rain. Scott and Bowman begin to stir as weary Marines pull more believers forward to be united with the others.

"Drew!" Scott awakes, stunned. "What happened?"

I keep looking at the believers' boot soles as I speak. "Don't know. I think we got overrun last night."

"What do you mean, you don't know?" Scott says, anxiously.

"I mean, I kept passing out. I only remember parts of it. There was this big fire when they dropped the palm. That's all I remember before waking up just now."

I look to my right and see Dusty approaching our foxhole. "Drew, whatever you do," Scott pleads, "don't tell Dusty you passed out! He'll waste you."

Dusty stops in front of our foxhole and peers down at us. "All right, you grunts, let's get moving." He sounds energetic. We stand and silently look at the bodies of the believers in both reverence and disbelief. Dusty suddenly changes the tone. "Looks like we get to pump their wives when we get home, guys," Dusty says, laughing. His words tear through my gut. All of us try acting callous by forcing some nervous laughter. "Get your gear together, grunts, 'cause we're moving out. Got some Mike boats gonna pick us up on the beach at 1100 hours and take us out to the carrier. Don't you know what day it is, ya'll?" Dusty's still smiling. "It's fucking Christmas Eve. Don't wanna keep Santa waitin'."

We gather our gear, speak a few words of encouragement to each other, and leave India Company to deal with their believers. We walk across the perimeter and back into the woods leading to the South China Sea. I once again have cheated Old Man Death out of his share of me; however, it's becoming obvious that none of us have much time left. Today is Christmas Eve, though, and there will be another sugar report for me when I get onboard the carrier. I can't wait for Christmas now. We reach the sea, board the Mike boats, and head out to the carrier leaving hell in our wake.

We eat a magnificent Christmas Eve dinner in the mess hall. I have never seen so much food in one place in all my life. After dinner we go into a large auditorium to see a performing group that had been flown in to help us celebrate Christmas. Maybe for a short time we can forget about the war. Cap walks around wishing everyone a Merry Christmas and passes out letters from home. He hands me the sugar report which I have been waiting for from Gayle. It has been at least a month since I have heard from her. I open the letter, but there are none of the usual hearts and kisses on the envelope. I read the first few lines: "Dear Drew, I'm sorry I haven't written for some time. I have been really busy and lots of changes have taken place with me recently. You still mean a great deal to me, though. However, I can't continue waiting for you any longer. I have met someone else and . . ." I put the letter down. My heart sinks. I walk up to the dark carrier deck in a daze. A tropical breeze blows into my face as I look out over the starlit sea. I hear the group singing "Silent Night" from beneath the flight deck. Ever so slowly, small groups of Navy seaman standing on top of the carrier, join in singing the carol. Eventually, they all sing together and sound like a choir of angels over the dark ocean. It's surreal and I don't feel a part of it. I stay on the carrier deck until the wee hours listening to carols and wondering whom Gayle is celebrating Christmas with. I look out beyond the flight deck, past the glistening sea, to the world of the Nam where Charlie is awaiting our next move. Merry fucking Christmas.

CHAPTER IX

Blue Eyes

December 26, 1967

As we prepare for our second beach landing in Quang Tri Province, the scuttlebutt onboard ship is that Charlie has amassed large forces along the coastline, and we're in for one helluva fight. However, Cap says Charlie's on the run and our battalion's in for a skate. Nobody really knows what's going on, but we hope Cap is still in his right mind. We carefully check over our gear in the confined quarters of the ship. We sit sideways on our bunks, four high, our legs dangling down on top of one another. Cars passes a news article from the States down to me. "Damn Commies!" he shouts while puffing on a cigarette and cleaning his rifle. A bunch of us cheer. "Take a look at this Stateside shit my brother sent me." His words are wired with contempt. The headlines read: "ANTIWAR EFFORT GAINING STRENGTH." There's a picture of young people with long, straggly hair, carrying signs protesting the war.

"Just what we need—more help from home," I comment, shaking my head in disgust.

"Yeah, I wish they could join us on our next beach landing," Cars retorts. "That would turn 'em into real believers, huh? I mean the kind that become pacifists for the duration. Maybe they could march down the beach protestin' that Charlie uses sapper squads as an unfair advantage. I can hear 'em now: 'Stop the sapping! Stop the sapping!' I'm sure Charlie will be moved."

"Yeah, he'll be moved enough to bust some cherry's ass," I laugh. "Maybe they should all go to John Wayne High School where Dusty went to school. They could take courses like "Becoming a Gungy Lifer" or "How to Become a Trained Killer." Dusty'd have 'em wastin' each other with a smile before their first day's up. Pogues!"

"I'd say you guys ought to get with the program like Killer over there." Scott's sitting on a top bunk kicking his legs and pointing down at Killer who's busy sharpening his K-Bar. "That's what I call l-o-o-o-ve. Killer can't wait to get some."

"Yeah!" Killer shouts. He moves his thumb lightly up the blade of his knife. "I think it's time we get some payback for those guys from India Company that became crispy critters the other night."

"They sky'd out the hard way." Cars' voice is low and even. "We're supposed to be linkin' back up with them today in the bush."

"I think it's bad luck to be runnin' with India Company," I say. "They're always gettin' rat-fucked. I don't like the feel of havin' to go back out in the boonies with 'em."

Fuller and Caldwell have been listening to us a few bunks away. "Dusty says we're gonna be workin' in a no-fire zone with Lima Company, so it'll be a lick." Fuller tries to sound confident.

Caldwell answers in his southern drawl, "Y'all outta look on the good side of it. We could do some Zippo raids if it gets real quiet. Then, I'm AMF, 'cause I'm gettin' really short and the Ultimate Weapon will have to do without one crunchy hillbilly."

"Sorry 'bout that, Caldwell, but ya still got a month of humping to do for me!" Minch exclaims, while swabbing the inside of his rocket launcher. "Besides, you better hope that Mr. Charles has moved north, 'cause this time when we hit the beach, we're heading south. Delta and Kilo Companies are heading north. I can tell you this—Charlie doesn't celebrate Christmas, so he'll be itchin' for a fight."

"At least we won't have to spend another Christmas in this hole." Bowman shoves C-rats into his pack as he speaks. "When I get home, I'm never gonna complain about anything. I mean this place is lower than whale shit."

"Drew, I heard you got a Dear John the other day," Red says, while cleaning a mortar tube.

My heart sinks. "Yeah, it was definitely a number ten." I keep my eyes cast at the floor. I envision Gayle's blond hair and blue eyes and I know they are no longer mine. I would do anything for one minute with her lush fragrance. The thought of her with another guy drives me crazy.

Red speaks curtly. "My wife ever messes me over, she's dead meat."

The black guys howl. "Red, you honky!" Taylor chuckles, flashing his pearly whites. "My old lady's out humpin' right now and that means I'm gonna have one helluva bank roll when I get back to the world." They gave each other high fives. "Drew's got plenty of girls waitin' for him. Don't ya, Drew?"

"Damn right, I do." I point at Taylor.

Cap, Dusty, and Sarge come busting into the cube. "Get geared up!" Dusty grunts. "We got Mike boats pullin' up to the carrier in one hour. I want to see forty-five swingin' dicks on deck number two at 1200 hours."

"What the hell's going on out there, Dusty?" Corporal Phillips sounds moody. "Where we headin'? What kind of zone we headin' into, and where's Charles?"

"Yeah, baby! I hear that," Taylor quips.

"You guys worry too much. If you'd spend more time thinkin' 'bout killin', y'all wouldn't care 'bout dyin'. You're gettin' to sound like a bunch of rear-echelon motherfuckers. Charlie just wants to kill, that's all! You know what Quang Tri's all about? A lot of guys go in and few come out. Now, let's get shaken." Sarge stands behind Dusty, and nods enthusiastically. They quickly turn and walk out of the cube, leaving us with a tense silence.

In the afternoon, we board Mike boats and head toward Quang Tri Province. Gigantic waves toss us across the sea as we heave our guts out on one another. We circle out at sea for hours, smelling puke and awaiting word to hit the beach. It's evening when we struggle off the Mike boats through the shallows and onto the barren beach. With unsteady sea legs, I walk up the dunes and into the trees. The ground has an odor of chemical defoliants and burned gunpowder, welcoming me back to the Nam. Orders and more orders move us inland to familiar battle terrain. It's dark when we reach our night-defensive perimeter. It looks all too familiar. The barren terrain is surrounded by forested hills, old foxholes, and the charred remains of the devil's groundwork. Two platoons of India Company are already manning the inner perimeter foxholes as their defensive position. Now, it's our turn to defend the outer foxholes through the ominous night. We're back in the exact perimeter that got overrun the night before Christmas. Scott, Bowman, and I dig holes 40 yards away from the trees, allowing just enough distance to see them coming at us. I wonder if the guys from India Company had much time to think about it—the danger, I mean—the moments we spend imprisoned in our minds before the battle is fought—the moment before the napalm hits, the bullets strike, or the swarm of NVAs attack. All the training on earth can't prepare you for that moment. The snakes in your gut squirm so hard, it squeezes your nuts up to your throat. Your mind races uncontrollably because you know there's no way out. Get ready! Now, you can be wasted.

At first we decide to let one sleep while two remain awake. Instead, we decide all of us should stay awake through the night. Every 15 minutes or so, an illumination round pops, flares, and hisses across the jet-black sky. The earth glows and spooky green trees cover the bogeyman. For hours, I strain to see the unseen but nothing happens. "Scott, whadaya make of all this quiet, man?"

"All I know is I can almost touch 'em," Scott says. "Can't ya feel 'em?" "Damn right I can. Charles is everywhere tonight but I can't hear a thing."

"He's up to somethin' big. Don't know what it is but it's gonna be soon." Scott shrugs.

We keep an all-night vigil looking for spooks in the night, listening for the bogeyman, and preparing for God. I wait so hard, I almost see them attacking us. It's a long, fortuitous night. Finally, the moon slips from the sky and the sun peeks over the horizon. My heart settles knowing I have survived another night, but Charles' presence is still in the air. "Guess he'll wait for another night, huh, Scott?"

"This area's sure different from back around DaNang. You can feel that Charles has a lot of numbers out here. He oozes power. Let's stick close today and keep on our toes."

"Yeah, I think we ought to keep our eyes on Dusty, too. I think he's still out to get us."

"Whadaya mean Dusty's out to get us?" Bowman says as he struggles to wake up.

Scott responds gruffly, "Bowman, you know what's been goin' on back at battalion with Dusty. Now wake up! Let's get our shit together, because the platoon's movin' out."

Cap, Dusty, and Sergeant Tanner walk around to each foxhole, passing the word. They reach our foxhole and Cap's face narrows as he speaks. "We'll be sweepin' southward along the coastline workin' with Lima Company. Our platoon will be walkin' point until noon. Keep on your toes 'cause word has it there's some 2,000 NVAs dug in somewhere in the area. We'll hump to the sea and then move southward. Let's get a move on." The number "2,000" reverberates in my head. Months of combat conditioning move us forward. It's December 27, 1967, and Christmas has passed with the blink of an eye. I have fleeting thoughts of past Christmases when falling snow, the smell of holiday pine, and opening presents on Christmas morning made everything beautiful. I wonder if I'll ever see Christmas again. Today is turning out like many other days in the Nam. The morning sun has begun its slow slide across the blue vaulted sky. The tormenting heat, flies, and pounds of gear remind me that it will be a torturously long day. I have chosen not to eat my morning C-rat and reward myself with two this evening, but something tells me to eat it now. Our platoon turns 30 abreast as the sacrificial point lambs of the battalion. Like brooms, we sweep a line from the edge of the sea outward about 200 yards. There is a mechanical precision with all our moves. I take long strides, leaning my shoulders forward into the straps of the pack, one arm swinging with a tight hold on my M-16, the other hand pumping with a clenched fist. It's easy to miss seeing Charlie through all my anguish and anxiety. We hump on line for a few grueling hours, firing at ghosts, blowing hidey-holes, and calling in recon-fire. Charlie is nowhere.

We quietly sweep through the ville of Thon Trung An and are held up only by wait-a-minute bushes. Finally, Cap passes the word downline to hold up in a gully 400 meters ahead of another large ville. I gratefully drop my rucksack on the incline of the gully and lie back on it. "Where are we?" I ask Sarge, as he walks by.

"Tham Ke," he snorts. He stops and looks over our heads at the ville. "India Company swept through there yesterday. Didn't find Charlie, so this is a skate. Lima's comin' up now to sweep it. We get to wait this one out."

"Hey, I can hear that, Sarge," I smile.

Point platoon of Lima Company tromps by and a tall, young Marine with a sun-baked face and blond hair catches my attention. He has piercing blue eyes and looks like he could have been a surfer from California. Now he wears the thousand-yard stare in those deep blue eyes, a gaze brought on by too many near misses. He walks with a long heavy stride with his fist clenched around the stock of his M-16, a picture of a pretty girl donning his helmet. He doesn't bat an eyelash. His features are filled with horror. He's a good Marine on another mission that could end his life. I stare at those deep blue eyes as he pounds by me. There's something very icy about his gaze that mirrors my own personal hell. I want to wish him good luck but nothing comes out. Good fortune is had by no one in the Nam. As he walks past me, I whisper, "Good-bye." I wish I had said it louder.

Five minutes pass. I lie on my back and study the patterns of clouds in the sky. They seem so close I can almost touch them. The silence is nice. Suddenly, there's an explosion near the ville. A split-second later, an all-out thunderous roll of automatic and small-arms fire rips the air. "Shit!" I holler. Scott hits his legs with both fists, knowing the fighting has begun. Bowman blinks his eyes wildly, his face is red, and he clutches his M-16. I look along the gully where the rest of the platoon huddles, peeking out toward the battlefront. Stray bullets swish over our heads. I stay tucked below the edge of the gully in a temporary safe zone, dreading the moment I will have to face the barrage of bullets. Sarge walks by our position, then reverses direction. With arms pumping, legs churning, and fire in his eyes, he races toward the radio. Cap's already there with Dusty listening to the red phone chatter. Cap speaks sharply, "Just lost communication with Captain Martinez of Lima Company. Lima's RTO said Martinez took a head shot. He said it's a cluster fuck. That's the last communication we had with 'em. Guess the RTO got it."

The furious pitch of the battle keeps us frozen in the ditch. Cap, Dusty, and Sarge stand tall and stare intensely at the ambush site, looking frustrated and confused. The radio clicks. "This is Lieutenant Frashmier," says a breathless voice.

Cap interrupts. "This is Bolt from Mike Company. What the fuck's happenin', Frashmier?"

"Ambush! Everybody's gettin' it! Bunkers, RPGs, machine guns, mortars, they got it all! Looks like a couple of NVA companies are dug in with a matrix of caves. The whole damn ville's sittin' on top of an underground fortress! We're gettin' overrun! I'm callin' in palm on us! You guys start your assault after the palm hits!"

"Hang in there, Lieutenant," Cap says, calmly.

I'm stuck on the word "palm." The volume of bullets swishing over our heads increases with each passing minute, indicating many more NVAs are assaulting the small force of Marines. Cap is still on the radio talking to Battalion CP. He starts heading down the gully with Cars as his RTO by his side. Dusty waves us toward them. We creep along the side of the gully, keeping well below the hail of stray bullets swishing a few feet above our heads. The firing sounds like vats of popcorn going off as hundreds of NVAs fire assault weapons on the point elements of Lima Company. We finally reach the end of the gully where our whole platoon is closely lined up, and wait for orders.

Dusty takes charge. "Lima's gettin' massacred! Air strikes are comin' in on em'!" My heart starts pounding, knowing that napalm is on its way. "We're gonna get on line and assault 'em. Phillips! Your squad will be to the left. I'll be between your squad and second squad. Red, take your squad to the right of us. Fix bayonets and get on line." I barely hear Dusty's voice. The snakes start squirming in my gut and a burning sensation runs all the way up to my brain. I'm losing ability to think on my own. Dusty's combat orders are clear. I'm about to have a meeting with Old Man Death. Get ready, now it's time to get wasted. Dusty's voice is hammering at me. "Drop your packs and get on line. Move out! Move out, I said!" My body is taut and I feel weak and dizzy. My legs slowly begin moving mechanically forward with the others. I enter into a different dimension of combat. We are moving directly into the line of fire, which puts us in the middle of the killing zone—the zone where nothing survives but a few lucky casualties. You're at point-blank range of 6.2mm bullets that can literally rip a person in half. Few live to tell about it. Those that do live probably wish they hadn't. My main thought is why are we doing this? Why don't we just set in and wait for the air strikes to work it out. Then we could go in slowly with precision accuracy and take them out one at a time. That's the way to do it. This is nothing more than mass suicide!

I look to my right where Bowman and Scott are clanking along firing their M-16s. We're about 200 yards from the battle zone when bullets start snapping around us. Two Phantoms streak across the sky at treetop level, dropping canisters of napalm on the positions in front of us. The metal canisters glisten in the sunlight and glide toward the ground. Several NVAs jump out of their bunkers firing AK-47s at the streaking Phantoms. A gigantic burst of fire from the napalm erupts across the battle perimeter directly in front of us, consuming the fighters. The intense heat causes me to halt and raise my arms to protect my face. Then, to my right I spot an enemy soldier's arm poke out of the ground. I run forward firing down into the enemy spider hole, killing the NVA soldier inside. I continue forward, hardly missing a beat, and find myself in the middle of the battle zone.

Little fires burn around us. The sharp cracks of so many rifles and automatic weapons all firing at once within a 100-yard radius is deafening. I have never heard such earsplitting noise in all my life. It's like being in the middle of 100 sledgehammers all pounding away. Enemy RPGs, mortars, and our own 3.5 rockets explode around me. A light, hazy smoke engulfs the perimeter with the stench of human incineration and gunpowder.

The NVAs open up on us. A moan erupts from the squad of Marines to my right as a barrage of bullets rip through them. They crumble like clay pigeons. Scott and I dive forward behind a small mound to use as cover. The screams of wounded Marines pierce the air. Bowman is to our right front, lying in the killing zone where he's been hit. Most of the Marines from Third Squad to the right of him have gone down in the line of fire. Those who are still able are crawling for cover as they continue to be shot at. Everything's happening so quickly it's difficult to comprehend. To my right front, two enemy bunkers pour a tremendous amount of fire power at us.

I hear a voice to my left. "Drew! Get up there in that position!" I turn to see Dusty leaning over a slope just 5 yards away. He's pointing his rifle at a spot about 15 yards in front of me in the killing zone. It's a flat piece of land in the open and is directly in front of one of the enemy bunkers. He's got to be making a mistake. I look back at him in astonishment. He points his rifle at the spot and yells, "Move it!" I turn to my right and look at Scott in shock. Scott looks bewildered. I look back at Dusty who now raises his rifle and points it at my face. I freeze in disbelief. "I said, move it!" He points his rifle at the barren spot in the killing zone and then back at my face. I look back at Scott and our eyes meet for one brief moment as we both realize what's happening. I look back at Dusty. He tightens the grip on his rifle, points the barrel at my face, and prepares to fire. I can't hesitate another second or he will shoot me. I rise and bolt forward, zigzagging to a spot just in front of the enemy bunker, and dive onto the ground. I quickly fire a whole clip into the front of the bunker. Several enemy rifles swivel and point directly at me. I see a small embankment to my left front that could provide cover. I put my left hand down and push up to one knee. Suddenly, a horrendous electric shock explodes in my wrist. I scream! I look down at my wrist where a bullet has ripped through me. I scream again! My left hand is dangling, connected only by one white bone, and blood is pouring onto the ground. I scream in agony and grab my arm below the elbow. Little fragments of bone stick out from the gaping wound and one strand of skin holds what's left of my wrist together. My wrist has almost been severed in half. I shout, "Scott! Scott!" I look down at my arm again in disbelief. The pain radiates up my arm as if I'm holding onto a live electric wire and can't let go. All the pain I have experienced in my entire life can't equal one moment of the misery I am feeling now. I'm about to pass out when I feel a hand on my left shoulder. I look to my left and see Scott kneeling next to me. He has followed through on his promise to never abandon me. His eyes glare and shift from one point to another trying to determine our next move. At that instant, Scott twists violently to the left and screams, clutching his chest. He hollers again as his whole upper body catapults back the other way from a second hit. He screeches and clutches his chest in agony. I realize we have only a few seconds to live when everything goes silent. There's no more horrendous noise. The throbbing in my arm leaves. A protective veil settles over me as if my spirit is preparing to leave my body. Then everything moves in slow motion. I look back at the bunker complex and see rifle barrels pointing at us. I glance to my left and see a narrow ridge about 15 yards away that could provide some immediate cover. I look at Scott and yell, "Run for it!" I turn and crawl with one hand as fast as I can toward the small embankment. There's no sound, only the awareness that Old Man Death is about to take me. I have a few short yards left to exit the killing zone when I kick my legs and dive forward over the ridge. I'm in midair when I feel a hot ball slowly rip across my head, splitting my scalp and skull. The impact of the bullet knocks my head forward and I roll over the embankment and onto my back. Then, Scott rolls over next to me.

I lie on my back looking up at the sky and realize I'm still alive, the sound of a hundred pounding sledgehammers and explosions going off in every direction returns. I look to my left over the small embankment and can see some of the guys in Third Squad still trapped in the open. Bowman is one of them. Every time he tries crawling toward a safe position, NVA soldiers shoot him in the hand, foot, or leg. He screams and stops moving. The NVAs are trying to lure other Marines into the open to help the wounded so they can bag more game. I look back at Scott just as his eyes close. Suddenly, an NVA machine gunner opens up on me with a hail of kill-fire. Dirt spews onto my face as bullets ping off the top of the mound a few inches above my head. I turn my head to the left to stay as close to the ground as possible. The machine gunner is trying to pulverize what little protective cover I have left. The earth is quickly disappearing around my head. I inch to my right to keep some cover above me. The merciless fire follows me every time I move. My muscles begin to quiver uncontrollably from the near misses. I am running out of cover and my arm and head are bleeding profusely. There's another little dike a few feet to my right that could provide better cover but I'll have to roll over in the open to make it. I have no choice, since the earth is disintegrating above me. There's an instant lull in the machine gun fire, so I quickly roll over to the other ridge. I come to rest on my back as the machine gunner opens up on me once again. Just when it seems there's no way out, an explosion blows the enemy bunker apart and the machine gun fire stops. A Marine rocket team must have pinpointed the machine gunner's position and come to my aid. I might have a little more time to live.

I rest my arm on my stomach which is drenched in blood. The electrical throbbing is excruciating and I'm losing so much blood, I might bleed to death. Out of sheer panic, I reach around to the back of my clutch belt and pull out an ace bandage and slide it under my gaping wound. Holding one end of the bandage string with my teeth and the other with my good hand, I tie a knot locking the bandage down on my wound. The pain from the pressure of the bandage is agonizing, but the bleeding seems to slow. I reach up and feel the area where the bullet grazed my head. There's a deep slice in my skull and it feels like a hot iron on my head. Blood is everywhere. I close my eyes and start praying.

The battle rages all around me. Bullets crack and whiz by me. The NVAs have started a counterassault. To my right, five NVAs jump out of a camouflaged cave opening, and assault a lone foxhole. A Marine who looks like Killer jumps up, firing a 45 and holding a K-bar as they swarm over him. All I see are weapons thrusting downward into the foxhole. Little fights like this are happening all around me. Demonic screams echo from nature's walls. The NVAs are everywhere and I am wounded prey. I look around for my rifle to defend myself, but I have no protection other than the grenades that hang from my clutch belt. I reach down and unhook one of the grenades and bend the cotter pin for easy removal. I decide to blow myself up and take the NVAs with me if I'm attacked. I set the grenade down next to me and wait.

The throbbing is driving me into a semiconscious state of agony. Suddenly, someone is shaking my shoulders. I open my eyes to see Corporal Phillips staring at me, his hands firmly grasping my shirt. "Fuckin' come to!" he yells.

"My arm!" I cry out.

He stops shaking me, draws his fist back and belts me on the chin. I snap into consciousness and begin getting my bearings. He looks into my eyes and pulls me up close to him. "Take it! *Take the pain!*" he orders. I hear what he's saying and realize it's the only way to stay alive. He slowly lets loose of my shirt and reaches into his aid pack and pulls out an ace bandage. He wraps it around my arm, and with a forceful jerk, tightens the bandage over top the other one. I let out a yell, but quickly shut up. Phillips quietly surveys the battle scene with jumpy eyes, rolls over, and scampers away.

Minutes, hours, days could have passed. I am once again losing consciousness when our rocket team of Minch and McGuire dive next to me. I am barely awake but I can hear them talking. They don't seem to be aware of me, probably thinking I'm just another dead body.

"They keep popping up from that bunker like there's an endless fuckin' line of live bodies to take the place of the dead ones." Minch says, in frustration.

McGuire snaps, "I heard Cap say we're on top of an underground city. He said there's a fuckin' tunnel system supporting the ground-level bunkers so the NVAs can reinforce or withdraw in any direction. Plus, they're so well fuckin' camouflaged, it's hard to make anything out for certain. He said Battalion is tryin' to decide whether to get the wounded out or just call in B-52s and waste the whole mess. We've stepped into a world of shit, Minch." "Yeah, well that bunker in front of us is history." Minch sounds angry.

McGuire stokes a rocket into the launcher saying, "Blast the motherfuckers." Minch raises up exposing himself to gunfire, takes aim, and squeezes the trigger. A flash of light explodes out the rear of the launcher. My body lifts off the ground a few inches. Then every NVA within a 50-yard radius opens up on us. Bullets pop through the tin canister of the rocket launcher like it's paper. I prayed for them to get away from me. Minch blares, "Let's get out of here!" They crawl off to the right as the hail of bullets follow them.

The NVAs retaliate with a thunderous mortar barrage. I am lying on my back looking up at the sky when one of the descending mortars sounds like it's going to slam directly onto my head. I close my eyes and cringe. Bam! A mortar explodes a few precious yards away, lifting me off the ground like a feather. I feel a burning sensation in the back of my arm. I reach around and feel a hole where shrapnel ripped into the back of my already-wounded arm above the elbow. I moan in disbelief. My hand is covered with new blood. My head's swirling with thoughts of dying. I regain some control by clenching my teeth, saying, "*Take it!*" I desperately try to keep my mind off my wounds.

Everything is happening so quickly, it's difficult to remain focused on any event longer than a few seconds. Minch and McGuire raise up to fire the rocket launcher again and both of them get hit at once. Minch yells and grabs his arm. McGuire falls backward clutching his chest. About the same time, I see Bowman lying in the open, still hollering for help. He gets shot every time he hollers. Bowman is lying on the other side of Caldwell who has bullet holes all over the front of him. Caldwell cautiously flicks his wrist a few times signaling to Marines undercover not to give up on him. I see Sarge and the other Marines lying flat under cover of a small dike trying to decide what to do. They are pinned down by relentless fire and unable to move. Other Marines who had tried helping the wounded lie dead, bent over the dike inches from their futile attempt. Some Marines that had gotten hit by the initial fire lie wounded behind the dike and are still fighting. I spot Red who is also wounded. Trying to fire his jammed M-16 unsuccessfully, he grabs a discarded rifle, fires, and it blows up in his face.

I take my eyes off the battle by looking up at the sky. The constant sound of explosions, swooping aircraft, screaming demons, and a thousand other noises split through my gut. I hear NVAs shouting in Vietnamese to one another. I hold the grenade close to my body. Then someone grabs my ankle. I look down and see Doc has hold of me and is reaching around to his first-aid box. He jabs me three times with shots of morphine. For one brief moment, I feel some hope that the terrible electrical impulses in my arm will ease. Doc pats my leg and quickly crawls away, dragging his first-aid box beside him. I wonder how long he will stay alive amidst such a fusillade of fire.

I still hear Bowman screaming. Finally, Sarge can't take it any longer. He raises up, braving an intense volley of fire and runs out into the killing zone to get Bowman. He dives next to him and then lifts him up and places him over his shoulders. He awkwardly runs in as the Marines on line give him covering fire. NVAs cut loose with kill-fire of their own. Bowman is hanging over Sarge's shoulder when a bullet blasts into his head. There is an explosion of blood and the back of Bowman's head comes off. Sarge dives over the dike with Bowman falling on top of him. The farmer's son from Iowa is gone.

I turn and look up at the sky again. My heart is beating hard. Bowman and Scott are dead. Killer probably went down by the blades of NVA bayonets. Half the platoon is wasted. I wonder about Cars. There's so much firing going on I can't think straight. I stay frozen in what little safe zone I have left. It's beginning to seem like I will never get out alive. The throbbing is so intense, I again feel consumed by it. I wonder why the morphine hasn't taken effect? I close my eyes and start to lose consciousness when I feel someone shaking me. I open my eyes and see Dusty. He has one hand on my shirt and the other is clenching a bayonet bathed in blood. His M-16 is strung around his shoulder. He's crouched low and his eyes shift from one spot to the other like he's formulating a plan.

"Drew! You got one chance to make it. There's a stream bed up ahead, but we'll have to run across this open area to get there." I look over my shoulder and across the open area where several bodies lay sprawled over the ground. We'll be committing suicide trying to run across that open area. I wonder why he's even there to help me. It all seems so crazy.

"Dusty, we'll never make it! Everybody's gettin' it!"

"Let's go!" he hollers. He jerks me up to my feet and I see the stream bed about 25 yards away. Not a long way, but we will have to cross through the killing zone to get there. Each step will be an eternity. Dusty puts my arm around his shoulder and carries me forward. I keep thinking about Bowman's head exploding in half. I sense that a round is going to burst into me at any moment. I feel like I'm running through a twirling fan blade without getting cut. I focus on the edge of the stream bed, praying that we will make it. Dusty bends forward, dragging me through the crossfire.

We finally make it to the edge of the stream bed and Dusty yells, "Dive!" I take one giant step and dive over the edge of the stream bed, closing my eyes in anticipation of a hard landing. I fall onto something soft and open my eyes. Not more than three inches from my face are two steely blue eyes staring at me. It takes a moment to gain my senses. I try to understand what I'm seeing. I look again at those blue eyes. The spiritless gaze is all too familiar. There's a bright red, dime-size hole where the bullet had entered the Marine's head. A trickle of blood flows down his cheek onto the ground where a small red puddle has formed. He has short, blond hair and a tanned face. A picture of a pretty girl is attached to his helmet. Now, I remember him. He's the would-a-been surfer from California who walked by me before the battle began. He's handsome even in death. He would have probably married that girl, but instead, he owns the death stare. His eyes are still open as if he had died instantly. Head shots are definitely the quickest way to go.

I raise my eyes from the stone cold face of the blue-eyed Marine. Above and to the right of him are at least 20 bodies of Marines from the point element of Lima Company who had walked unsuspectingly into the ambush. All of them have been shot in the head.

Dusty and Cap are standing in the midst of the bodies peering out at enemy positions, exposing themselves to incoming fire. They show no concern for their own safety, only the desire to get us through the next few moments. The battle has been raging for about two hours and I now clearly see the extent of the carnage. The dry stream bed runs along one side of the ville all the way to the South China Sea, which is to my left about 300 yards away. We own the stream bed but it has been hard fought. There are at least 50 NVA and Marine bodies strewn to my left on the bedrock where they had fallen in battle. From what I'm able to discern, there's another 70 or 80 wounded Marines pinned down around the ville or entrenched within the stream bed. The front incline of the stream bed provides cover for the survivors. Most of the remaining Marines who have not been wounded keep their heads down holding rifles above the edge of the incline, blindly firing at enemy positions. You risk getting shot in the head by raising up. Those who took the risk lie dead as witness to the others.

Cap yells to the Marines who are pinned down along the far edge of the stream bed, "Help the wounded!" I crawl over and lean against the steep incline of the stream bed where everyone is gathering. Corporal Phillips is in charge of getting the wounded out. He crawls over and gives me the plan. "There's still a chance we can get out of here alive. Dusty says that a medevac will be landing back over that ridge." He points back beyond the open area which we had run across during our initial assault. "First we gotta get there. We're gonna crawl along the stream bed until that ridge is directly opposite us. Then we'll have to run across the open area to get to the ridge. Drew, since you can still walk, you go first." My heart sinks. "If you make it to the ridge, we'll follow. Get movin' along the stream bed, Drew." It's fitting that I am chosen as the expendable one. The point man always goes first because he clears the way for the others.

I start crawling toward the South China Sea, using the incline of the stream bed as cover. Marines are hurling grenades, firing rockets, M-16s, and machine guns. Mortars are skyrocketing down around us. At times, I just want to give up. I am feeling weak and sick to my stomach. My arm throbs but I keep crawling forward. I finally reach the area along the stream bed which places me directly across from the ridge. The ridge is about 200 yards to our rear and will provide enough cover for a medevac to land. I wait for the rest of the wounded to catch up with me. Some of the more seriously wounded are being dragged on ponchos or carried by other Marines. Phillips makes his way up to me. "Okay Drew, go for it!"

I crawl up the backside of the stream bed braving enemy fire, not caring any longer if one of their bullets has my name on it. I muster all remaining strength and begin zigzagging in a crouched position across the open area toward the ridge. I glance back and see the first Marine to follow get shot in the back and collapse. I feel like my legs are going to give out. It's a long run, punctuated by bullets snapping around me. The closer I get to the ridge, the more I want to live. Guys along the ridge that hadn't yet advanced into the battle are waving me forward. I'm getting painstakingly close. I'm going to make it! Then, as I near the ridge a chopper takes off in a barrage of enemy fire. I dive to the ground looking up at the chopper. It tilts a few times and then crashes onto the beach of the South China Sea. No one is getting out of here alive. I get up and run over the top the ridge, tumbling to the ground on the other side.

Within minutes, other wounded Marines pour over the ridge. Marines who haven't yet entered the battle come to our aid. One of them comes over and holds me while we await the arrival of a medevac. I am so exhausted, I can't keep my eyes open. He keeps pouring water over my face and shaking me so I won't pass out. "Come on, stay awake," he says. "You're almost home free." I know if I fall asleep, I might not wake up.

Then I hear the distant thunderclap of an approaching medevac. I look across the South China Sea and see a huge CH-46 Sea Knight chopper flying toward us. Will he get shot down like the last one? Will we make it out of this hell?

The big chopper tilts upward and lands about 20 yards to our right. The tail of the chopper drops open so we can climb aboard. I hear thuds of mortar erupting from enemy positions. The NVAs are cutting loose with a mortar barrage on us. I am so close to getting out alive, yet still so far away. The first wave of mortars whistle down exploding about 40 yards to our left. The more seriously wounded are dragged onto the chopper first. I realize the NVAs are making adjustments in their line of fire and the second wave of mortars are about to come.

As I'm being helped onto the chopper, mortars start exploding around us. The engine of the Sea Knight chopper roars and we lift into the air. Bullets snap through the paper-thin walls of the chopper. NVA snipers are having a field day with us. The chopper continues to rise. About 15 of us are packed into the back of the chopper like sardines. The guy next to me suddenly screams and grabs his shoulder. None of us budge. I keep praying for us to get out of this hell as bullets continue to pop through the walls of the chopper. Finally, the chopper tilts downward and accelerates forward. The deafening sounds of battle trail off as we race across the beach of the South China Sea toward an aircraft carrier.

I lie back on the floor of the chopper and take a deep breath in relief. I close my eyes and quickly fall into a semiconscious state, the sights and sounds of battle still churning in my head. My friends are still stuck on the battlefield. Then, the image of the blue-eyed Marine who lies dead in the stream bed comes back to me. I remember how I backed away from him in shock. Now, it's as if an earthbound spirit is calling out from his soul, speaking through my crazed thoughts. I hear him saying, "Why didn't you say something to me before we got ambushed? Remember when I passed by? Now it's too late, and I'm gone forever. My parents will miss me. They will never know how the war changed me—how it changes all of us. I didn't really want to go on like this any longer. By the way, I heard something before the bullet hit. You know how all the grunts say you never hear the head shots? That's bullshit! I heard it the instant it hit. A deep, weakening feeling shot through me from my head down to my toes. I knew it was serious as I fell to the ground. It was a long fall and I was able to see my life all over again. My life was too short. There weren't many memories to bring with me—family, friends, going to school, and growing up in California. My girlfriend, Lisa, will miss me. We were going to get married after I got back from the Nam and live out our dreams. Now, she'll have to marry someone else. My spirit lifted out of my body when I hit the dirt. At that moment, I no longer cared about the horror, the hard luck, or my family. I am free! I'm sorry you're not with me. It's really nice over here, but some of us have to live to let others know what happened in the Nam. There are men and nations who profit by selling arms for war. God is not happy with them. They see lesser people as expendable—you, me, and the gooks. We are all one in death and we will all meet again . . ."

I agree with his vision of war and death. I snap back to reality as the chopper slows, making its descent onto the aircraft carrier. It lands smoothly, the back hatch drops, and hospital personnel jump onboard. Two corpsmen put me on a stretcher and carry me to an elevator which takes us down to the surgery rooms. Hundreds of sailors line the ship's planks and look on in silence. I feel like I'm about to pass out when a priest kneels over me, making the sign of the cross. I hold tightly onto my scapular as he anoints me with holy oil, praying in Latin. I realize he's giving me my Last Rites. He compassionately moves on to another Marine. The ship's elevator slowly descends into a hospital prep room where two nurses and a corpsman begin cutting off my fatigues, searching for wounds. The corpsman comments, "Looks like we're in for a long day. They're sayin' this is a Widowmaker battalion. Reports are estimating at least 55 guys killed and 90 wounded outta the first couple hundred guys that went in. The whole battalion's gonna be wiped out soon."

A door opens from an adjoining operating room and a surgeon walks in. He quickly discards his bloody gown and gloves for new ones. He's a small guy with dark curly hair and deep brown eyes. He bends over me and looks into my eyes. "We'll be putting you to sleep, son," he says, softly.

"Will I lose my arm, sir?"

"No, you won't," he replies emphatically. "I can also say, you'll never see war again."

My eyes close and I leave the Nam.

CHAPTER X

War Lepers

December 28, 1967-August 1968

I'm in a black void and my left arm feels like it's immersed in a pot of boiling water. I want to scream but can't muster the effort. I remember I had just gotten off the battlefield and had been seriously wounded. I take a deep breath of antiseptic air and open my eyes. Blurry images of wounded Marines and ghastly cries echo through the brightly lit passageway.

I am lying on a bottom bunk in a narrow hospital corridor of the ship. The bunks are stacked three high along the bulkhead. I feel cramped and burning with fever. I look across the aisle to see a wounded Marine lying on a bottom bunk staring blankly through me with pitiful, dark eyes. His hair is straggly and he needs a shave. He's covered with blood-soaked sheets that drop to the bed just below his mid-section. Where are his legs? I look at his upper body where the sheets are tucked in unnaturally along his shoulders and chest. They're tucked in so close to his body, it gives the appearance of an upper torso without appendages. The reality of what I'm seeing begins to sink in as I look him over again. He seems consumed by pain. I am sickened by the sight of him yet amazed he lived through whatever blew him apart. What if his family would see him like this? I'm sure they never considered he would be coming home without arms and legs. The Marine Corps is supposed to produce heroes—not freaks. Tears fall down his cheeks like a dreary autumn rain. Now he must come to grips with the reality of being a freak, a war leper destined to live in a country where beauty and strength are worshipped. He's distant, remote, and totally alone. He probably would have been better off dead.

As my mind clears, I become aware of constant screaming from the bunk above him. I glance up where a black Marine is strapped down to the bunk with his hands tied to the side rails. He's screaming at the top of his lungs and his face is contorted like a demon. He wears only underwear and doesn't appear to be wounded. Where is his pain coming from and why is he screaming so insanely? I cringe each time he jerks up and lets loose with his loud, blood-curdling scream. Suddenly, it dawns on me what's going on. In the field, when FNGs come under fire for the first time, or when somebody begins to unravel after getting too close to Old Man Death, they would freak out and run around in circles, break down and cry, or bury their face in Mother Earth like a little kid looking for Mom. Most combat Marines have come close to it or have done it at one time or another. This guy definitely saw something that nearly scared him to death. I can only guess what horrific event sent him over the edge. As the blood-curdling screams continue, I wonder if his mother will ever know her son again.

A guy on the top bunk above him sits up and yells for a corpsman to do something to help the crazy Marine, but no one comes. His upper body is wrapped with bandages, so I surmise he had been shot in the chest.

The intercom on the far wall bellows, "Incoming medevac—team three—red-alert!" More wounded are being brought onboard.

I am sick to my stomach and my arm feels like a fire is raging inside of it. I have never felt such terrible throbbing in my life. I lie on my bunk for about 15 agonizing minutes listening to the screams from the crazy Marine. Finally a doctor and corpsman walk into the ward and administer a sedative to him, and the demented Marine instantly passes out. Then they move on to the Marine across from me who hasn't any appendages, and give him some morphine. Mercifully, his eyes close. As the doctor walks by my bunk, I grab his wrist and plead with him to give me something for pain. He bends and looks into my eyes, saying, "I'll give you the relief you need, but only ask for this drug when you absolutely can't handle the pain any longer. These drugs are really addicting, Marine." For a millisecond I consider what the doctor is saying about addiction and shake my head in agreement. I realize he has never known such pain. My eyes follow his hand as he reaches into his pocket and pulls out a syringe. He inserts it into the IV tube in my arm and slowly pushes the morphine solution into my vein. A warm feeling immediately shoots through my body. The terrible burning in my arm disappears and a great peace settles over me unlike anything I had ever experienced. All the horror is gone and life becomes a beautiful experience. I try to stay awake to relish the rapture of the moment, but my eyes close and I fall asleep.

It seems only a second elapsed, and I open my eyes. The incredible fire in my arm returns, and I feel consumed by pain. I again see the horrid image of a torso and head on the bottom bunk across from me. He's still starring blankly at me as though I don't exist. His family and friends would be shocked to see him without arms and legs. It will take a whole lot of love to nurse this Marine back to life. Only a mother has that kind of love. My wounds seem minuscule compared to his.

"Incoming medevac—teams two and three—red-alert!" The blaring intercom reminds me that my buddies are still fighting a war. If they only knew what's awaiting them in these hospital wards, they would probably stop the fighting. I hear voices within the small confines of the trauma unit crying out, "CORPSMAN!" Behind each voice is a wounded Marine begging like a dog. The whimpering sounds rip through my Marine Corps heart. We are fighters! This isn't supposed to be our fate.

The burning moves through my arm and into my body like a firestorm. "Corpsman!" I beg. "Corpsman!" I repeat, in a high-pitched scream.

A corpsman suddenly looms over my bed with a beet-red face. "It's not your time!" he snaps. "You still have two more hours until your next shot, so don't be callin' out. I'll be back when it's time."

"Corpsman!" the dismembered Marine on the bottom bunk across from me yells.

"Fuck it!" the corpsman snorts. "Your turn to give him a fuckin' shot. I'm tired of his ass. Every goddamn day it's the same friggin' shit from him. No arms, no legs, no peter. What fuckin' good is he anyway?"

"Hey, he ain't my patient," another corpsman responds in an angry manner. "I got my own assholes to deal with. You take care of your shit, and I'll take care of mine."

"Incoming medevac—team three—red-alert!" The intercom blares.

"Fuckin' no end to this shit!" the corpsman snorts.

Am I really in a hospital? I have the sense I'm nothing more than a slab of meat on the chopping block. Will I ever get out of here alive? There is a different kind of war going on deep in the bowels of this hospital ship. This is the war against pain. You live from minute to minute by the rules of the corpsman. The corpsman is fuckin' God down here.

The burning in my arm increases with every passing second. I wait for the corpsman to return, praying for time to pass more quickly. "Corpsman!"

I finally holler in desperation. He doesn't come and my worst fears are realized. Should I beg? No, I must hold out! More time elapses. The burning furnace in my arm is now out of control. "Please help! Corpsman! I can't take it!" I plead. He doesn't come. The Marine across the narrow aisle is still starring at me. Lifeless, mournful eyes appear sick and tired and, for the moment, far beyond the point of begging. "Corpsman!" I scream. The Marine across from me doesn't blink. Will I ever get beyond the point of begging?

"Incoming medevac—team two—red-alert!" The intercom blares.

Finally, the corpsman makes his rounds again with the long, glistening needle from heaven. The Marine across from me once again closes his eyes when injected with the morphine. Then the corpsman inserts the syringe into the tube in my arm and slowly pushes the magical solution into my vein. A few seconds later a beautiful warmth settles over me and the fire in my arm disappears. I could care less about anything now. A few minutes later, I pass out from the powerful drug.

It seems only seconds elapse when I awake to the instant searing in my arm. I cringe. "Incoming medevac—team two—red-alert!" The intercom blares in a monotonous tone. "God, doesn't it ever end?" I mutter. My arm still throbs. The demonic screams of the insane Marine pierce my ears. Each time he wails, I wonder about what kind of horror drove him over the edge. The Marine above him is still calling out, "Help this crazy motherfucker!" No one comes. All of us start pleading again for help from the corpsman. Hours of hell pass and the intercom continues to blare. Finally, the corpsman makes his rounds. He inserts the long, glistening needle from heaven into my IV tube and all the horrendous pain disappears. I stay awake for about five minutes, relishing those precious moments of pain-free existence before drifting off to sleep.

The scenario repeats six times a day. Each time I awake the intercom welcomes me back to reality, "Incoming medevac—team three—red-alert!" The pain never goes away except when I pass out after each morphine shot. Sometime after one of the shots, they remove the crazy Marine from the hospital bay. I feel relieved that I no longer have to listen to his demonic screams. He's being shipped off to some VA psychiatric ward where doctors will try to make him human again. I hope his mom will not have to see him in this condition. The Marine on the top bunk keeps exclaiming, "Thank God that crazy fucker's gone."

The dismembered Marine on the bottom bunk has the thousand-yard stare most of the time. He never acknowledges anyone's presence other than the corpsman. His face remains expressionless, then suddenly he roars, "CORPSMAN!" with such ferocity, it sends a shock wave through the whole unit. For that one instant, a couple of times a day, he shows his insides to all of us. A momentary hush briefly settles over the unit as we contemplate his horror. The corpsman usually doesn't show up and the Marine's face once again turns to stone.

Four horrible days elapse. Finally, I start feeling some relief from the horrendous pain. The corpsman removes the IV tube from my arm and at about the same time my fever breaks. I sit on my bunk and begin eating real food. Many other Marines who are not seriously wounded also begin coming back to life. Grunt chatter fills the room.

Unexpectedly, one of the guys in my platoon pays me a visit. Red is smiling as he approaches my bunk. I remember he had picked up a rifle on the battlefield and it exploded when he shot it. "Can't believe you're still alive," he says, putting his hand on my shoulder and smiling. "I wanted to stop by and thank you, 'cause when I shot your rifle, it blew up and I got the million-dollar wound."

"Oh, that was my rifle you picked up?" I see dark specks of shrapnel in his face.

"Yep! That was my third wound, so I'm AMF outta the crotch." Red's so excited I thought he might jump right out of his shoes. This wound qualifies him for a ticket back to the States.

"What happened to the rest of the guys in the platoon?" I ask.

Red's eyes narrow and his eyebrows furl as he speaks. "A lot of guys didn't make it. They still can't find Scott's body. He might have been incinerated when the palm came down. Or, shit, it could have been a direct hit from the B-52s that came over the perimeter later that night. God knows what. Bowman, Indian, and six other guys from our platoon went down hard. Just glad I wasn't with 'em, ya know?"

"Yeah, I know what you mean. It was bad enough where we were," I respond, feeling grateful to be alive.

Red shakes his head saying, "There was a total of 55 or 60 of our guys killed and about 100 wounded from our company and Lima Company. That's why they're startin' to call us the Widowmaker. Won't be long before everybody in the battalion gets it. I'm just glad my time in hell's over. I wanted to stop by and thank you before they ship ya outta here. Can't believe I got my third Heart."

"What about Cars?" I ask.

"I heard he's okay for now." Red begins to pull away but I grab his wrist.

"Red," I whisper, "Dusty got me and Scott shot. He forced us out into the killing zone."

Red frowns and backs away saying, "He'll get his, Drew, don't you worry. I wouldn't want to have to go back out there like he's going to do. I'll try to get in touch with you back in the real world. By the way, what's your last name?"

"My name is Drew Martensen," I say emphatically.

Red leaves as a corpsman gives me another shot of morphine. "You'll be gettin' shipped to DaNang for the New Year," says the corpsman. "That's tonight. This shot should hold you till you get there."

The time has come for me to leave the hospital ship. As they put me on a stretcher to leave the unit, I look one final time at the dismembered Marine. He's 18 or 19 years old, but his eyes are ancient. Like most of us, he hadn't planned on ending up like this. No matter how long I live, I will never forget his icy stare, stone face, and dismembered body.

About 10 of us are moved up to the top deck of the carrier. A storm has blown in from the north, producing huge waves across the ocean. The temperature has dropped into the 50s and it's unusually cool for the subtropics. Marines off-shore are still buried in foxholes holding up through the storm. I'm sure they're cold out there waiting for Charles, and thinking about Old Man Death. I feel grateful I'm not there, but also guilty since I'm not with them. However, the war has broken my spirit and I just want to get home alive.

Over the ocean I see an incoming chopper bearing a red cross coming toward us. It makes a graceful descent and lands on the carrier. The ugly sight of freshly wounded Marines spills out the back of the chopper. Then we're put onboard the chopper and we head back over land toward DaNang. I look out the window and see villes scattered within the trees below. At times, I see people moving among the trees. I pray that we're high enough not to be shot at. I remember the doctor's promise that I will never see war again, but it seems the nightmare won't go away. Eventually, we land safely at the hospital at DaNang and I'm one step closer to getting out of Vietnam. We are transported by ambulance to an infirmary where I'm assigned a hospital bunk and given some pain pills. The next thing I do is write a letter to Mom and Dad about what had happened:

Dear Mom and Dad,

Well, by now you have probably heard I was wounded. I hope you haven't been too worried because it isn't that bad. I was pretty lucky compared with most of the guys. You probably read about the battle we were in. I was shot in the lower part of my arm near the wrist. When the bullet came out, it did a lot of damage by busting out my bones. It will be awhile before they can tell if any nerves in my arm were messed up. I also have a small wound in my elbow and one on the top of my head where a bullet grazed me. These really don't amount to much. I will be sent to a hospital in Guam and then to Bethesda Naval Hospital close to Washington D.C. Right now, I'm eating like a king and will have nurses to pester when I get to Guam. Please don't worry about me and excuse the shaky writing. I'll write soon again when I find out anything new.

All my love,
Drew

P.S. Tell Gayle I said hello and will write her soon.

At about the same time that I write this letter, my parents are notified by the Marines that I had been wounded. I never really gave much thought to how they would be notified until I later received an account of the event written by my little brother, Mark, for his fifth grade class. He writes:

The Marine

This was a one-day affair. I was 13 at the time of my brother's mishap and it brought out the emotion, fear. This took place when my brother was in Vietnam for about a half-year. A Marine came to our door and the following is what happened:

As I sat watching TV with my sister, I heard the doorbell ring. I ran to the door immediately and swung it open. As I looked out the window of the storm door, a Marine stared at me. I went into a daze, because if you have a brother in Vietnam and a Marine at your door, he was either injured or killed. As I stared at the Marine's face, I saw my brother's whole life in one moment. I thought of how much I loved him for all the things he had done for me. All of those little things that we take for granted. Then, I thought of what it would do to my mother. I thought that she might have some sort of nervous breakdown or something just as terrible. I considered what it might do to my little sister or my older brothers. It could change their whole outlook on life. So, as not to keep the Marine waiting, I ran upstairs to get my mother.

As I entered my mother's room, she was relaxing on her bed reading a book. I walked to her slowly and told her there was a Marine at the door. At that moment, she started to shake violently and tears came to her eyes. For a moment I thought she was going to faint. She got up from the bed and started to shake even more. I knew she was thinking about our family's life, and that this could be the end for all of us. Then, my mother told me she'd be down in a minute.

As I started down the stairs, I tried to think that maybe my brother wasn't hurt at all. But, there wouldn't be a Marine at our door if he wasn't at least injured. Maybe he came to tell us that my brother was coming home from Vietnam, but that left my mind because no one comes home until he has been over there for thirteen months. And so, with fear in my mind, I went to tell my sister.

I entered our back room and found my little sister watching TV. I sat down beside her and calmly told her that there was a Marine at our door. She started breathing heavily and almost started to cry. As I looked at her, I could see my brother hurt badly but not killed. I could tell that she was thinking the worst. I told her not to worry because everything would be okay. We walked toward the living room where the Marine was waiting.

As we entered the living room, my older brother came out of his room to see what was going on. When he saw the Marine, he sat down and stared at him. Then, my mom came down the stairs. Everyone must have had a million thoughts going through their minds at that moment. The Marine said to my mom, "Is your son Victor Drew Martensen?" Mom replied, "Yes, he is." Everyone tensed up even more. The Marine finally said, "First of all, he's all right."

This was a very hectic time in my life. I never want to forget it, because I grew up a little more.

Mark Martensen

It's New Year's Eve and I'm lying on my bunk praying for more pain pills when all hell breaks loose outside the hospital in DaNang. Mortars whistle down and explode within a mile radius of the hospital. Guns are firing, machine guns and rockets are going off, and people are frantically yelling in the distance. I am visibly shaking. I hear chatter from the hospital personnel in the background. "They're saying that parts of DaNang are under siege! Hue has been hit and Saigon is also under attack! Hope they can hold them off here in DaNang!"

"Corpsman!" I cry out. "Get me a rifle!" Many of the other wounded start calling out for weapons.

"Get under the bed if you like, but we can't issue rifles," the corpsman orders.

I have lived by the code that my M-16 is my closest friend. Now, I feel stripped of all identity. Like scared rabbits, most of us crawl under our beds to wait out the night. The gunfire lasts throughout the long night and into the morning, tapering off by afternoon. Word has it that there's a major NVA offensive building in all of South Vietnam and the heavy fighting could last for months. Charlie is definitely trying to change the tide of the war and the Tet New Year is only a few weeks away. No telling what might happen then? I pray that I just get out of here alive.

Finally, on January 4, 1968, I'm transferred by plane to a hospital in Guam. Once we lift off the airfield in DaNang, I sense the horrible nightmare really might be coming to an end. Most of the trip is spent adjusting to the feeling of having a safe zone around me. It's hard to adapt to not being constantly at risk for your life. Once we arrive in Guam, I feel like a huge weight has been lifted from my shoulders, and I realize—*I have survived Vietnam.*

Safely on the ground, hospital personnel meet our plane and move about 20 of us into the hospital on wheelchairs and gurneys. We are transferred to beds in a long, narrow ward of the hospital. A group of doctors and nurses walk in with bandage carts and surgical equipment and position themselves around the patients in the first two beds at the front of the unit. Some of us sit up to see what's going on. There's an eerie silence in the ward. Suddenly, a ferocious scream erupts from one of the patients who is surrounded by a team of three nurses and a doctor. A patient next to him, who is also surrounded by a medical team, starts thrashing about, hollering, "No! No!" They hold him down and strap him to the bed. By this time, the guy next to him is screaming his lungs out. I realize they're changing bandages. Why don't they give them pain shots?

The guys next to the first two beds are getting nervous. Two corpsman are positioned at each end of the infirmary as guards. I look at my arm and wonder how long it has been since I had a bandage change. I vaguely remember having it changed when I came out of one of my slumbers on ship. It's also been close to eight hours since I've had any pain pills and my wrist is already burning with pain. I envision them pulling the bandages off my wound. Screams explode from the first two bunks, I look at the other patients to see how badly they are wounded. One of them, lying a few bunks down from me, is wrapped like a mummy. He keeps trying to raise his head to see what's going on. Best he not see.

Once they complete the dressing changes on the first two guys, one of the nurses administers pain shots to each of the patients. Why didn't they give them pain shots before the procedures began? This makes no sense. Looking more closely at the medical teams, I notice one of the nurses is in the role of observer. Everything seems staged for her benefit. It's becoming clear what's going on—they are using us as guinea pigs to help desensitize the RN trainee to pain.

They move systematically from one bed to the next and the excruciating screams move along with them. When they reach the guy wrapped like a mummy, there is hell to pay. He screams so loudly it's like listening to a banshee. At times there are moments of total quiet when he passes out. I look at him and cringe. There is hardly any skin on his arms and legs. It looks like an explosion of some kind had ripped or burned everything away except muscle and bone. I can't believe they're doing this to him, especially since he's already in such bad shape. When they finish with his bandage change, the doctor says, "Good job, Marine." Then, the doctor pulls a syringe out and gives him a shot of morphine. I am powerless to do or say anything. I am a lowly grunt that has been taught to "take it."

A lifetime later, they reach my bed. I close my eyes and start praying. The whole procedure takes only a few minutes but it seems like forever. I let loose with a few cries as they pull the bandages from my skin. When all the bandages are removed, I open my eyes and look at my wound. There's a large gaping hole that extends from just below my elbow all the way down to my hand. I cringe as the doctor tells me I'll be having a skin-graft operation to close the wound in just a few days. I'm given a pain shot and the experiment is finally over.

A few days later, I have the skin-graft operation. I lie in a recovery bed for about a week with a high fever. I'm once again given morphine to ease the physical pain, but I'm also finding the drug eases the vivid memories of combat still fresh in my mind. Those terrible memories are never far away until I'm given morphine. I'm developing a special love for this drug.

Once I recover from the skin-graft operation, I'm flown to Bethesda Naval Hospital with a refueling stop in Hawaii. We are on the ground in Hawaii for only a few hours but it's long enough for the Marine Corps to award all of us a Purple Heart. It's a quick informal ceremony on the tarmac where a colonel pins the medal to our robes, saying the usual, "Job well done, Marine." He never makes eye contact with us and is so terse, he gives me the impression we have interrupted his afternoon golf game. I feel let down and discounted by the insensitivity of the affair. We reboard the plane with our Purple Hearts dangling from our robes and depart for Bethesda Naval Hospital.

It's a cold, windy day in early February when we arrive at the Naval Medical Center. It makes the grueling heat and humidity of Vietnam seem like a distant nightmare. The hospital looks like a small skyscraper rather than a traditional hospital. It's a tall, narrow structure that overlooks a golf course, beautiful homes, and thoroughfares—a sharp contrast to the concertina wire and fortifications that surround the hospital at DaNang. There are no gunshots, mortar tube thuds, explosions, or yells of "incoming!" Instead, car horns are blowing and shoppers scurry about wearing winter coats and gloves. Once we arrive at the hospital, gorgeous women in high heels and mini-skirts take my breath away. I have finally made it back to the real world and it's time to get readjusted!

I'm put on an orthopedic ward where about 40 other wounded lie in beds, filling the entire length of the room. A nurses' station is in the center where at least four nurses are on duty at all times. This is only a step-down unit and we will be transferred to permanent wards after being evaluated. About half the guys in the room are ambulatory patients like myself. Most of us will rehabilitate in the hospital for a few months and be transferred to Headquarters Marine Corps in Washington, D.C. for final discharge. The other more seriously wounded patients will never fully recuperate. They are destined to rehabilitate in VA hospitals far from the eyesight of others. There are lots of war lepers on the unit who are missing arms or legs. The more seriously wounded have multiple amputations and wounds that make recovery more difficult and gruesome.

A guy a couple of beds down from me is missing his right leg, half his left leg, half his right arm, and all the fingers on his left hand. His face was also hit by exploding shrapnel and he's missing an ear, his nose, and one eye. One day his parents come to visit him. They cry most of the time standing beside his bed and holding what's left of his right arm in a vain attempt to comfort him. He's married but his wife didn't make the trip to be with him. The scuttlebutt is that she's a 19-year-old beauty queen and couldn't bring herself to see him. She's in the process of divorcing him because of his injuries. No one blames her because the reality of his injuries is hard for anyone to take. We sometimes whisper about his state of being, like he's a freak we can no longer relate to. It's hard for any of us to comprehend the kind of life he's facing.

Many such cases are on our floor. There's a young man who walks around the unit with literally half his head gone. It looks like a piece of shrapnel sliced off the entire right side of his face and head. He has only one eye and a huge skin-graft covering the area where his face and head are missing. I wonder how he lived through the ordeal, since part of his brain was sliced away. He'll go through the rest of his life like that.

Many guys strain to hear sounds because their eardrums were blown out. Some stare endlessly at the ceiling, having been blinded by a close encounter with a booby trap or some other explosive device. Others are learning how to use wheelchairs or beginning to use artificial limbs. Some are beginning to speak again since the shock of combat has worn off.

I think I've seen just about everything until one day, I stop in horror while walking through the unit. There's a Marine who was flown directly in from the field after being found lying on the concertina wire at an outpost near the DMZ. The NVA had tortured him and left him to slowly die for all to witness. Unfortunately he's still alive, lying naked in a bed with a curtain surrounding him. The front of the curtain is open as I pass by. I freeze when I glimpse what's left of this young, once vibrant, Marine. He has no eyes, ears, nose, or lips. Most of the hair has been pulled from his head, not unlike being scalped, leaving open areas where the skin had been ripped away. There are gashes on his face. Both hands are cut off at the wrists. Both feet are cut off. He has no penis or scrotum. He has huge gaping holes on his midsection. He lies on the bed squirming his head as if straining to see something or to understand the horror. Later that afternoon his parents rush onto the unit to be with their dying son. I'm shocked they let them see him in such a hideous condition. From my bed at the end of the ward, I hear his mother let out a blood-curdling scream. She falls to the floor, unconscious. I am so upset I leave the ward and walk around the hospital in disgust. Mercifully, the Marine dies later in the day. He will always remind me of the real horror of war.

I get my first weekend liberty from Bethesda Naval Hospital in March. I take a bus to Georgetown University with another Marine named Ray Gallenstein from my hometown. We have short hair and our faces are dark and gaunt from the long hot days in Vietnam. Ray walks with a limp because his legs have been shredded by a close encounter with a mortar round. My arm is in a sling and wrapped tightly to my body. It's obvious that both of us are wounded war veterans, since the Naval Hospital isn't far away. We walk down a side street near the campus and a group of students spot us. They start yelling, "Fuckin' baby killers! Women killers! Rapists! Sonsabitches!" Then they pelt us with eggs. I run from the scene, full of shame and confusion. I am stunned at the level of hate they vent at us. I'm also surprised they know of some of the things that has been happening in Vietnam. I believed these were war secrets only vets knew about. I feel so ashamed after the incident, I decide to hide any connection with the military. I will let my hair grow and keep my casted arm hidden under my coat on future liberties. I will also never admit to having served in Vietnam. I'm beginning to learn that being a Vietnam veteran is less than honorable. A few weeks later, I go home on a weekend pass and find that time has cruelly slipped away. I meet some of my old friends at the Varsity Club on The Ohio State University campus and catch up on current stuff. Most of them have progressed on in college and I'm far behind. They're talking in a language I don't understand—there's this "prof," that "elective," and a maze of words and syllables that don't make sense. The upcoming spring break is being planned with a trip to Fort Lauderdale, Florida. I'm surprised to hear that Mark had gotten married to Rosey. My old girlfriend, Gayle, is definitely seeing someone else. Stumpy has bought a new Volkswagen. Pig has avoided the draft through a medical deferment. Johnny is planning to go to law school. They talk about how their softball teams have done this season and how the Buckeyes are definitely going to beat Michigan this fall. Reiner and Zeik are making plans for everyone to hit the winery at Kelley's Island. Some of the guys who are about to graduate from OSU have good jobs lined up. They talk about management styles and how to run a company. My brother, Hank, has been offered a job as an auto plant manager in Flint, Michigan. Everyone is excited about the future.

I listen to their chatter, drinking a beer, and become more and more withdrawn. I want to tell them about what had happened to me in the Nam, about the danger and the insanity of it all, but I sense that no one really cares. They have no connection with the words "grunt," "fire in the hole," "Zulu," "Charlie," "palm," "kill-fire," "frag," "LZ," "Mr. No-shoulders," or "Widowmaker." I will have to keep these words to myself because they don't make real world sense. My world is still the world of the Nam—the pain, the suffering, the torment, and the horror.

After returning to Bethesda from the weekend furlough, I realize that life in America in 1968 is totally different from the America I once knew. I have returned to a country in turmoil rather than at peace. Televisions are mounted on the ceilings of our unit which each day delivers more bad news about the war and the effect it's having on our country. The brutal sieges at Hue, Conthien, and Khesanh are being televised to the world. The discovery of nearly 3,000 South Vietnamese executed by the Communists shock the nation. Weekly casualty figures reaching as many as 300 Americans soldiers killed and 1,000 wounded take its toll on the U.S. psyche. Buddhist monks burn themselves to death on national television in protest of the South Vietnamese government. The Communists in Hanoi parade dazed and tortured American pilots in front of the camera for all the world to witness. A South Vietnamese general coldly executes a young Viet Cong suspect on live television. The news reports often portray Americans engulfed for days in useless firefights, where the enemy will simply reclaim territory after we have moved out. Costly night ambushes and jungle booby traps are evidence that we are fighting a no-win war and it's time to get out. On the evening of March 31, 1968, President Johnson announces to America that he will not run for reelection. His Great Society has been gunned down on the battlefield of Vietnam. A few days later, Martin Luther King is shot down in Memphis. Antiwar demonstrations are breaking out on university campuses all across the country, while the "silent majority" stands up for law and order.

Each day I watch the insane scenario unfold. However, the intense combat I experienced in Vietnam is still fresh in my mind and daily life in America seems somewhat remote and foolish to me. I'm a little more concerned with getting through my third operation which has been scheduled for late April. The purpose of the surgery is to explore and possibly repair the median nerve in my left arm. Shrapnel had severed the median nerve, making repair or regeneration doubtful. The movement and feeling in my left hand depends upon this operation. I'm told that I will have only one bone extending into my wrist. The ulna bone had been completely blown away by the impact of the bullet, limiting movement and strength in my wrist.

However, none of these injuries really bother me much. It's amazing how huge events like the operation I am facing and all the craziness in society seem minuscule compared to what I had experienced in the Nam. Vietnam had taught me there aren't any normal boundaries left to establish good from bad, right from wrong, or sane from insane. An atom bomb could drop on New York and I might wince a few times and that would be it.

I once overheard a patient trying to explain to a nurse how he just wasn't able to feel much of anything since coming back from the Nam. She was trying to encourage him to get on with his life and go back to school. He told her a story about a man who had survived the fire bombings in Dresden during the Second World War. "He awoke in the corner of a basement under some pilings after the night of bombing had ended," the patient said. "He peeked out and saw that every structure within sight had been incinerated and nothing was left standing. He then looked over to another corner of the basement and saw an adult male lion that had escaped from the zoo, cowering like a pussycat. The man understood why the king of beasts had lost his primeval power. War does something to you that only another survivor can relate to, so stop telling me to go back to school!"

I'm no longer trying to make sense of the way I feel. Like the lion, I have been beaten to a pulp and stripped of my identity. The only thing that makes any sense is wanting to escape and feel good. I have already learned that nobody cares to listen to the Vietnam vet because they think we're part of the problem. If we stand up for the war, we are hated by the antiwar groups. If we protest the war, we are labeled long-haired hippie freaks by the silent majority. The best way for me to survive is to ride the middle of the road and keep my mouth shut. Anyway, alcohol and drugs can remove the pain. I'm sick and tired of "taking it" and the drugs at the hospital make me feel damn good.

I have my final operation in mid-April and it fails to repair my median nerve. I'm cut open from my wrist all the way to my armpit. There's lots of bleeding and plenty of pain following the operation. I'm put on a new synthetic narcotic called Talwin. I easily fall in love with the dope and find myself again counting the minutes between fixes. My days and nights are measured by pleasurable hallucinogenic dreams that quickly fade when the Talwin lets up to a world filled with physical pain. The nurses become gods, and I pray constantly for their quick return. My life is revolving around drugs.

Once I recover from the operation, I continue asking for pain killers even after a nurse tells me to stay away from them. She spends hours trying to get me to talk about Vietnam to ease the emotional pain and to quit using drugs. She gives me Viktor E. Frankl's book, *Man's Search for Meaning*, on his survival in the Nazi concentration camps. However, I am still so consumed by my own grief, I can't see beyond the words on the pages. All my coping skills are rooted in three words—piss on it!

Back on my feet a few weeks later, I start going out with other patients to drink at the local bars. It's quite a relief to sit in a barroom sipping beer and not having to worry about where the next gunshot's coming from. We talk in grunt language and share war stories in an attempt to re-create the camaraderie we had in the Nam. There's something very special about being around other combat vets. We share the common bond of having "seen the elephant," which is to have survived being under fire. You can look these guys in the eyes and feel some pride. They know what you have experienced and respect you for it. No one outside the military really understands or recognizes the value of this bond. When people realize we are patients from the Naval Hospital, they look at us like we're freaks or war lepers to be avoided like the plague. Most Americans seem to be washing their hands of the debacle in Vietnam. Fighting a respectable war is one thing, but what's happening in Vietnam is part of the darker side of human nature. America is simply not ready to own its part in the war, and is washing its hands of the collective evil by singling us out as the real sinners. It's a stark contrast to all the other wars where combat veterans are held in the highest esteem by all of society. I feel rejected and angry about all this societal bullshit.

Shortly after my final operation, I'm moved to a step-down unit to begin the transition out of the military. During this time, I discover there's a huge black market of pain drugs flourishing at the Naval Hospital. Talwin, Demerol, and morphine are drugs of choice for many of the ambulatory wounded. One day I'm offered some free Talwin by a patient who works part-time in the pharmacy. I literally have no defense against that first hit of illegal Talwin. I learn quickly how to inject the magical potion into my arm, groin, or leg. I'm limited only by the amount I am able to procure. Life is beginning to take on a totally different perspective for this Marine. I start running with the guys who hang out in the stalls of the bathrooms since it's the only safe place in the hospital to shoot-up drugs. We place guards at each entrance to watch for the nurses and medics who roam the wards. I shoot up and stagger back to my bunk where I lie low until my next fix. The euphoric pilgrimages to the bathroom last throughout the day and into the night. Late evenings are spent doing the bar scene. This is heaven compared to Nam.

During the final months in the hospital, I keep up on events with my old unit through incoming patients and a couple of letters I receive from Cars.

I am told by some of the new patients that our special landing force had been wiped out several times through a series of 14 field operations during the months of December 1967 through May 1968. We have unfortunately earned the nickname "Widowmaker" by sustaining a 90 percent casualty rate during these months. Recruits in boot camp are being told if assigned to our SLF unit, it's a death sentence. Ironically, they are also being told stories of heroism about our battalion. In one of the letters I receive from Cars, he briefly describes the end of our old platoon. He writes:

May 3, 1968

Drew,

How is everything going for you in the hospital? Last time I wrote, we were at the Cu Lu Valley doing operations. Thank God I pulled mess duty onboard ship and missed those operations. Most of the guys from our platoon who were still left got killed during some of the battles. Red got his third Heart on the day you got wounded, but the assholes on ship claimed they didn't have any record of his previous wounds. They sent him back into the field and he got killed a month later. That same day, I had to go up on deck to identify the bodies of Taylor, Andy, and all the rest of the guys. They were pinned down all day by two 50-caliber machine guns. They finally tried to make a run for it, but none of them made it.

Right after that, I got off mess duty. We went to Camp Carroll up near the DMZ. While we were there we went on a three-day operation in the mountains. For a change we didn't hit anything. Then we went to a position called Alpha-3, which is 300 meters from the DMZ, between Conthien and Gyo Lien. We were there for about one week and then we went back to Camp Carroll. Also, Fuller and Dusty went home in February. Can you believe that? They were the only ones to make it out without getting hit.

My brother came over here January 26. He is a water supply engineer and is stationed at Dong Ha. He doesn't even have to leave the perimeter. Thank God for that! Oh yeah, these assholes finally made me corporal.

On April 22, I went on R&R to Hong Kong. Boy did I have a good time!!! You can imagine what I was up to. Here's some more good news. I'm going to Okinawa for the rest of my tour since my brother is over here. How's that for lucking out?

When I was on R&R, the battalion had another operation in the mountains. It was another bad scene, and they almost got wiped out. From the 50 grunts that were in our platoon when we left the Philippines, only Potts and myself are left. Now, I'm leaving.

Well, Drew, that's about all for now. Write when you can.

Your pal,
Cars

I decide not to write back to Cars. I just want to put the thoughts of those guys behind me as quickly as possible and get on with my life. Thinking about the horror and all the loss of life only seems to add more misery to my already overburdened heart. Most of the guys I served with are dead and the survivors will go on to other things. It's time for me to forget the whole mess and start anew, but I'm in no hurry to get a job or go back to school. The Veterans Administration will temporarily send me monthly checks for 100 percent disability which will provide badly needed time to find myself. There are places back in Columbus I can visit that will help me make the adjustment—The Varsity Club, The Silver Fox Lounge, Micky's Bar, The Press Grill, The Thunderbird, and many other "thinking" places. These barrooms will be good places to get on with some serious soul-searching about life and what to do with myself.

In August 1968, I'm finally transferred to Headquarters Marine Corps for discharge from the military. On my last day of military service, I sit in a lounge in Washington National Airport awaiting my flight to Columbus. Surprisingly, a guy sitting next to me at the bar begins buying me drinks to celebrate my discharge from the Corps. Our deep discussion about the dismal state of affairs in our country and the beauty of military service causes me to miss my flight. Of course, that gives me more time to think about things. One thing is really clear, though—Old Man Death is no longer hanging around me. What isn't so clear is the gnawing sensation in my gut that I haven't seen the last of him.

Widowmaker, Part II

"There is no coming to consciousness without pain."
— Carl Jung

CHAPTER XI

Homecoming

1968-1976

A year of drinking and drugging has passed since my discharge from the Marines. I am sitting in a neighborhood bar on the west side of Columbus, Ohio, on a Saturday morning, sipping Echo Springs with water, and listening to a Vietnam vet tell me his tale of woe. We are slouched on stools at the end of the bar and I look at him through the bar mirror. The vet's pudgy face is dripping with sweat and his VA cap tilts down over his forehead. He's peeling and scraping the label off his bottle of beer with his thumbnail. A clump of shredded paper fills the ashtray next to him. Four double shots of liquor are lined up on the bar to serve as boilermakers. The vet grabs one of the shot glasses and, after a deep rumbling burp, chugs the whiskey. He suddenly protests, "I can't believe that cop didn't give me a break. You'd think he'd have more respect for a disabled vet!" He slams the shot glass down on the bar in disgust.

The bartender, who's talking to a customer at the center of the bar, glances at the vet with a furled eyebrow. "Keep it down, pal," he orders.

The vet lowers his voice and continues peeling the label off his bottle of beer. "I told the cop that my left leg was blown off in the war. Think he gave a shit? He said it wasn't a war. The fucker called it a police action!" The vet snaps his words in anger and looks over at the bartender for reassurance that he isn't talking too loudly. Then he rubs his artificial leg as if it is aching. "I asked him how he'd dodged the draft to stay out of the police action? That really pissed the cop-fucker off. He dragged me out the car and handcuffed me." The vet grabs another shot glass of liquor and heaves it down. He puckers his lips in satisfaction, "I'm movin' out to the woods next month. Wanna join me?"

"I can't. I've got a job," I say, in disgust.

"What the hell kind of work are you doin'?"

"Ah, deliverin' frozen food around the state. I'm havin' trouble pickin' up the boxes though, 'cause of my bad arm." I pull my sleeve up and point to the gunshot wound on my arm. The vet shakes his head in recognition. "I'm too slow haulin' the food off the truck. I don't know how much longer my boss will keep me on." I take a swig of Echo Springs and swallow hard. The liquor burns away the thought of getting fired. "I'm thinkin' about goin' down to Florida for a break. Maybe I'll come back after that and start school." The vet responds with a head shake and a smirk.

I look into the bar mirror and think about the past year since my discharge from the Marines. I've been staying at my parents' house since I haven't been able to afford my own place. All the hopes I had about having a decent job and a good woman in my life are going down the drain. Most days are spent in bars trying to fuzzy up my brain and wipe away memories of combat. Even in my sleep, I'm having recurring nightmares about Vietnam. In one of the more persistent nightmares, I am redrafted into the Marines and sent back to fight in Vietnam. Scott, Bowman, Roberto, and Cars are alive and walking the jungle trail next to me. It's good to see and feel them close by once again. As we stalk through the jungle, huge booby traps hang from trees and trip wires run across the trail. The enemy suddenly ambushes us from behind trees and the familiar sound of gunshots and explosions begin going off. A sickening feeling shoots through my gut as I hear my buddies screaming and see bullets ripping into their flesh. They turn into skeletons and crawl underground leaving me to defend our position. Hundreds of NVAs with big red stars on their foreheads attack. I sense it is just a matter of time before they overrun my position. My gun suddenly jams and NVAs rush toward me screaming and firing their rifles. I pass out as bullets hammer into my body and I wake up in my bed sweating and shaking in terror. The nightmare stays with me throughout the next day or until I fuzzy up my brain again.

On one particular day while walking near a tennis court with my brother, Mark, a car backfired and I lost all contact with reality. Once again I became an animal on the fringe of the herd fighting for my life. I dove onto my hands and knees and crawled around in circles looking for cover. Still panicked, I body-crawled into the fence of the tennis court thinking Charlie was firing at me. I clawed at the metal fence, gasping, my heart pounding. When I came to my senses, I saw tennis players looking at me in dismay. Embarrassed, I walked over to my brother and tried to explain what had just happened. Although he was supportive, it's difficult to understand that kind of behavior when you've never been under fire.

I experience other bizarre post-war reactions. Having slept with "one eye open" while in Vietnam, I was always hypervigilant after the sunset. One night at my parents' house, Mom walked into my bedroom while I was in a twilight sleep. I heard her footsteps as she approached and thought she was a VC attacking my foxhole. Instinctively, I jumped out of bed, grabbed her by the neck, and began strangling her. She screamed and I woke with my trembling hands around her throat. "Mom!" I sobbed, "I thought you were an enemy soldier!" She looked at me in horror trying to comprehend my actions. After that incident, Mom never came into my room at night.

Living at home, I realize that Mom and Dad are having their own problems. Predictably, Mom has slowly progressed over the last five years into daily drinking. I say predictably, because Mom had several hospitalizations due to bouts of binge drinking and depression when I was growing up. I remember Dad taking her to the hospital and leaving her there for weeks at a time. Like her own mother who died from alcoholism, Mom is unwittingly doing the same thing. She seems humiliated and frightened by the insanity created from all the drinking. Dad is no help because he has been a daily drinker as far back as I can remember. Dad is on the verge of losing his food brokerage business and Mom is trying to keep the business afloat by making phone calls to customers in the mornings before their heavy drinking gets started. The biggest decision of the day is deciding who is going out to get the liquor.

My younger brother and sister are in their junior and senior years of high school and witness all the drinking and mayhem. They come home after school to find Mom and Dad passed out on the living room couch. Cynthia is thinking of quitting the cheerleading squad and getting her diploma early so she can get married and move away from home. Mark has begun experimenting with alcohol and drugs in an attempt to escape the day-to-day insanity. Mark and Cynthia are probably the ones who suffer the most from all of our drinking.

I'm incapable of helping any of them since I have been hanging around the neighborhood bars and living from one drunk to the next. Every morning, I awake with a hangover from an all-night bender, which

I temper with a morning drink. My only possessions are a '68 Oldsmobile Cutlass and a Harmony guitar that I can't play because of my war wound.

I have also begun to grasp the reality that I might not be able to get a good enough job to support myself. Over the past year, I have sold magazines door-to-door, delivered telephone books, and have run errands for people. At times, I would attempt to write a book about my experiences in Vietnam, but always gave up after a sentence or two. Dad made the effort to help out by calling a food broker friend who offered me a job delivering frozen food around the state. Since it took me so long to unload a truck, I constantly ran late for appointments and knew it was just a matter of time before I lost the job. The only real hope I have is going to school through the Disabled Veterans Assistance Program. The VA will pay for a technical or business education and will also give me a stipend to live on. Before considering school, though, a short trip to Florida might be the cure I so desperately need.

I'm still looking in the bar mirror thinking about how my life is crumbling when the disabled vet sitting next to me taps my arm and says good-bye. I feel very alone as he turns and limps out the door. I have a few more drinks for the road and leave the bar making the decision to change my life for the better.

The next morning, I call an old boyhood friend, Mark Tonti, to see if he wants to go with me to Florida. Mark and I grew up together and he had been my closest friend throughout school. Mark's a high-energy kind of guy who thrives on doing things for family and friends. He looks up to me for going into the Marines and fighting in Vietnam. Mark is now facing his own conflict of wanting to drop out of college and serve in the Army. He's a hopeless romantic who believes in God and country, and avoiding the draft is just not his cup of tea. Mark's desire to serve is further stimulated by my own tour of duty despite my attempts of telling him it isn't anything like the movies have made it out to be. Nevertheless, he seems determined to go to Vietnam.

Mark agrees that a trip to Florida will be a welcome change from his daily grind. A few weeks later, I quit my job before getting fired, and we head south to Florida. We stay with an old high school friend, Lisa, who has an apartment in Ft. Lauderdale. Lisa is glad to see us and gives us free reign of her apartment during the day while she's at work. Mark and I sleep off our hangovers and spend afternoons on the beach sipping beer and watching girls. Evenings are spent doing the bar scene, going to jai-alai games, or the dog races. As usual, there's plenty of alcohol and pills to go around. After a few weeks of insane drinking and drugging, I see that nothing has really changed. I am still the same person trying to avoid the reality that my life is going nowhere and the year-and-a-half of daily drinking since my discharge from the Marines is making me physically sick and extremely depressed.

It all comes to a head one morning when I discover I'm broke and out of booze. In desperation, Mark and I decide to sell our blood to a local blood bank to get some badly needed cash. In the process of giving blood, I become dizzy and pass out. The nurse takes my vital signs and wants to admit me to a hospital for observation. Of course I won't hear of it, being more concerned about losing out on the badly needed cash. I struggle back to Lisa's apartment and fall quickly to sleep for what seems like an eternity. When I awake, I'm shocked to see a beautiful young woman standing next to my bed. She begins asking me a series of intrusive questions.

"Why have you been sleeping so long?" she queries.

"Who are you?" I ask, defensively.

"My name is Lynn. I got here from Philadelphia a few days ago with a friend of mine. All you have been doing since I got here is sleep. I've never seen anyone sleep for two straight days. So, what's your problem?"

Lynn's brown eyes, shapely figure, and quick mind is very intimidating to me. I hesitate and then rub my head. "Are you sure I've been sleeping for two days?" I ask, with alarm.

"I've been here for two days and slept on that couch over there and you haven't moved an inch." Lynn points to a couch on the other side of the room.

I answer impulsively, "I've been partyin' too long. Guess I just couldn't take it any more."

"Don't you have better things to do than drink?" Lynn snaps.

"Well, yeah," I mutter, feeling embarrassed and ashamed.

"Think you could get up and do something worthwhile?" Lynn grins whimsically. "Why don't you get dressed and take me to an art exhibit that I heard about in Palm Beach? We can get something to eat on the way."

I'm startled but pleasantly surprised by her interest in me. Fortunately, my last check from work had arrived, and Mark had placed it on the night stand next to me. I sense things might change for the better.

We head for West Palm Beach and have an early dinner on the patio of a restaurant that faces the ocean. A warm breeze blows in from the open sea and a light surf caresses the beach. Lynn looks out at the ocean and her brown frosted hair blows in the wind. Her lively face is copper tan against a deep blue sky, and her brown eyes sparkle when she laughs. She is wearing a low-cut white blouse and red mini-skirt that highlights her smooth, delicate skin and pretty legs. She's cheerful, witty, and kind. She is as much interested in the wealth at Palm Springs as she is in a homeless guy who sleeps on the beach or the shadows that are cast on the walls of the restaurant from the ocean sunset. I have never known anyone so confident and beautiful. My fascination quickly turns to infatuation and I can't help but wonder why she's spending time with me.

She is full of interesting stories about her family and friends. She had just graduated from Moore College of Art and Design in Philadelphia and is taking a break before beginning to look for work as an artist. She speaks highly of her father, a physician, who died a few years earlier from a heart attack, saying that he cared more about his patients than he did about their money. Her mother remarried another physician, but Lynn seems unhappy about it, since she's still grieving the loss of her father. She talks a lot about her two brothers, who are in medical school and how they are aspiring to be physicians like their father. She has a younger sister in college with whom she keeps in regular contact. Lynn is very close to her family and takes pride in their accomplishments. I'm beginning to feel out of her league.

After dinner, she bluntly asks, "What happened to your arm?" I'm wearing a short-sleeved shirt which exposes the gunshot wound on my lower arm.

"I was in the Marines and got shot in Vietnam about two years ago." I wait for her response, hoping she will not reject me for having been in the military.

"How did you end up there?" she asks.

"That's a good question. I guess I was feeling at the end of my rope. There was nowhere left to go but in the service," I say with finality.

"Yeah, but why did you go into the Marine Corps? Why not the Army or Navy?"

Her question caught me off-guard. I hesitate and answer honestly. "I wanted to prove that I could do it. I mean, do something I could be proud of," I say with conviction.

"Yes, but couldn't you have just continued in school and succeeded like that?" Lynn smiles inquisitively.

"School hasn't been my thing since third grade," I say, wondering again if she will reject me.

"You mean you've never liked school?" she asks, with interest.

"No, it wasn't always like that. I failed third grade and that changed the way I felt about school. I guess I always wanted to prove something since I hadn't done well in school." There's a pause, and I still wonder why she's so interested.

Lynn turns and looks out at the ocean. "Is that why you went to Vietnam, because you wanted to prove something?" she asks.

I hesitate in deep thought. "I think it was all part of a secret plot the CIA had to turn me into a killer-spy."

Lynn laughs. "Let's go to the art show and we can talk about that later."

"You may not want to hear about it," I caution. She smiles and looks lovingly at me. There's magic in the air, and at that moment, hope enters my life for the first time in years. For some odd reason, I know our relationship is destined to happen. Later that night, we go back to the apartment and I tell her about some of my experiences in Vietnam. She has an uncanny ability to unlock the depths of my secretive soul. It's the first time I open up to anyone about the horror. She listens intently, always responding with admiration and support. I feel a sense of validation from her that I had never known. I want to reach over and kiss her but I'm afraid she'll reject me. At that moment, she leans forward and places her lips on mine and kisses me so deeply, I feel like I'm being embraced by a flock of monarch butterflies. For the first time in years, my heart pounds with passion and not with fear. We make love through the night and, the next morning, I am fully christened a man.

We stay in Florida for another week going to movies, lying on the beach, and sightseeing. I have stopped drinking and am experiencing a renewal of energy and excitement—like a kid with a new bike. We're love-struck and decide to travel to New Orleans for the Mardi Gras. Mark and Lisa decide to join us rather than miss out on any fun in the Big Easy. We are invited to stay with my grandmother who lives at Basin and Conti streets on the fringe of the French Quarter. The Mardi Gras is unlike anything any of us have ever experienced. People are crammed shoulder-to-shoulder in the streets, drinking booze, smoking weed, touching and grabbing one another in a full-scale assault on anything considered normal behavior. Lynn and I stay on the fringe, observing the mayhem and holding onto one another like there's no tomorrow.

After Mardi Gras is over, we stay a few more weeks at Grandma's house and go to many of the exciting restaurants and clubs within the French Quarter. As our relationship continues to grow, Mark and Lisa begin feeling abandoned by our obvious love affair. Eventually, they decide to go back to Florida and leave us to do our own thing. Mark is somewhat hurt and irritated by my hopeless attraction to Lynn; however, he accepts my apology and we agree to get back together in a few months in Columbus.

Lynn and I are now on cloud nine and decide to continue our travels through Texas and farther south into Mexico. A few weeks later, we end up in San Miguel, a little artists' colony about 100 miles north of Mexico City. Since we don't have much money, we pick up a book on how to live on five dollars a day which encourages eating certain local foods. One morning we go on an excursion through some back roads in the mountains and come upon a small town. We hadn't eaten anything since the previous afternoon, so we stop at a small Mexican diner and try some of the local food. Once inside, we scour the menu like vultures trying to find anything that looks close to being omelets, grits, bacon, or sausage. Finally, I recognize the word chili and quickly order two big bowls for us to devour. Within minutes, a smiling, toothless waitress brings out two large, steamy bowls of chili and sets them on the table in front of us. It smells good, but I notice some crusty little shells floating on top of the concoction. Curiously, I turn a shell over and see tiny legs sticking up in the air. I turn a few more shells over and see more legs. We realize the crusty shells are the backs of roaches that have somehow dropped into the chili. It's amazing what you'll do when sufficiently tired, hungry, broke, and isolated in a foreign country. With little forethought, we remove the little critters and quickly eat the chili. The toothless waitress is in the background smiling, either brimming with pride about her delightful dish or mocking us as American suckers who dare to eat the concoction. We leave her a quarter tip and spend the afternoon popping antacids and burping our way through the mountains. The next day, we come down with Montezuma's Revenge, with Lynn contracting the worst case by far. I must have had some immunity from the parasites still hanging with me from Vietnam because I wasn't affected too much. However, Lynn is so ill, I call a Mexican doctor in San Miguel who comes to our hotel room and gives her a shot. Her condition greatly improves within a day and shortly thereafter, we leave Mexico for a healthier culinary life.

We have been traveling together for three months and are beginning to talk about getting married. Lynn's everything I could have ever hoped for in a woman and I'm crazy about her. We decide to go to Philadelphia to meet her family and then to Columbus to meet mine. This leads to us moving into an apartment together near The Ohio State University. We get married on July 27, 1969, amidst the turmoil of the "love generation," and one week after, the astronauts land on the moon. We buy into the American dream of having a good job, owning a house, and eventually having children. A career as an attorney will be the way to go, but first, I will have to attend college and earn a degree.

There has been divine intervention in my life at very critical stages. Getting off the battlefield in Vietnam was one such occurrence. The second was with marrying Lynn at a point when sheer survival was at stake. The third is when I experienced an awakening while attending school at Franklin Business University in Columbus.

I had no prior success experiences in school on which to build. My father had always tried to discourage me from attending college saying I wasn't college material and would never succeed. I believe he felt let down since I hadn't done well academically in high school and had dropped off the track team. However, he wasn't alone in this assumption.

The VA decides to run a gamut of tests on me to determine if I am more suited for a traditional college or some type of technical training. Following the tests, a VA psychologist concludes that I should attend a computer school or at most, a business college. If I do well at this level, there will be an opportunity to transfer to a four-year college. I lack confidence in my abilities but Lynn's encouragement and support spurs me on.

With much trepidation, I enroll in Franklin Business University in Columbus in hopes of getting a degree. Predictably, my first year is wrought with academic difficulty and I struggle to keep my grades up. I have very little experience on how to study, take tests, or write term papers. No matter how hard I try, I can't catch on to school. Eventually, I reach the point where I am about to drop out when a professor by the name of Dr. Bunte makes a lasting impression on me.

Dr. Bunte teaches economics and criminology and has a reputation as the most demanding professor at the University. I'm taking his course in economics and as usual not doing well. One morning during his lecture, he walks over to a window and observes the people on the street below. He tells a story about how Adam Smith developed his theory of economics from watching people's behavior. He makes a point that Adam Smith possessed an intense hunger for knowledge and that he spent most of his life forming his theory of economics by finding out why different cultures behave in certain ways. Dr. Bunte suddenly turns and looks at me as if I'm the only one in the classroom. Stunned and mesmerized by his demeanor, I feel something very strange happening to me. I can't say exactly what it is, but

I feel a burning desire to understand the human condition as Adam Smith must have. It's the first time I've ever felt enthused about school. From this point forward, I am obsessed with learning as much as I can in all of my subjects. I had heard that one teacher can change a life, but I never thought it would happen to me. One year later, after having achieved all A's in my subjects, with the help and encouragement of Dr. Bunte, I transfer to Ohio State to pursue a bachelor's degree in social studies, education.

Unfortunately, Dr. Bunte died of cancer sometime later, but he left me with a priceless gift of academic achievement for which I will always be grateful. I'm in love with learning now, but the old alcohol nemesis begins to rear its ugly head again.

Lynn and I have been married for two years and are still madly in love. I am going to school at Ohio State and working part-time in the transportation department at the University. Lynn has a job at one of the local boutiques during the day and is also doing some freelance painting. We spend most evenings and weekends together doing the normal kinds of things newlyweds do. The few times I drink alcohol is on Friday nights when we grill steaks or fry fish. We have a few glasses of wine or daiquiris with dinner, which is strictly social drinking and not an issue in our marriage. Lynn has no idea that my history is riddled with alcohol abuse until an unfortunate incident occurs.

I receive a letter from my good friend, Mark Tonti, who is now serving in an infantry unit in Vietnam. Mark had dropped out of college a year earlier and received his Army draft notice within a few weeks. At this point, Mark has served in Vietnam for about three months and the tone of his recent letters is dark and foreboding. I'm concerned about him because he has experienced battle and is well on his way to cultivating the thousand-yard stare. On the same day I receive his last letter, I get a call from my brother who says Mark stepped on a land mine in Vietnam and was killed. This big-hearted 19-year-old boy, who had a great family and a bright future ahead of him, is now a grim statistic. I am devastated with losing another close friend to the Vietnam nightmare. His death brings back buried memories of all the guys I served with in Vietnam. In late afternoon, I have flashbacks of the battles when Scott, Bowman, and Roberto are killed. I think about the other platoon members and wonder if any of them survived the battlefield. I had been trying to forget about Vietnam and now it's all back with a fury.

I drink into the late evening hours and, at some point, I black out and demolish our new apartment in a drunken rage. Lynn powerlessly witnesses the whole episode. The next day she is still stunned and horrified by my insane behavior. She realizes there is something very different about the way alcohol affects me, and our relationship begins to change.

My drinking slowly and methodically increases over the next few years of our marriage. It eventually takes on a life of its own, independent of the Vietnam nightmare or any other reason to drink. Once I touch the first drink, I can no longer predict with any certainty how much I will drink, where I might end up, or what I might do. Lynn makes the common mistake of focusing all her energy on trying to control my drinking. She's caught in a vicious trap of trying to make sense of why I drink. When I don't drink, Lynn feels our love for one another is winning out. When I do drink, she feels hated and unworthy of my love. She has no concept that no power on this earth could cause, control, or cure my drinking. We spend most of our productive energy fighting to resolve this issue.

As the years roll by, Lynn begins to lose hope in our marriage and starts calling me an alcoholic who is just like my father. I respond by becoming more defensive about my drinking. I hide booze so she won't know how much I'm drinking at any given time. She finds bottles of beer and wine stashed behind the commode, in closets, and under furniture. This becomes a constant source of unexpected fights. Lynn gets to the point where she distrusts my every move. I start lying about where I'm going in order to go out to the bars. At times, she secretly follows me into a bar and pulls me off the bar stool to make her point. It makes me more determined to get away with my drinking.

Some days, we battle about things of which I have no recollection, because I was in a blackout the night before. I have no comprehension that I am destroying our marriage. My denial system is so strong I can't see anyone's perspective except my own. I believe straight people are prudes who don't know how to have a good time. This kind of reasoning has become more a product of my cellular craving for alcohol than any kind of misguided thinking.

Lynn's stepfather makes an attempt to crack through my denial system one holiday weekend when we travel to their home in Cherry Hill, New Jersey. He has a large bar in the den of his home where, on this particular evening, he's entertaining family and some close friends. Everyone has a drink or two and is enjoying one another's company but as usual, I continue drinking long after the party is over. My drunken behavior gets out of control and I am ushered to bed by one of Lynn's brothers. The next morning, I awake with a terrible hangover and wonder if I had made a fool of myself at the party. I decide to face the music and go downstairs and into the kitchen where everyone is gathered for a late breakfast. When I walk into the room, everyone immediately stops talking and looks up at me. You can hear a pin drop. After I sit at the table, Lynn's stepfather looks sternly at me and says sharply, "Drew, you're such a nice guy but every time you drink, you get drunk!" I interpret his concern as a personal attack. I look at him, feeling defensive and ashamed but think, what right does he have to criticize me? Doesn't he realize that I drink to get drunk? I've never known any other purpose to drink alcohol. Social drinking has never made sense to me.

I am unable and unwilling to make any changes in the way I drink. My drinking escalates and our marriage deteriorates to the point of divorce by the time I complete a master's degree from Ohio State. One fateful morning after one of my all-night benders, with tears in her eyes, Lynn tells me she can't take it any longer and demands I leave our apartment. A locksmith is coming to change the locks on all the doors and she has called an attorney to proceed with a divorce. I finally realize our six-year marriage is over. I gather my belongings and leave the apartment thinking Lynn has just lost the best thing she ever had.

Alcohol had dulled my senses, killed my feelings, and given me a rosy view of the world when, in reality, everything has been caving in around me. Alcohol is one of the greatest widowmakers on earth. It has just removed one of the finest persons I have ever known.

CHAPTER XII

Mr. Light

1976-November 1978

I reluctantly move into my parents' house—unemployed, penniless, and depressed. I am 27 years old and back in the same state of despair and confusion as when I returned from Vietnam. Once again, I obsess about Vietnam unless I fuzz up my brain with booze. I still cling to the hope that Lynn will change her mind and come back into my life. I stay in the house most evenings, drinking and watching the arms of the clock go around, anxiously awaiting a call from her. Of course, she never calls. I finally accept that the marriage is over although it will take another four to five months to finalize the divorce. Now, I have to do something with my life.

Grudgingly, I begin looking for a teaching job in secondary social studies. I quickly find there are no positions available due to the large number of college graduates who already have garnered the available jobs. I am resentful that there are no priorities given to Vietnam veterans for employment. In fact, most vets are finding it more difficult to get jobs if you mention being a Vietnam vet. In desperation, I answer an ad to teach schools for a book company called Grolier, out of White Plains, New York. I'm interviewed by a man who becomes my boss and savior, Vern Nepple.

Vern is in his mid-thirties and has been selling encyclopedias door-to-door since high school. He's about six feet tall, thin, has curly brown hair, and smiles like a Cheshire cat. He has a crooked neck, which forces his head downward sometimes when he's making a sales pitch. He tells me it was caused by an old football injury in high school but I suspect it's a stress-related condition. Vern is the consummate salesman and easily convinces me there is plenty of money to be made by teaching classes in elementary schools, which generates leads to sell encyclopedias and reading programs. All I have to do is simply go into classrooms and teach library science to grades 3 through 8. In the lower grades and preschools, I'll present a 30-minute magic show to create enthusiasm for a magical character known as "Mr. Light." Mr. Light is a magic pen that lights up whenever a child touches the right answer in the accompanying pre-reading book. The Mr. Light reading program is designed to help children learn how to read or to improve their reading ability. After class the children take a letter home inviting their parents to inquire about reading programs and encyclopedias. Once I procure the leads, it's a simple matter of scheduling appointments to sell the various programs to the interested families. Vern makes it sound like the million-dollar job, but I also believe in the reading programs the company is promoting.

I enthusiastically take the job and begin working for Grolier in September 1976. I spend the first few months learning how to teach the various classes and sell the reading programs. Initially, things go well and Vern is impressed by my sales talent. I make good money and plan to move out of my parents' house and into my own apartment. Vern drives to Columbus once a month to go out on appointments and observe how I am doing. I respond by turning in high-volume weekly sales reports and consequently I'm considered for a promotion to District Manager of Central Ohio. Everything looks quite promising until I start drinking again.

I had been so busy trying to make a good impression on Vern, I hadn't spent much time partying. By the time Christmas rolls around, I become somewhat complacent with my job and begin stopping off at some of the local taverns after nightly sales calls. It's also the holiday season, which gives me an excellent excuse to begin drinking again. However, it's not long before the holidays are over, and I'm still laughing and cheering in the bars and wondering where everybody has gone. All the boozing begins to impact the quality of my work and sales slowly decline. I fall into the trap of lying about the number of my sales calls so I can spend more time in the bars. After a few weeks of this nonsense, Vern becomes suspicious and comes to Columbus weekly to put the pressure on me to get the job done. It's in early January 1977, a month before my scheduled divorce from Lynn, when things really go haywire.

It's an unseasonably mild winter, but on this particular day, the weather reports indicate that blizzard conditions are moving into the Ohio Valley from Canada. I'm working on the west side of town picking up leads from schools. I decide to stop by my parents' house and have a few drinks with them to invigorate my day. It's about 11 a.m. when I arrive at the house and Mom and Dad have already started drinking. This is just the excuse I'm looking for to tie on a good drunk. One thing leads to another and before I know it, we are all three sheets to the wind. By afternoon Mom and Dad are passed out on the couch from all the booze, so I decide to visit a bar close to the house. When I walk out the door, the temperature had dropped sharply and a light snow has begun falling. I drive down Sullivant Avenue toward a red-and-yellow blinking sign marking the front of the establishment—Mike's Bar.

I open the door to the bar and inhale the stench of stale cigarette smoke and ale. The bar is in a dark, narrow hallway on the first floor of an old apartment building. It has been transformed into a watering hole for west-side drunks and has a bad reputation for fights. I recently read in the paper that a guy had been shot here just a few days earlier. I wonder what I'm doing in this wretched place. However, the idea of cheap booze and low-bottom entertainment is simply too much to resist. I slink up to a bar stool and order a double Scotch and soda. The bartender slides a shot glass in front of me and measures a triple into my drink. I like him right away. I stir the drink with my index finger and stare at the liquid like it's gold. I gulp the entire Scotch and soda and, like magic, I feel content with my life. I look into the bar mirror and see a few other people seated around me. There's an old woman sitting a few stools to my left with one hand clinging to a drink and her head resting on her forearm. She can't handle her booze and ought to get some kind of help for herself. To her left is a fat, bald guy in a T-shirt, who puckers his lips in satisfaction with each swig. He stares solemnly into the bar mirror in deep drinker's thought. To my right is an aging couple, smoking cigarettes and smooching to their hearts' content. I look around for someone young and pretty in the bar but there is no one. "Bartender," I call, "bring me two Scotch and sodas this time."

The bartender limps over and sets two more glasses on the bar in front of me and fills them to the rim. He's skinny and frail with a wrinkled face and hollow cheeks. An ash-laden cigarette dangles from his lips. I keep an eye on the long ash, hoping it won't break loose and fall into my Scotch and soda. "Kind of a rich man's drink, ain't it, boy?" He speaks sarcastically while stirring the drinks and inhaling his Camel cigarette.

"Ah, yeah," I say, feeling defensive. "I learned to drink it just before going to Nam. I was at Camp Pendelton out in California and it was overstocked at the clubs. Shit, they were practically giving it away. I don't turn down free shit, ya know."

"I had a nephew that served over there. What did you do over there, boy?"

"Went up to the Widowmaker and dodged bullets most of the time. What happened to your leg, old man?"

"Circulation problem. They had to cut it off at the knee. Shit, doc told me to quit smokin'. Hell, next they'll want me to quit drinkin'. Then they'll tell me to quit havin' sex." He laughs and coughs, blowing the cigarette ash all over the bar. "I say, the hell with that! Shit, if I'm gonna die of some rat's-ass disease, I'll at least have fun. You see much action over there, boy?"

I look into the mirror. "Yeah, I saw more than my fair share."

"Do much drinkin' over there?" he asks.

"No, tried to stay away from it. You took a chance every time you drank."

"Whadaya mean?"

"Like the night I helped get four good Marines wasted on the Riviera. I mean, blown to smithereens. It didn't take long for 'em all to die. That is, of course, unless you consider a couple of minutes long. I mean, do you think two minutes are long?"

It must have been r-e-a-l long, huh, boy?" He looks hard into my eyes and I can tell he wants to know what happened.

"There's a difference between being afraid and being fuckin' terrified. I thought that fear was all there was until that night," I say in a sharp tone.

"What happened? Tell me, I want to know." The bartender plops a bottle of Scotch on the bar saying, "This one's on the house. Now, tell me about it."

I grab the bottle of Scotch and take a swig that goes down easy. Now I'm ready to tell him the story, plus I want to show him I'm not the young punk he thought walked into the bar. I begin telling the old bartender the story of how I helped get four good Marines wasted that horrific night on the Riviera. He rests his elbows on the bar and looks into my eyes. I notice the old woman next to me has passed out has started snoring. The couple on the other side is still smooching and fondling one another. The fat bald guy is eavesdropping, but about five minutes into my store, he slams his drink on the bar and storms out the door. "The fucker probably never served in the military," I say to the bartender. I continue telling him all the grisly details until the story is finished. This is but one of a hundred stories

I can tell on any given drinking night. I look up at the old bartender and say, "Well, who gives a shit now, huh?"

"I don't think you ought to blame yourself for what happened that night. I mean it was a good-for-nothin' war anyway. All you guys got fucked over by just bein' there. You're lucky you didn't get killed that night."

"Sometimes I think it would have been better if I had, old man. I gotta go."

"Come back and tell me more some night. Be careful cause there's a big storm brewing out there. They say it's turning into a blizzard."

"Yeah, right. I'll see ya around." I stand up and steady myself, then leave the bar.

I walk outside into a horizontal sheet of snow that belts me in the face. Stoplights and street signs are swaying in the howling wind. It's just another drinking night as far as I'm concerned. I get into my car and drive down a side street at about 40 miles per hour—too fast for the icy road conditions. I'm lost in thought about that fateful night in Vietnam on the Riviera when suddenly, my car starts sliding uncontrollably toward the curb lane where several cars are parked. I sideswipe the cars and run over a curb, spinning full circle into someone's front yard, then crash into the front of their two-story house. The impact of the crash hurls me into the windshield and I break the steering wheel with my chest. I fall back onto the seat, stunned and bleeding. I'm in a semiconscious state but comprehend that I'm drunk and in big trouble. My only thought is to get away from the scene of the accident, so I leap out of the car and run. I jump over fences and run through huge snowdrifts toward my parents' house, only about a mile away. At some point I become aware of how treacherous the weather has become and how dangerous it might be if I fall and am unable to get up. I keep putting one foot in front of the other praying to make it home. Finally, I burst into the front door of the house and see that my parents are still passed out in the living room. I run upstairs and into the bathroom and look in the mirror. I have several facial cuts and some big bumps on the top of my head. I quickly wash my face and put Band-aids on the small cuts. My chest is bruised but, miraculously, I'm otherwise unscathed. I change out of my wet and blood-stained clothes and put on some pajamas.

A few minutes later, the front door bell starts ringing. I look out of the upstairs window and see the red flashing lights of two police cruisers. I hear Mom trying to awaken Dad. She then opens the door and lets two policeman into the house. I tip-toe to the top of the stairs and listen. The cop bellows, "We're looking for a Drew Martensen and we were told by his wife that he's living here."

Jesus, now Lynn's involved and knows I'm in trouble.

"This was listed as his last known address. Is Drew Martensen here now?" the cop questions.

"Yes," Mom responds, not knowing I had left the house earlier. "He's upstairs asleep, officer. Is there something wrong?" she asks.

"Has he been here all evening, ma'am?"

"Officer, he came over this morning and has been here all day." "Could you go up and get him, ma'am?" the policeman asks.

I immediately get into bed as Mom walks up the steps. I pretend to wake up as she approaches me. "Drew, there are two policemen downstairs who want to talk to you. Have you done something wrong? What are those Band-Aids doing on your face?"

"Oh, nothing, Mom," I say, rubbing my face. With trepidation, I get up and go downstairs.

As I enter the living room, the cop blurts, "Are you Drew Martensen?"

"Yeah, that's me," I say, trying not to slur.

"We talked to your wife and she told us you were living at this address. What are those cuts on your face?" the cop asks, peering into my eyes.

"I went outside earlier and a branch from a tree hit me in the face."

"You shouldn't have gone out this afternoon, Drew, especially in this weather," Mom says sincerely.

The cop speaks sharply, "Mr. Martensen, your car is a few streets over, plowed into a home. Where have you been this evening?"

I run to look out the window, pretending to be in a shocked state. "Mom, he's right, my car's not here. Somebody stole it!"

The cop interjects, "Would the two of you swear in a court of law that Mr. Martensen has been here all evening?"

"Yes sir," Mom says emphatically. I know he hasn't been out of the house all night. I just can't understand why anyone would steal a car on a night like this?"

The cop looks at me suspiciously but reluctantly takes our statements. He tells me that I will be hearing from them the next day concerning the investigation of the accident. Then, they finally leave the house. Mom never figures out that I hadn't been home most of the evening.

The next day, I'm terribly hungover and guilt-ridden by my behavior. Trying to figure out why it happened is fruitless, since the only sane answer is to quit drinking. Of course, my only urge is to run to the nearest bar.

Then I receive a call from a detective saying there are several discrepancies in the police report and he wants to see me in the evening to answer some questions. Obviously, they figured out what had happened and are about to spring a trap. I immediately call an attorney who recommends she meet me later at police headquarters. Later in the afternoon, I meet with the attorney and she asks me to tell her everything that had happened. I tell her the truth and that I reacted out of fear and automatically went along with the way everything developed. The accident ends up costing me well over $5,000 in repairs to the house, cars, attorney fees, and high-risk insurance. I have to carry bond money for several weeks in case the police decide to arrest me. It seems the ordeal will never end, yet the true insanity is that I continue to drink and drive after the accident.

My job with Grolier is also beginning to fall apart. As the months roll painfully along, encyclopedia sales fall off and I'm once again lying to Vern. He calls nightly trying to keep me on track with opportunities, having no idea that my drinking is the real problem. I simply lie about being on sales calls, so I can go to the bars. At the end of the week, I cover my lies by telling Vern I'm not able to collect the full deposit from a customer so the sale no longer exists. I also report to Vern that I'm calling on schools during the week to generate lead flows, teaching classes, or phoning a certain number of customers for evening appointments. Vern is never able to verify these activities unless he actually comes to Columbus and works directly with me. There are times when I stay drunk the entire week, thinking I'll go out on the weekend and make up for lost sales. By the time the weekend arrives, I'm usually so sick from all the booze, I'm unable to work at all. It's an endless cycle of lies and deceit.

To add insult to injury, on a bleak, rainy Monday in March, I meet Lynn at the courthouse to finalize our divorce. I am, of course, hungover, tremulous, and sweating profusely. The judge asks if we are sure our problems are irreconcilable? I listen carefully for her response. She states emphatically, "Yes!" I cringe, but agree our problems are beyond hope. The judge dissolves the marriage with the bang of his gavel.

As we leave the courthouse, Lynn asks me to join her for a late breakfast at a nearby restaurant. It's her way of trying to part with honor and dignity. During breakfast, I try to create a strong image that everything is going well with me. She asks about the accident since the police had called her in the middle of the night looking for me. She wants to know if I was driving the car and had left the scene of the accident. I can tell she knows the truth but wants me to admit to it. I bow my head and tell her what happened.

Lynn thanks me for being honest and strongly suggests I quit drinking. Her words go in one ear and out the other. When I look up at her, I think about our first meeting and our dinner at the restaurant along the ocean. She's still as beautiful as when we first met. I want so badly to be with her, but the harsh reality is, I won't ever see her again. We shake hands and part for the last time.

I'm emotionally devastated following the divorce. Alone in my apartment, I keep playing the same tune by the Ink Spots, "I'll Never Smile Again," while drinking wine and crying. After several weeks of whining, I muster the strength to get back out on nightly sales calls. However, sales are hard to come by and the urge to drink never leaves. It's about a week later when I enter a neighborhood nightclub looking for a woman to take Lynn's place. One of the things I had always told Lynn was that she didn't know how to have fun. Well, this night in the bar I meet a girl from California named Debbie who's also coming off a divorce and likes to drink as much as me. Debbie is just the kind of girl I'm looking for.

Debbie and I begin spending evenings together and partying until we pass out. I'm in heaven because we both share a common love for booze. Underneath all this, I have an inkling we just entered the eye of a monstrous hurricane and it's only a matter of time before hell unleashes its fury. In one of our delusionary states, we decide to move into a roach-infested apartment on the poor side of town. I believe we can happily transform this sleazy spot into The Ritz with a can of Raid. Debbie gets a job working as a bar waitress, and I still attempt to work for Grolier two or three nights a week. However, I begin hanging out in the bar where Debbie works until closing, then we go out slumming until the sun comes up. I begin missing work for weeks at a time and eventually get to the point where I don't care if I'm working or not. Vern calls me nightly until I just stop answering the phone. By the end of June, I have no more contact with Vern and I stop working altogether. At this point, I'm drinking about a fifth a day and still unable to keep up with Debbie. The girl of my dreams is turning out to be the Alcoholic from Hell. Our binge lasts almost four months when I slowly start running a low-grade fever and feeling chilled all the time. Debbie finally gets to the point where she has enough of me and decides to go back to California to visit her ex-husband who is in a veterans' alcohol rehabilitation center. I tell her she is wasting her time with the loser, since he's an alcoholic and can't handle his booze. She says I'm becoming a lot like him and she's getting sick and tired of hanging out with guys like me.

Debbie piles her belongings in her Volkswagen and leaves for California without saying good-bye.

I spend the next couple of weeks inside my apartment drinking, fighting a fever, and trying to figure out what's causing my problems. The more I drink, the more confused and paranoid I become. I stay inside the apartment, afraid to go outside or answer the phone or even open the curtains. I watch people on television and wonder how they are able to stay sober from one day to the next. Going more than a day or two without drinking is impossible. I even ponder the idea that I had been killed in the car accident and I'm now in hell. I know there's something desperately wrong with me but still believe it's much more than simply the drinking.

Eventually, the high fever forces me to call my family doctor who puts me on an antibiotic. He says the medicine should take care of my illness in short order. I lie in bed for another week, suffering with fever and drinking only enough to stop the shakes. I again call my doctor and he decides to admit me to a hospital because of my ongoing high temperature and failure to respond to the medication. After being in the hospital a few days, the test results come back revealing that I have alcoholic hepatitis. I stay in bed for eight more days recovering and trying to figure out why I have this strange illness. On one occasion, my doctor walks into the room and asks how much I've been drinking. I tell him the heavy drinking has been going on for only about three years. He asks what exactly "heavy drinking" means to me. I lie to him, saying only about three or four beers after work and nothing on Sundays. He then tells me I should not touch a drop of booze for one year or I will definitely have liver failure and die. I ask him how a young guy of 29 could have such bad luck with a liver. He says it's genetic and nothing can be done other than to avoid the alcohol. Well, it's really too bad that I was born with a weak liver. I'll just stay away from alcohol for two or three months and my liver should be healed. I remember how my ex-father-in-law also would jump to conclusions about my drinking.

After release from the hospital, I give up my apartment and stay at my parents' house for a couple of months to recuperate from the hepatitis. Vern had hired a crusty old encyclopedia salesman to replace me as district manager in Columbus. It's finally obvious that I haven't done even a minimally acceptable job. I call Vern and ask if I could have another chance working somewhere else within the organization for him. He reluctantly offers me a job traveling on the road with him within the tri-state area of Ohio, Kentucky, and Indiana. By the time winter hits, I am recovering well from the hepatitis, so I drive to Cleveland to meet Vern to begin working the area of northern Ohio.

In January 1977, winter descends upon Cleveland with a vengeance. Vern and I are staying in a cheap, damp, and drafty motel outside Lorraine, Ohio, right on the lakefront. We teach school during the day, trying to generate leads to sell encyclopedias in the evening. I'm driving a '72 Vega after wrecking my car the previous year, and am having great difficulty starting it in the subzero temperatures. Vern suggests I set my alarm for two-hour intervals during the night and go outside and start the engine to make sure it will turn over in the morning. To make matters worse, the furnace in our motel keeps going out during the night. In the middle of the night, Vern wakes up and turns on the hot water in the shower to heat the room. In the morning, my clothes are musty, the toilet seat is frosty, and the air in the dingy room is freezing.

Vern becomes despondent when the schools close for a week due to inclement weather. Inevitably, our encyclopedia leads run out and we have no source of income. Vern's wife, Gloria, keeps calling, because she hasn't seen him since Christmas and wants him home. Vern proposes that I move down to Louisville where the weather is milder and set up a one-man encyclopedia operation. He will go to Cincinnati and see his wife and join me in Louisville in six to eight weeks. It seems to be a good solution to our problems and I will have the opportunity to prove myself once again to Vern in Louisville. The only problem is, I had already started drinking again on weekends and alcohol is beginning to preoccupy my time.

I arrive in Louisville at 5 a.m. on a Monday with a hangover from a weekend bender in Columbus. I teach my first school at 8 a.m. to generate leads so I can begin selling reading programs and encyclopedias by the next evening. All goes as planned and by the second day, I collect all the leads by late morning and get on the phone booking appointments for evening sales. Since my afternoon is free, I decide to stop by a go-go bar near the motel and have a couple of drinks. A young, scantily clad dancer in the bar catches my attention. I start buying her drinks at about 12:30 p.m. until my first appointment at 6:30 p.m. I'm having way too much fun to leave, so I call my first two families and tell them I'm having car trouble and will visit them the next evening. That still leaves me with a 9:30 p.m. appointment, which I believe is a sure sale, and will give me at least one sale to call in to Vern. No problem, I've got myself covered.

I end up dropping $70 in the go-go joint, which is about what I make from an average sale. Once my money is gone, the pretty dancer doesn't want anything else to do with me. I leave the bar at 10 p.m., a half hour late for my appointment. When I walk out of the bar, it's snowing and by the time I get to the house, there's about an inch of the white stuff on the ground. As I walk up the snow-covered driveway, I begin weaving and slipping from all the booze I had consumed. I pull a sales slip out of my pocket that has the family's name of John and Betty Sullivant. I try pushing the doorbell with my index finger but keep missing the button. Just when I think I had better not go on this appointment, the Sullivants open the door.

"Hi folks," I say with a smile. "My name is Mr. Light! Just kidding folks," I say with a giggle. They don't laugh. "My name is really Drew, and I am scheduled to show you folks our incredible Mr. Light reading program!"

"Are you the man that called this morning from the school for Mrs. Redmond, our principal?" Mrs. Sullivant asks, inquisitively.

I thought for a moment about which sales pitch I had used on her this morning. I can't remember if I led her to believe I was representing the principal, my company, or the whole Catholic diocese? I take a chance, saying, "Folks, your child's principal, Mrs. Redmond, specifically told me I should call you because of your keen interest in the education of your child. Now, let me just get the request form from my briefcase that you folks sent back to Mrs. Redmond to make sure that you are in fact the ones she was talking so highly about."

I reach down and grab the handle of my briefcase to get the form, when Mr. Sullivant interjects, "Look, I really don't think that's necessary. I'm sure we're the ones." He stops talking in mid-sentence when I jerk the handle of my briefcase, accidentally flipping it open. All my presentation materials fall onto the snow-covered porch, and in the middle of everything is a fifth of Smirnoff Vodka that I keep hidden in a side compartment. I quickly drop onto my knees trying to conceal the bottle of vodka, and awkwardly scoop up the wet props and the vodka and put everything back into the briefcase. I stand up, dust the snow off my pants, and brazenly walk through the front door. The Sullivants are wide-eyed as they step back out of my way. I walk toward the living room couch to my right, saying, "Folks, I think you're really gonna like the Mr. Light reading program that Mrs. Redmond asked me to show you."

"Ah, Drew, I think it's too late for us to see this program this evening. Why don't we call Mrs. Redmond tomorrow and reschedule our appointment?" Mr. Sullivant requests politely.

"Can I call the two of you John and Betty? I mean, you folks know Judy as well if not better than me. You know that Judy Redmond would never put anything before a child's education, now would she?" I ask with sincerity.

"Well, sure, education is really important to us," says Mr. Sullivant, "but . . ."

I interrupt. "John, Betty, I know it's late but I have 50 other families on Mrs. Redmond's list to visit. All I want is five minutes of your time to show you one of the finest reading programs this country has to offer. Folks, I've been running to families' homes all evening and I am really tired, so need I say more?"

"Well, just five minutes," Betty sighs. "Then we have to get ready for bed because we have to get up early tomorrow."

"Folks, I promise, you won't regret this night. Let me show you just what I mean." I pull out a reading prop and fan it out onto the floor. "This is it!" I say with confidence. I kneel in front of the Sullivants, who are sitting on the couch. There's a big, colorful picture of our cartoon character, Mr. Light. I point at the prop waiting for the usual positive response that customers have so I can continue my canned sales pitch. The Sullivants remain silent. At that moment, I feel myself begin to lose my balance. I start to sway and try to catch myself by putting my right hand on the floor. They look at me in shock as I fall over on top of my props. They both gasp. I quickly push up onto one knee, trying to remain steady. I grab my wet demonstration book out of my kit to continue the botched presentation. The Sullivants sit on their sofa with dropped jaws. I walk on my knees toward them and put the demonstration book directly in their face like the pitch calls for. "Betty and John, as you can see, this is the most well-illustrated set in the country." The Sullivants sit back on the couch as far away from me as possible.

Betty grimaces. "What is that smell?!" she shrieks. "Have you been drinking, young man?"

"No ma'am!" I say, shaking my head.

"Then what's that awful smell?" she asks, giving John a wild-eyed glance.

"Betty, I swear I don't smell a thing," I say, looking puzzled. I start swaying again. The Sullivants look on in amazement. I fall again, landing on top of my demonstration book, wrinkling and crushing the pages. "Folks, I'm not feeling well this evening. I think I have a bad case of the flu. I better take the rest of the night off."

"I think that's a good idea," Betty exclaims.

I gather my wet and wrinkled props and put them back into my briefcase. I manage to stand up and stagger toward the door. John is well ahead of me and opens the door for my departure. Betty bids me farewell by saying, "I will be giving Mrs. Redmond a call in the morning about your visit!" Great, now I'm in big trouble. I leave the house and return to my hotel room where I proceed to get obliterated on wine and beer.

The next morning, I have a message from the hotel operator to call Vern in Cincinnati. He is probably checking on how I did with sales last night. It's 10 a.m. and I have a terrible hangover, but decide to call Vern back in case I start drinking again.

"Vern, this is Chet calling you back." Vern likes to refer to me as Chet Huntley and to himself as David Brinkley.

"What the hell's going on over there?" Vern screams. "I have been getting calls all morning from the company about this Judy Redmond there in Louisville. What the hell were you doing last night in that home? The president got a call from our vice president, Sam, this morning and they called me to get to the bottom of this mess. Now, what the fuck happened there last night?"

"What are they saying, Vern?" I act surprised.

"Look, I told you before I wasn't going to put up with this shit! They said you were drunk last night when you went into a family's home. Let me see here . . ." He pauses, and I hear him shuffling through papers. "Their names are Betty and John Sullivant. They say you were in their living room, drunk and falling all over the place."

"Vern!" I say with all the sincerity I can muster. "I had a few drinks last night before I went out on my appointments, but I mean—these accusations are a little unreasonable! Remember the time you told me that you had visited a real religious family and mentioned to them you drank alcohol and they kicked you out of the house? This was probably the same kinda shit. Hell, I had a few drinks and this family is probably a bunch of teetotalers that just want to burn my ass in Hell. What pisses me off is now they're getting their way. I mean, if this is the way the company is gonna keep treating me every time a family gets a notion that I'm trying to hard-sell them, well, what is this world coming to? Hell, it wasn't like this when you were out there selling your heart out, was it, Vern?"

"Drew, Sam said this family reported to the school that you were drunk on your ass!"

"Vern, I *swear* to you, I was not drunk! Now, I did go back to the room last night and got pretty shit-faced *after* the presentation."

Vern interrupts, "You know I don't care what you do on your own time, but anyway, didn't your doctor tell you to stop drinking?"

"Vern, you know how those doctors are. Hell, they're always trying to ruin a good time. By the way, when are you coming down to see me?"

"Hell, if I get any more calls like this, you ain't gonna be alive to come down and visit. I'm telling you, Drew, I don't want any more fuck-ups or you're history. You hear me?"

"Yeah, I hear you."

"Okay, I'll see you in a few weeks." Vern hangs up the phone.

I sit speechless trying to comprehend the seriousness of my situation. There seems to be no way out of my desperate state of affairs. I'm spinning a web of deceit which will eventually snare me. I know it's just a matter of time.

I pick up the phone and start booking appointments for the night. I call the next lead, saying, "Hi, Mrs. Jones, this is your friend, Mr. Light, calling on behalf of your principal, Mrs. Redmond, concerning the reading program!"

"Who is this?" she questions.

"Mr. Light." I repeat.

"Who?"

"I said, Mr. Light!" I say loudly.

"Who are you?" She sounds confused and puzzled.

"I am Mr. Light."

"Are you the guy who visited the Sullivants last night?" she questions.

"Oh, no ma'am! I'm representing the diocese and Mrs. Redmond."

CHAPTER XIII

The Blackout

December 1978-May 23, 1980

Vern gives me one more chance to pull things together as a manager in my hometown of Columbus. The incident with the Sullivants in Louisville focused negative attention on me with the vice president of the company, so Vern forces me to take a promotion as manager in order to become a viable producer, or leave the company. My skills are above average as long as I'm not drinking. That's why Vern keeps believing in me. He sees periods when I outsell everyone in the country, while at other times, when bingeing on alcohol, I go for weeks without a sale. Vern is absolutely baffled by my behavior, because he believes a man should be able to handle his booze. Therefore, I try hiding the amount and frequency of my drinking to prove I still have control.

I return to Columbus in December 1978, and it seems the Snowbelt has moved south. It's frightfully cold, way below zero, when the winds blow across the cornfields and into the shopping malls, obscuring the lights of the city. I wear a waist-length leather jacket with a thin silk lining, more suited for autumn than an icy Ohio winter. A hefty four-fingers of Southern Comfort usually keeps me warm while driving my '72 Vega to homes to sell encyclopedias. At first I sell many sets of encyclopedias, because the kids and parents like my looks, sincerity, and fortitude to brave the wintry nights. I smile and laugh to keep the pitch smooth and relaxed. I'm naturally dark-complected, have a mustache and brown eyes, have long black hair that curves softly to the left over my eyebrow. I lost weight since my divorce and recently was fitted for a 30-inch-waist size. Sometimes I'm asked in the middle of a sales pitch if I know I look like Tony Orlando. "Yes," I say in a discouraged tone. "But, I can't sing and I'm poor!" Then I will sing off-key, "Tie a yellow ribbon 'round that old oak tree . . ." The customers always laugh and I use my dreadful singing as an opportunity to gain control of the pitch and close the sale.

I push my luck one snowy Christmas Eve by having booked a suspicious appointment with a couple where I can sell one more set of encyclopedias. Of course, Vern will be proud that I forced myself into a home on this holiday night. My appointment is with a couple who is drinking heavily when I arrive at their home. The husband, Mac, sells pots and pans door-to-door and I figure I have my work cut out to sell Mac a set of encyclopedias. His wife, Sally, is petite and quiet. They sit on opposite ends of the couch observing my presentation and sipping martinis. I sit in a chair across from them pitching the *Americana,* Grolier's adult set of encyclopedias. I keep trying to figure out how Mac is going to get out of the sale, since they don't have children and have sent their lead back with a neighbor child, probably just wanting to have me over for some Christmas Eve laughs. Mac is having fun popping ridiculous objections, trying to embarrass me and ruin the pitch. I've been through this sort of thing before, so I'm not much rattled. Sally is still sitting on the sofa being pleasant and quiet. She jumps up a couple of times to fill Mac's glass with martini, but never speaks a word throughout the presentation. Neither of them ever offer me a drink. I pitch for about half an hour without getting anywhere when Mac suddenly bends forward looking at one of the pictures I turned to in my presentation book. He says, "Look, Sally, that's a picture of the hospital where I was born." Sally doesn't budge and obviously couldn't care less. Mac is so excited, he asks to page through the book himself. Of course, I am very pleased to hand over the book, thinking I have inadvertently sold him on the encyclopedias. Mac begins showing Sally the presentation book, pointing to pictures and commenting on the high quality of the *Americana.* Both of them are still gulping martinis like water which was fine with me. I have been in the house for close to an hour and have to close the sale or lose it. When it seems Mac is sold on the *Americana,* I ask my closing question: "Well, folks, now that we have determined that you're in love with the program, all I need is your okay to sign you up on one of our convenient payment plans. Now which one is most convenient for you?" I hold my clipboard out in front of them showing the payment plans. Mac looks at Sally and nods pointing to plan number three, which is $30 down and $30 monthly. I say, "Great!" Then, little Sally frowns at Mac and suddenly jumps up, hollering, "You son of a bitch! You promised not to buy a fuckin' thing tonight!" Then she heaves her martini glass at the wall, shattering it. Mac has his hands in front of his red face anticipating Sally might try to hit him. I begin scurrying around on the floor gathering all my props to get out of the house without getting assaulted by Sally. Once everything is in my briefcase, I bolt out the front door. Sally's still screaming at Mac as I get into my car and I figure it was the only way she could get out of the sale. After my presentation, I go to a nearby bar and spend the rest of Christmas Eve getting hammered.

On Christmas morning, I have difficulty remembering what had happened at Mac and Sally's house due to all the booze I drank afterward. I often wonder what it would be like to live from one day to the next, remembering everything that takes place. Life has become one daily blur after another. On this special morning, I go to my brother's house where our family has gathered to celebrate Christmas. Mom and Dad have also pulled themselves together enough to be with everyone. When I walk through the door, my brothers and sister are all there with their families. I slowly walk around the room with a drink in my hand, greeting everyone. I haven't seen many of my nephews and nieces since the Christmas before. At one point, it occurs to me there is something very wrong and frightening about my life compared to the rest of my siblings. They have decent jobs, children, and financial stability. I am stuck in a grandiose world of alcohol delusions punctuated by the reality of an occasional encyclopedia sale. I feel bewildered and scared amidst the joy of Christmas. I leave the house in a state of despair and loneliness.

I spend New Year's Eve by myself at Mike's Bar. The narrow corridor of the bar seems more like a coffin than a place for fun, but the more I drink, the more hospitable the place becomes. After a half-dozen or so drinks, I make a move on one of the local barflies who has been giving me the eye from the far end of the bar. A good-for-nothing boyfriend walks in and takes offense to my overtures by pulling out a gun and sticking it in my ear. "Fire the motherfucker," I spout, without batting an eyelash. The bartender grabs the guy and makes him put the gun back in his pocket. In frustration, the boyfriend yanks my drink out of my hand and throws it to the floor. Then he pulls the girl off the bar stool and belligerently forces her out the door. I sit on the bar stool trying to hold myself up and figure out who is left in the bar, but images are blurred and it's difficult to stay awake. I don't know how much time elapsed, but I hear the bartender say,

"This fucker needs some help." I lift my head up and focus on a clock that shows it's 2 a.m. The new year has come and gone as a lonely affair with no resolutions. With great effort, I get up from the bar and stumble out the door to my car. That's all I remember until I wake up the next morning and start drinking all over again.

On New Year's Day, I barely recall watching a replay of Woody Hayes punching a Clemson player during the OSU bowl game on TV. In my confused state, I wonder if it really happened. My world has become a kaleidoscope of unreal events. I wake up each morning over the next two weeks with every intention of getting back to work, but my first sip of booze always ends in another drunk. Finally, I become so sick and tired of all the booze and the constant liver pain erupting from behind my right rib cage, I stop drinking and force myself back to work. The next several days are fraught with alcohol tremors, depression, and futile attempts at regaining control of my sales pitch. When my life seems to be at its lowest point, I once again get a glimmer of hope.

It's late one evening in January after one of my shaky sales presentations that I meet Linda. My sister-in-law, Cathy, arranged for us to meet on a blind date. Cathy and Linda are friends and work as secretaries for a cardiology practice close to one of the local hospitals. Cathy knows I have been drifting and drinking heavily since my divorce, and thinks Linda might help put some badly needed direction into my life.

I'm wearing my lightweight leather jacket in the blowing snow when I call on Linda in her cozy apartment. She answers the door and I'm surprised by her pretty face, hazel eyes, and long blond hair. She's petite, only 5-feet tall, and has a beautiful smile. Her sexy features obscure any thoughts I might have about seeing her once. I nervously enter her apartment, since I haven't been on a real date in at least a year. However, I'm quickly put at ease by the comfortable atmosphere of Linda's living room. We make small talk about the weather, and she guides me past her aquarium to the patio door at the end of the room. She points outside at the railing where snowdrifts hang from the roof and a bird feeder sways in the wind. "That little bird feeder has saved a lot of birds from starving this winter," she says.

"I guess I haven't really paid much attention to how hard this winter has been on birds," I say, feeling somewhat lost for words. It's as though I've been suddenly thrust into a world of sensitivity I had long forgotten. I look out past the railing where a light snow is falling. Linda's warm spirit and bright smile radiates throughout the room. I have been living out of a suitcase for two grueling years and traveling from one city to another, selling encyclopedias. Home for me is a Red Roof Inn when I have the money and the YMCA when I don't. Friends are passers-by from the bar scene and girlfriends are not more than one-night stands. I'm sick and tired of all the loneliness, daily drinking, and running from one town to the next. For the first time in two years, I feel safe.

We go out to see the movie *Saturday Night Fever* and then to dinner. Eventually, we go back to Linda's apartment and talk and listen to music. I tell Linda I am making good money, have a great job, and well on my way to an auspicious career. I'm drinking wine and believe every word of what I'm saying. By the end of the night, I have her convinced that I am a responsible, aspiring salesman. She thinks I'm worth investing more time in, because she asks when we might get together again. I tell her that I would like to see her as much as possible, but in the back of my mind, I'm wondering how I will have enough time to drink.

I leave Linda's apartment and feel a sense of urgency to make this relationship work. She's attractive, has class, a decent job, and is independent. She has all the attributes I desire in a woman which could help motivate me to make changes in my life. Linda and I start talking to each other almost daily after our first date. I'm still living at my parents' house and start back to work on a regular basis for Grolier. After a few weeks of dating and staying sober, we make love for the first time and I become crazy for her. However, as in past relationships she doesn't realize I have a drinking problem. Our relationship grows deeper over the ensuing months, and Linda eventually invites me to spend weekends at her apartment. We have a great time in the evenings cooking, going to movies, visiting her friends, and dancing. Other areas of my life are also developing well. I have hired some people to sell encyclopedias in the Columbus market and Vern is calling again on a weekly basis to congratulate me on the increase in sales. It seems I can't do much wrong, until I once again have to face problems brought on by my secretive drinking.

By early spring, I'm staying at Linda's apartment on weekends and living at my parents' house during the week. This has its advantages because I live a sober lifestyle at Linda's place and do my secretive binge drinking at my parents' house. However, as the months roll by, Linda begins asking why we can't spend more time together. She wants our relationship to progress, but I'm more concerned with not being able to hide my drinking from her. It's an inevitable situation where I have to make a move or run the risk of losing her. In the end, we decide I will move into her apartment and develop our relationship more fully.

The problems start when we begin spending most all of our time together. Linda usually comes home from work at 6 p.m., often to find that I have just gotten up to go out on sales calls. I tell her I work in the morning and take a nap in the afternoon. Of course, I'm drinking in the morning and am passed out in the afternoon. At this point, she still doesn't suspect anything. Sometimes I go to my parents' house in the morning and drink all day. Then, I go back to Linda's around 11 p.m. and tell her I had gone out for a quick beer after my last sales call. After a month of this sort of thing, she becomes suspicious about my drinking and begins watching me more closely. That's when things really start to go awry.

I'm always looking for what I believe is an acceptable reason to drink. It could be a certain television show, sporting event, dining in, dining out, the weather, a hard week, a slow week, someone's birthday, a special holiday, a good day, a bad day—it doesn't really matter what the reason is so long as I can use some off-the-wall excuse to drink. Sometimes I won't show up in the evening because I'm out late at a bar and crash somewhere else, or I'll come back to the apartment real late and pass out in a stupor. Eventually, I regularly drink in the morning, pass out in the afternoon, and wake up when Linda comes home from work. She finds beer and wine bottles stashed everywhere in her apartment. Finally, she announces that my drinking is out of control and I need to do something about it. We had been talking about getting married, but she says it's now out of the question unless I seek help. She tells me I really don't care about her and that booze is more important than our relationship. Linda believes that if I love her, I will stop drinking. However, as with my first marriage, love has nothing to do with it. I could just as easily have cancer, heart disease, diabetes, or some other incurable disease and be asked to make it go away. I lost all freedom of choice in my drinking a long time ago. I have a physical craving and a mental obsession to drink in spite of any consequences.

Linda tells me about a reprinted article she read by Jack Anderson about Alcoholics Anonymous where people with drinking problems could go for help. She strongly suggests I call AA to get the help I need. I'm absolutely shocked by her suggestion because I believe AA is for skid row bums, not social drinkers like me. However, I'm in a corner and don't want to lose her or my job, so in sheer desperation with Linda standing next to me, I call Alcoholics Anonymous. An AA member answers the phone and listens patiently to my story about how Linda is unhappy with my drinking and that I need to comply with her wishes to get help or leave. The AA member relates to my story by sharing his own experience of losing his wife to drinking. He says I don't have to live this way anymore and all I have to do is attend an AA meeting near my residence. After I hang up the phone, Linda gives me a big hug and kiss exclaiming that we are going to beat this thing! The next evening, I go to my first AA meeting.

The AA meeting is held in the smoke-filled basement of a local church. As I walk through the door, several members greet me with a handshake saying, "Welcome to AA!" I hesitantly shake their hands and quickly slink to an isolated corner of the room where I can avoid being spotted by someone who knows me. As luck would have it, a young fellow, to whom I once gave condescending advice on how to drink like a man, spots me in the corner of the room. He approaches and exclaims, "Glad to see you made it here!"

I respond with a tight smile and say, "I'm here for a friend who has a drinking problem and needs advice on how to stop."

"Oh, I see. Then you're not here for you?"

"Of course not." I reply, with all the sincerity I can muster up. "No, I'm doing fine. I'll be taking notes for my buddy, though."

The guy looks at me like he's studying a goldfish in a bowl. "Okay, just keep coming back," he says.

Yeah, right. I just want to get my ass out of here in one piece before someone else gets the notion this meeting is for me. I grab a seat in the corner of the room and the meeting begins with preambles, prayer, and a reading of this thing called the "Twelve Steps." The Twelve Steps from Hell as far as I'm concerned. I just want to get people off my back and cool their jets so I can get on with my life. To my amazement, a speaker walks to the podium and begins telling a very personal story about his drinking to everyone in the room. Doesn't he have any pride left in him? I listen but am much more concerned about who I might know in the room. The speaker loudly proclaims that he had been arrested 50 times for drinking-related offenses. This is just what I want to hear, since I've rarely been in trouble with the law. This guy is *truly* an alcoholic type. Matter of fact, this meeting is full of these kinds of people—*unlike myself.* I'm convinced my drinking is social but gone awry a little, and this is just the kind of thing I need to get it in hand. Anyway, I can't believe these people are really happy without booze in their lives. After the meeting is over, some alcoholic types approach me, shake my hand, and give me their phone numbers to call if I need help. They are probably after my money.

As I walk toward the door, a tall Irishman stands at the podium and tells everyone he loves them. Anyone that would say such a thing to such a large group is definitely gay. What other types of people hang out here? I feel humiliated that I have reached the bottom of the barrel. I trot to my car and speed home to tell Linda I'm now cured of alcoholism. Of course she asks when I will be attending another meeting? I respond that it isn't necessary since I will never drink again, and she believes me.

A few months later, I am craving a drink and fit to be tied but the thought of attending another AA meeting is just too degrading to accept. Instead, I decide to go to my family doctor and ask for help for my unsteady nerves. He's the same physician who had treated me when I was in the hospital for alcoholic hepatitis a few years earlier. The good doctor is only about 5 feet 4 inches and weighs under 160 pounds. He could easily pass for Mickey Rooney's twin and he bounces around the office with the same amount of energy. He smiles at me when I tell him I have quit drinking.

"That's good," he says, "so what can I do for you today?"

"Well," I respond with a raised eyebrow, "I haven't been feeling well since I quit drinking, doctor."

"What do you mean, not feeling well, Drew?" he asks in a caring voice.

"I mean, I've been real nervous and edgy. Sometimes I feel like I'm about ready to lose it or something." I grimace while stroking my hair.

"Well, how can I help?"

"I'm not sure but is there anything you can give me?"

He hesitates in thought and then smiles. "How would Valium be?" he asks, folding his hands behind his head.

"That would be just fine," I respond, feeling relieved.

"How many do you want?" he asks.

"How many can I have?" I blurt.

The good doctor reaches over and begins writing on his prescription pad. "Get this filled and it will do the job, Drew," he says with confidence as he hands me the prescription. I quickly scan the directions which indicate one hundred 5-mg. Valium, monthly, for six months. "How is your dad doing, Drew?" he asks.

"Dad hasn't been doing well at all, doctor," I say, while shaking my head. The doctor writes another prescription, which he hands to me. The second prescription indicates another one hundred 5-mg. Valium, monthly, for six months. I'm feeling more relieved.

"Thank you," I say politely. "This will really help old Dad!" "How's your mom doing, Drew?" The doctor asks holding his prescription pad in hand.

"She isn't doing well at all," I say, with excitement. The doctor scribbles again on the prescription pad. He hands me another slip indicating the usual one hundred 5-mg. Valium, monthly, for six months. I quickly put the third script into my pocket and pat it for safekeeping. "I should also tell you that my grandmother is visiting us and is extremely nervous by all the activities," I say, brimming with confidence.

"No need for that," the good doctor says with a smile. He hands me a fourth prescription for one hundred 5-mg. Valium, monthly, for six months. "Anything else I can do for you?" he asks.

"I will be just fine," I say. "Thank you for the help and I hope not to bother you again."

The doctor shakes my hand saying, "If this doesn't work, I'll prescribe something else."

I leave the office and race to the nearest pharmacy and get all four prescriptions filled. I overhear the pharmacist say, "Hey, we got four scripts for freeze-dried alcohol."

I don't care if it's spun-dried, oven-dried, or baked in the sun all year. Just give me the dope and I'm outta here!

Linda and I marry in August 1979, believing that I'm finally at peace with myself. As time goes on, I start smoking grass, using speed, popping Tylenol with codeine which I acquire from other doctors, and taking the Valium. I truly believe I am fully sober since I'm not drinking alcohol, but six months later, all hell breaks loose.

The combination of Valium, marijuana, speed, and all the other non-alcoholic drugs I have been taking begins to make me crazy. I can't get enough of anything inside of me to satisfy my craving for drugs. Eventually, Linda stops talking to me and makes plans to move out and live with a girlfriend and her husband. I am bewildered by what's happening and totally unaware of what the problem actually is. I slowly begin thinking about using my gun to end it all. I'm 33 years old and can't see any way out of the dark life I've created for myself. But first, I decide to have a drink before doing anything drastic.

If I ever have any doubt about what alcohol can do to me, I find out when I pick up the first drink. I don't have any control left in me and begin drinking around the clock. I awake at times in the sitting position with one foot on the bed and the other on the floor. I look out the window and see that it's twilight and don't know if I'm going to bed or getting up. When I'm out in the bars, neighborhood thugs begin targeting me. One night one of them calls me a fag, because I'm so drunk I can hardly stand up. I pick up a beer bottle to clobber him, but lose my balance and fall helplessly to the floor. They laugh and leave me there, knowing I'm not worth the trouble. I awake in a stupor, wishing I could just hold my booze again. I am so behind with sales, Vern has stopped calling. Then Linda tells me to get out of the apartment. She heard some alcohol counselor on TV talking about "tough love," and making drunks accountable for their actions. I sincerely believe the whole world is out to get me.

The next thing I remember is waking up at my parents' house on May 23, 1980. I awake from a deep sleep and my eyes slowly focus on a blaring television in the corner of a small room addition of the house. The reporter on TV is standing in front of a distant volcano that is spewing enormous amounts of smoke and ash into the hazy sky. He says, "It's May 23, 1980, and Mt. Saint Helens has been erupting for a solid week."

What did he say the date is? The last day I recall is Wednesday, May 16, a week earlier, when I returned to my apartment in Columbus, Ohio from an overnight sales trip to nearby Zanesville. I had stopped at a state liquor store, purchased a fifth of Jack Daniels and guzzled half the bottle before arriving home. I continued drinking all afternoon and popped eight Valium and three quaaludes to increase the buzz. I vaguely remember calling Linda at work and disturbing her in some way. Then I watched The Deer Hunter on TV and recalled my nightmarish experiences in Vietnam. I laughed and cried through the whole thing. After that, I must have blacked out. I now have no idea how I ended up at my parents' house or where I have been for the past week.

I feel bewildered as I look around the room of my parents' once-thriving household and smell the pungent odor of dog and rotting food. My dad is passed out in a recliner with his stomach bulging between his boxer shorts and tank-top T-shirt. His head is cocked back over the arm of the chair and he's snoring loudly. His hand clutches a shiny can of Budweiser that has spilled onto his lap. Empty beer cans and quart bottles of liquor litter the room. I see through the doorway into the kitchen where newspapers and dish towels are strewn on the burners of the gas stove. A clock on the smoke-singed wall behind the stove reads 3 p. m. The day is almost gone and I'm just getting up. To the left of the kitchen, I look into the living room where Mom is passed out on the couch. Her once-beautiful, jet-black hair falls gray and limp over the edge of the armrest. She's breathing heavily, almost snoring, with both hands under her chin as if in prayer. The years of drinking wine and smoking cigarettes have caused her soft, lustrous skin to become coarse and wrinkled.

Around the couch, I see dog crap and puddles of urine on the floor. Crimped cigarette butts dot plates, spoons, beer cans, glasses, and the tops of end tables. The back door is open a crack, allowing a streak of sunlight into the dusty room. Flies buzz paper plates of half-eaten fried chicken while red ants crawl over the rotting food. I glance down to see ketchup splattered all over my jeans and T-shirt. Little squares of tinfoil containing small amounts of cocaine and a high-powered sedative known as quaalude powder are on the sofa next to me. Shadows of mice dart around corners and under chairs and tables. Am I seeing things? Our little beagle, Winnie, cowers in the corner, peeping at me with dejected eyes.

I rub my face with trembling hands and realize I haven't shaved for days. I feel bugs crawling over my body, so I keep brushing my arms and legs to make sure the bugs aren't real. I reach over and take a big swig of warm beer and quickly puke onto my shirt. I just sit there for a few minutes, wiping my shirt and trying to hold down the rest of the beer. I look at my arm where a huge scar from the gunshot wound reminds me once again of the horrors of Vietnam. Flashbacks of battles are constantly on my mind. Now the alcohol is making the memories more unbearable instead of dulling my senses. I glance down at the side table where my wallet lies open, displaying a picture of my wife, Linda. I suddenly realize I haven't been in contact with her for over a week. This could be the end of my second marriage as a result of drinking. Then the thought hits me that I haven't worked for over a week and have probably been fired from my job again. I am 33 years old, have no money, no idea where my car is, and once again, am relegated to living in my parents' home.

I walk to the bathroom and look into the mirror. My face is pale and gaunt; my eyes, red and swollen. I stand there a long time thinking about facing another divorce. The next stop for me is the streets or a VA psychiatric unit. It's now time to get my gun, put it to my head, and squeeze the trigger. I break down and cry uncontrollably. In my anguish, I recall the smiling faces I had encountered at my first meeting of Alcoholics Anonymous. I remember a sign at the meeting which read, "Hope is found here!" Hope is what I so desperately need. Then—as though God reaches down and touches me—I make one final commitment to stop the insanity and give AA a real effort.

That night I attend an AA meeting and, for the first time, and listen with an open mind to what the recovering people are saying. The AA members hold my trembling hands, console my bewildered spirit with loving laughter, and begin to heal my broken heart. It's the beginning of a bittersweet love affair that could save my life.

CHAPTER XIV

Recovery

1980-2000

Linda has reached the point of sheer desperation and wants to file for divorce. This leaves me no alternative but to leave the apartment and hopefully give her some time to heal. I call Vern to see if he will consider letting me work for him again in Cleveland. I level with him by explaining most of the problems I had in the past were because of my drinking. He listens in silence as I recount one incident after the other which were brought on by my drunken behavior. I tell Vern I am determined to beat my drinking problem with the help of Alcoholics Anonymous. He asks if I'm sure that I should be going to AA. I tell him it's my only hope and that I'm afraid to think of what might happen to me if I don't go to AA. Vern reluctantly agrees to let me go back to work for him, but only under the close supervision of a coworker in Cleveland by the name of Cindy.

I had known Cindy and her boyfriend, Sonny, since I first went to work for Grolier. They had always been very kind by letting me stay with them whenever I needed a roof over my head. I call Cindy and explain my predicament and ask if I can stay at their place until I am able to arrange with Vern to live in the back of one of his offices. She agrees to help me and says I can come to their place at any time.

I travel to Cleveland on a Friday just when Cindy and Sonny have left for Toronto, Canada, for the weekend. They have given me full reign of the apartment until their return on Sunday night. At first I think it will be nice to be alone but I quickly begin ruminating about all the failures in my life. They say God will give us only what we are able to handle, but at this point, I am feeling so overwhelmed by guilt and remorse for what I had done to myself and Linda, I wonder if life is even worth living. I try desperately to keep my mind focused on positive thoughts and begin planning to attend an AA meeting on Saturday night.

The evening and next day pass very slowly. By Saturday evening when I'm getting ready to leave for the meeting, I walk into Cindy's bathroom and open the medicine cabinet looking for some mouthwash to freshen up. I'm surprised to see a prescription of Tylenol with codeine on the shelf beckoning me to the world of instant relief and pleasant hallucinogenic dreams. I'm here alone and no one will ever know if I take a hit. Then, a voice in my head speaks sharply, "*You* will know, Drew!" I close the medicine cabinet and gaze at my face in the mirror. For the first time in many years, I feel a sense of pride knowing I had finally made the right choice.

I leave the apartment and go to my first closed AA discussion meeting. I had heard that closed AA meetings are for people who willingly admit they are alcoholics. Open AA meetings are usually lead meetings where a person tells his or her story and the meetings are open to anyone, not just alcoholics. I nervously enter the brightly lit room where about 15 people are conversing in small groups. I'm tremulous and sweating and still have blurred vision from all the drugs that are still in my system. Oddly, as I look around the room and see so much happiness, I wonder if I truly belong here. How could these people be so happy without booze in their lives? I avoid shaking hands with anyone and sit down just as the meeting begins. The chairperson opens the meeting by reading *The Serenity Prayer:* "God grant me the serenity to accept the things I cannot change," he begins. I think about Linda and the fact I can't change her thoughts about me. " . . . the courage to change the things I can," he adds. I can change only the way I think, feel, and behave. "And the wisdom to know the difference. Amen." The chairperson introduces himself, saying, "My name is Bill and I'm an alcoholic." The group responds, "Hi, Bill!" Then, each person introduces themselves by giving their first name, followed by, "I'm an alcoholic."

When it's time for me to introduce myself, I hesitate, feeling embarrassed and ashamed and say in a whisper, "My name is Drew."

There's a moment of total quiet followed by voices bellowing in unison, *"What are you, Drew?"*

My head drops to my chest in shame and I force out the most important words I've ever spoken, "My name is Drew and I'm an alcoholic."

I slowly lift my head to see a room full of caring, smiling faces looking at me. They respond, "Welcome, Drew!" Like coming home from a long journey, I now know I've arrived at the right place. I meet many people who take the time to share their experience, strength, and hope with me. After the meeting, I go out with several AA members and have coffee and tell them what brought me to the AA meeting. I'm given several phone numbers to call if I need help or feel like I'm going to drink or take drugs. It's amazing at how freely the AA members give their time and energy to newcomers like myself. They believe helping others keeps themselves sober. I'm impressed by the honesty and for the first time in my life, I feel some hope for my future.

A few days later, I attend another meeting but this time it's an open AA meeting. A man shares his personal story of recovery and he stresses that the key to recovery is the Twelve Steps of Alcoholics Anonymous. I learn that the Twelve Steps can be condensed into a few basic concepts—admitting defeat, cleaning house, and helping others. He says the First Step of AA is to admit powerlessness over alcohol and that our lives as alcoholics are unmanageable. The Second Step is to believe a Power greater than ourselves can restore us to sanity. Sanity, I think, what does he mean by that? Then he says, "I thought about the time when I was being chased around a bar by a guy with a beer bottle who wanted to smash my brains out! That's alcoholic insanity!" I recall many of my drunken episodes and it finally dawns on me that I have been living a life of insanity. I listen intently to how he coped with the awareness of his own insanity. He said, "Only in these meeting rooms will you find sanity and sometimes, even serenity."

I continue to attend AA meetings and begin to learn there really is a way to live without alcohol. I find out that AA is simply a fellowship of men and women who come together to share their experience, strength, and hope with one another so that they may solve their common problem and help others to recover from alcoholism.

The first step in this new life of recovery is to admit powerlessness by attending 90 AA meetings in 90 days. I'm confused about this so I ask an oldtimer who had over 25 years in AA why I need to attend so many meetings. He asks me how much time I had spent drinking. I start to add up the hours in the days, weeks, and months, and the reality leaves me speechless. One hour each night attending a meeting no longer seems like such a huge commitment.

Another suggestion made at the meetings is the importance of getting a sponsor to help me learn what the AA program is all about. One night while attending AA, I meet a guy named Bob who gives me his phone number and tells me that he's willing to be my sponsor. He strongly suggests that I call him each day to develop a habit of reaching out for help. Bob also suggests that I get a home group where I can begin to get active in the fellowship of AA. I have no idea what this means until one night I see an old street wino serving coffee at one of the meetings. He shuffles around to each table with hands trembling, pouring more coffee onto the floor than into our cups. I ask an oldtimer sitting next to me why this man is being made to do this by the group. The oldtimer says he was given the privilege to stay sober by serving coffee at the meeting. It suddenly dawns on me I can also stay sober by getting active and helping other alcoholics. After that night, I start arriving early at meetings to help them set up and staying late to help clean up after the meetings. This provides me a few hours of relief from emotional pain by putting my own problems aside long enough to help someone else. The AA philosophy of admitting defeat, seeking help for yourself, and then helping others is beginning to make some sense. Slogans are posted everywhere: "Keep It Simple," as a reminder that our brains are our own worst enemy. "Let Go and Let God," another slogan reads. Each slogan indicates that right action is the only mode of success for the recovering alcoholic.

I begin calling my sponsor Bob every day as he had suggested. The conversation begins and ends in exactly the same way each day:

"Hello, Bob, this is Drew."

"How are you, Drew?" he asks.

"Just fine," I always reply.

"Good, give me a call tomorrow."

I think Bob was practicing tolerance and patience to put up with my brief daily calls. These calls continue like this for a few months, until one day, Bob asks me the usual, "How are you doing?" I hesitate and then tell him I have not been doing well for about a week. Bob asks what the problem is and I tell him I feel like I'm not capable of making the AA program. I say there is no love in my life, no friends, a pitiful job, and I have no money. I then break down by saying I have lost my will to live and have been thinking once again about getting a gun to end my life. Bob understands the seriousness of my situation and tells me to meet him for dinner.

During dinner we discuss what is going on with me, and Bob makes a few observations about my life. He reminds me that I was in the process of divorce when I came into the AA program but Linda hasn't divorced me.

He points out that even though we aren't living together yet, it's probably better that we're not. He also points out that I didn't have a job or any ability to pay bills before AA, but now I do have a job and can pay my bills. He then tells me he values me as a friend and that I'm working an excellent AA program. I just need to give it some time. At that moment hope enters my life like a man on a raft lost in a rough sea who spots a beacon of light in the distance. Nothing is assured but if I head in the right direction, there will be a great reward awaiting me. As I look at Bob, I begin to understand the benefits of opening up to others and sharing my pain. I also realize AA is no longer a matter of choice and that I have to develop a solid AA program in order to stay alive. Like the man lost at sea, I must immediately head in the right direction because I may not be given another chance. Bob says that I have another drunk in me but not another recovery, and I will be dead in short order if I drink again. After dinner I make another solid commitment to stay with the AA program.

After a few more months of sobriety, I have to face the great nemesis from my past—*Vietnam*. I still go to bed most nights thinking about Vietnam and waking up each morning with it on my mind. I know this obsession will cause me to drink if I continue to let it eat away at the fiber of my existence. Knowing my life depends on remaining open and honest, I overcome my embarrassment and turn to my sponsor, Bob, and share with him my innermost thoughts about Vietnam. This is a very difficult thing for me to do since alcoholism is a disease of secrecy and 20 years of keeping secrets is a hard habit to break. As usual, Bob listens intently without batting an eye and simply suggests I keep a copy of the Serenity Prayer with me and read it every time I think about Vietnam. I tell him that the Vietnam demon is much more complicated than this and a friggin' prayer is too simple to conquer it. Bob simply smiles at me and I get the message. I remain skeptical but willing to try anything, knowing my life depends on staying sober. I make a resolution with God that every time I think about Vietnam, I will attack my thoughts by saying the Serenity Prayer as many times as necessary.

I begin saying the Serenity Prayer the first thing the next morning before I even have time to think about Vietnam. The prayer keeps the obsessive thoughts away for minutes at a time. Once they return, I immediately begin praying the mantra. I spend every waking moment fighting this obsessive preoccupation with thoughts of Vietnam, and the raging battle with my mind goes on for three full days. On the fourth day, I'm driving my car with one hand on the steering wheel and the other holding a copy of the Serenity Prayer, and I pass a church. As if in a trance, I abruptly pull the car to the curb and walk inside. I scoot into a pew, get down on my knees, hold my hands in prayer and *beg* God to release me from the relentless thoughts of Vietnam. I feel a huge weight lift from my shoulders and the warmth of a bright, spiritual light filling my soul. My heart begins to slow and I sit back in the pew in awe of the incredible feeling of being exorcised of a demon. I leave the church knowing that God has preformed a miracle in my life.

The next day I awaken for the first time since returning from Vietnam without feeling the dark spirit of the war within me. I know life will never be the same again, because God is doing for me what I could not do for myself. I begin going to bed at night and arising each morning without any thoughts about Vietnam. The war is finally placed in the past, and I'm given another chance to establish a decent life here on earth.

I am coming to believe that it is only through miracles that this alcoholic can stay sober one day at a time. I am totally at the mercy of God and His devoted servants here on earth. As each day passes, I learn this lesson more fully, especially concerning my relationship with Linda. To this end, I have been overcome with grief about her since getting sober and want desperately to make amends so we can start a new life together.

These early months of sobriety are nothing more than a tug of war between *my* will and *God's* will. One day, I give into a tremendous urge to call Linda and plead with her to give me just one more chance. She is in no mood for forgiveness and says she wants me out of her life for good and to leave her alone. I ask her again to give our relationship one more chance by going to see a marriage counselor that I had heard about in Columbus. Because of my strong will, she finally agrees saying, "If this will get you off my back, then I'll see the counselor with you!" Three days later, I drive to Columbus to meet Linda at a treatment center to speak with the director and counselor, Dick Schnurr.

Dick is a small man with a legend a mile long. He had started one of the first alcohol treatment centers in central Ohio in 1976, called Talbot Hall. Dick is a recovering alcoholic and has just left the priesthood to marry a nurse by the name of Susie whom he had met at the hospital. He has cultivated a reputation as a tough, no-nonsense clinician who believes in promoting basic human dignity to all alcoholics, but also reserves the right to pry open their souls for a damn good housecleaning. Stories in AA abound about how most alcoholics who meet Dick never forget how they got their bell rung. Many got sober as a result of it. Now, it's my turn.

I travel to Columbus from Cleveland and pick up Linda at the apartment for our counseling session. I attempt to give her a hug but she pulls away saying, "This really isn't the time to begin being nice to me!" I apologize and we get into the car for a tense and mostly silent ride to Talbot Hall. When Linda and I walk into Dick's office, he stays seated behind a large oak desk and motions us to our seats. The room smells of incense, seems airtight and soundproof. A large crucifix hangs on the wall next to a picture of Sister Ignacia who had started the country's first treatment center at St. Thomas Hospital in Akron, Ohio. There is also a copy of the Serenity Prayer hanging crooked on the wall in a frame with a cracked glass. It seems odd that such a peaceful prayer hints of a violent episode. A statue of the Holy Mother stands on the windowsill next to the Big Book of AA. On one of the walls, there is a picture of the founders of Alcoholics Anonymous, Drs. Bob and Bill Wilson. They are distinguished-looking in their dark suits and wire-rimmed glasses, revealing no hint of their alcoholic past. One large window is the gateway to an early summer day that now seems a lifetime away.

Dick leans back in his chair and peeps over his reading glasses, asking, "What can I do for the two of you?"

I speak with a trembling voice, "Well, sir, I thought you could explain to my wife a little about AA and sobriety, since she doesn't understand what I'm all about now. What I mean is, she still wants to get divorced even though I'm sober and attending AA meetings each and every day."

Dick looks at Linda and asks, "And what is your side of all this?"

"I've been taking care of myself by attending Al-Anon meetings and learning about this disease," she says in an angry tone. "What he doesn't understand is that I don't *care* if he is sober or not! I just want him to get off my back and leave me alone! I want him out of my life!"

Dick holds his hands out as if in agreement. I then lean forward, expressing myself as forcefully as possible. "Dick, what she doesn't understand is," I look directly at Linda, proclaiming, "I promise you, I'll never drink again!"

I see Dick out of the corner of my eye swivel his chair and stand up. I am still looking at Linda, but can sense Dick is moving around the desk toward us. He stops a few feet from my chair, looking angry, with his fists clenched at his sides. He bends over, leans into my face, and yells, "How many times have you promised her that!? How many times have you promised her you would never drink again!?" My head spins with memories of making the very same promise to her and others. Then, he says, "You're a drunk! You hurt people!" The word, drunk, sends a piercing sensation of self-disgust through me and I begin to feel very hurt and angry. I have an instant flashback from twelve years earlier when the Vietnamese woman scorned, "You devil, Murine!" He shouts again, contemptuously, "You're a drunk! You hurt people!" The word "drunk" echoes in my head so loudly that I begin to tremble. "You're a drunk!" he proclaims, again. At that moment, I prepare to spring out of my chair and strangle him, when he backs away. He knows he has made his point by pushing me as far as he could.

Linda is sitting in her chair with her mouth open like she has just seen a ghost. Dick sits down in his chair and looks at her saying, "You're doing the right thing by staying away from him. Continue to attend Al-Anon meetings and the right answers will come to you." Dick slowly looks over at me and snaps, "You are also doing the right thing by attending AA meetings. Don't stop going to meetings or you'll get drunk." After a little more discussion, he shows us to the door and we leave his office.

This is the first time I realize the hypocrisy of my drinking. I tell Linda that I won't bother her again and apologize for my empty promises. Later, I go back to Cindy's apartment in Cleveland where I notice a sign hanging on the side of her refrigerator which reads: "If you have a bird in a cage, open the door and let it go. If the bird flies away and doesn't return, it wasn't yours to begin with. If the bird returns, it's yours forever." There no longer has to be a tug of war between my will and God's will. God's servant Dick Schnurr hit me between the eyes with a verbal two-by-four. I can finally get out of the driver's seat to let *God* decide whether Linda and I are going to get back together.

Two months have passed since visiting Dick Schnurr at the treatment center and I haven't heard from Linda since that fateful day. I have just about given up hope when the phone rings as I was preparing to go to an AA meeting. It is Linda and she says I can move back in the apartment with her. She tells me that through Al-Anon meetings she has learned that alcoholism is a family disease and she needs to focus on her own feelings rather than spending time blaming me for the way she feels. She has come to the understanding that she didn't cause, can't control, or cure my drinking, but that she *can* cope with the family disease with the help of the AA and Al-Anon programs. The same spiritual tools of meditation and prayer, getting a sponsor, and working the Twelve Steps will also help her find happiness for herself. We can start to build our relationship with mutual respect and courtesy. Working our individual programs can bring us together, but staying sober is my task, and she promised to leave if I drink again.

Two days later I move back to Columbus and begin attending an AA meeting every day. Linda is also very involved in Al-Anon meetings and is developing a recovery program for herself. The more meetings I attend, the more I realize how sick I had become through the years of heavy drinking. Fortunately, I learn to keep my focus on attending AA meetings and staying close to people in the program as my lifeline to getting well. Linda and I spend countless hours after meetings, associating with couples who have been in the program for many years. It is through these relationships that we are able to laugh at ourselves and our predicament and enjoy the camaraderie of recovery in AA. I am sure the close relationships we are developing will last for many years into the future. I also feel very blessed to experience this fellowship and acceptance by others since life was a lonely affair in the not too distant past. As a result of attending so many meetings and experiencing the fellowship of AA, every so often the alcohol fog lifts and I become more aware of myself and how the AA program is working for me.

Now, a year has passed since getting sober and with the help of my sponsor, Bob, I have been preparing to work on the Ninth Step of Alcoholics Anonymous which states: "Made direct amends to such people wherever possible except when to do so would injure them or others." I have been pondering which amends I should make first so I call Bob and ask for help. He suggests I start with what I had feared the most—the hardest amends.

I have already prepared an amends list, which is quite long, and find the one I didn't want to make. The first amends should be to my first wife, Lynn, whom I haven't seen or talked to since our divorce. Bob assured me that I needed to start with her, and I should begin praying for the strength to make this amends. For several weeks I attend AA discussion meetings to gain insight, strength, and the confidence to make this very important amends. The alternative to not making this amends is that I will be leaving a stone unturned and risk the sobriety I have so hard fought for.

Eventually, I find out Lynn has remarried and is still living in Columbus. One evening, before attending an AA meeting, I gather the courage to call her on the phone. I slowly dial her number, remembering that I am making this amends for myself and that she may not accept it. A deep voice answers "Hello, may I help you?"

"Yes," I respond in a tremulous voice. "My name is Drew Martensen and I am . . ."

"What do you want?" the deep voice interrupts. "You don't need to be calling here for anything!"

I respond, "I'm not calling Lynn for romantic reasons, but I really need to make an amends to her. Would you allow me to speak with her, please?"

He puts the phone down and I hear him telling Lynn that I'm on the phone. She picks the phone up saying, "Hello?"

"Hello, Lynn. This is Drew." There is a pause.

"What do you want? Haven't you done enough already?"

"I understand what you're saying. I'm calling because I recently got some help for myself. Please, I need to say something and then I will leave you alone."

"Okay, go ahead," she quips.

"I'm calling because I have stopped drinking." Lynn remains silent. "I just want to let you know that 85 to 90 percent of our problems during our marriage were due to my alcoholism."

"No kidding!" she says.

I'm speechless, trying to understand her response. It dawns on me that I am the last person to recognize the obvious. "Well, I guess it's wake-up time for me."

"Whatever," she replies. "Look, I'm glad things are going well for you and that you're getting your life together, so I'll be saying good-bye."

"Just one more thing I would like to ask?"

"And, what is that?"

"May I call your mother and make an amends to her as well?" "Absolutely not! She did not appreciate what you put me through and it would hurt her too much."

"Well, thanks for your time. Good-bye." I end the conversation in relief and confusion. I have faced an unconscious resentment toward Lynn for divorcing me. The Big Book of Alcoholics Anonymous states that resentment is the number-one offender and will kill more alcoholics than anything else. I am finding that another key to recovery is based on making amends to others so that we can forgive ourselves. However, I can't make the amends to her mother for the problems I had caused. I understand from Bob that making amends is a privilege and not a right. With some situations, becoming willing to make amends is the best we can do. I have to let the amends to Lynn's mother go and put it into God's hands . . .

CHAPTER XV

The Night is Over

The time I have spent in AA has been like a little toddler who reaches out to experience a new world and then rushes back into its mother's arms for security and the confidence needed to move forward again. AA has provided me that security and confidence needed to function without alcohol in an adult world. I have now moved forward into practicing the Twelfth Step of Alcoholics Anonymous, which is to help other alcoholics achieve sobriety like so many others have helped me. I have begun sponsoring newcomers, chairing AA meetings for a month at a time, and have become a secretary for one of the AA groups, responsible for organizing all activities at the meeting. I have immersed myself in the fellowship of AA. Linda has been at my side, offering encouragement and love. She has gone to AA meetings and has also been very active in Al-Anon meetings through this entire awakening.

Nearly three years into sobriety, we celebrate the birth of our son, Brian, with the people who have guided us through the years of early recovery. There were times when I was on the road selling encyclopedias and drinking that I wondered if I would ever have a wife and a family. AA and Al-Anon gave us back our lives and love for each other, and the faith and strength to have this delightful child. Brian has added a new perspective to our life together and has enriched our souls.

I am learning a little more about love and what it takes for a woman to bring a child into the world. If it were left up to me, Brian would be exposed to a tough, no-nonsense approach to life. The way I see it, there is only a right way and a wrong way and no gray areas to do things. However, Linda is teaching me that kids are sensitive little people who need empowerment, love, and clearly defined limits. She knows this intuitively and gives Brian the unconditional love he deserves. The love I once had for alcohol is being replaced by the true rewards of staying sober—my new life with Linda and Brian.

God never forgets anything nor does he leave us floundering in a world of chaos. He guides us on an eternal path toward righteousness here on earth with the people we love and provides us with assurance at all times. I'm truly aware of his presence only when remarkable occurrences open my consciousness to him, such as the time I was walking through a department store in Columbus. I turned a corner and ran into Lynn's mother who was visiting Lynn for the weekend from New Jersey. The chances of meeting her on this day and in this place, to which I rarely go—out of the million or so people in Columbus—and when she rarely visits her daughter, were a billion to one. God put her there for a reason. I took the opportunity to tell her about what had happened to me and that I was sorry for the hurts and disappointments of the past. She graciously accepted my amends and even made a few jokes about past experiences. I have since come to believe there are no coincidences in life—only God working anonymously.

God has worked in other mysterious ways in my life. About two years into my recovery, I reached a point of total frustration with my encyclopedia job. I began interviewing for various sales jobs but found I really wasn't interested in continuing in the sales field because of the uncertainty with income and the unpredictable hours. I felt very confused trying to figure out what kind of profession to enter.

One morning while going through the want ads, I came across an ad for an alcoholism counselor at Talbot Hall. Two years after visiting Dick Schnurr at his office, I interviewed with him for a job as an alcoholism counselor. He never acknowledged confronting me in his office on that summer day in 1980. I believe he didn't want to take any credit for my sobriety or for Linda and I getting back together. So, I went to work for Dick and learned the art of alcoholism treatment. In 1985, I was promoted to the position of Director of the Adult Inpatient Unit. I worked at Talbot Hall for seven years.

During my last year at Talbot Hall, Dick was diagnosed and died of lung cancer. He left me with insights into alcoholism and treatment which have taken me far into the field of chemical dependency. More important, there was a time when working steadily for more than a few months was an impossibility for me. Now, I have a *career*.

Around the time that Brian came into our lives in 1983, my father went back in the hospital for another alcohol-related illness. Mom and Dad had continued drinking after I got sober and I had to stay away from them for my own good. Dad lost his business and had gone to work for my brother's food brokerage company. After he was released from the hospital, dad immediately went back to drinking and not showing up for work.

In a final, desperate attempt to get him help, I gathered my brothers and some close friends together at dad's office to do an intervention. On this particular morning, Dad clawed his way into the office, hungover, and in desperate need of a drink. We were all gathered in a conference room where my brother, Bradley, ushered dad into the meeting. We took turns sharing incidences where his drinking had affected each of us in some way. After we shared our concerns, dad was given the chance to enter a 30-day treatment center or relinquish his job. Dad chose to go into treatment and after his release from the hospital, he began attending regular AA meetings. That was 17 years ago and he hasn't had a drink since. Shortly after dad's intervention, mom also stopped drinking. It's a tribute to Alcoholics Anonymous—and God—that we are all alive and well on planet Earth.

Another area of concern I had was my health, since I had continued smoking after getting sober and ballooned to well over 200 pounds. At some point when I was out of breath from climbing stairs, Linda suggested I go to a doctor for a physical. After running some tests, the doctor confronted me on my weight, high blood pressure, and high triglycerides. He said I needed to quit smoking, lose weight, and get into shape. Shortly thereafter, I was watching TV and saw Bill Rogers running the New York Marathon. I was so impressed by what I saw, I decided to quit smoking and set a goal for myself to run the Columbus Marathon. It took four years of consistent training to prepare my out-of-shape body for the 26.2-mile distance. I weighed 50 pounds less when I completed the Columbus Marathon in 1986.

In 1989, I read a newspaper ad placed by Veryfine Corporation asking for people to submit a short essay of their personal life story in order to win a trip to Boston to run the Boston Marathon. To my surprise, I was chosen as one of three national winners. I ended up going to Boston and running the marathon. I also had the opportunity and honor of meeting Bill Rogers. I have since come to believe in the power of never giving up on your dreams. As a result of that trip, in 1989, I began expanding the short essay on my life into a book. However, there was still a critical missing link to accomplishing this task.

In 1990, for the first time, I visited the Moving Vietnam War Memorial Wall when it came to a Columbus suburb. After nearly nine years of sobriety, I was finally ready to deal with the unconscious pain I still carried about Vietnam. I went to the Wall, not expecting anything unusual to occur. I began to page through the litany of names of buddies who were killed around me on the battlefields of Vietnam. My finger suddenly stopped beside Scott's name and I was transfixed for a moment. Time stood still as his face seemed to jump out at me from the written page. I could see him so clearly, so young, so handsome, and so alone. He had made the ultimate sacrifice by giving up his life that I might live. I dropped onto my knees next to the table and began sobbing. My sobbing increased to a wail and I started pounding the table with my fist. I kept shouting, "What a waste, what a *waste!*" Then, I felt someone's hand rubbing my shoulder. It was the same feeling I had when Scott reached out and touched me on the battlefield when I was wounded. It takes courage to reach out to another when a soul is dying and in need of help. There is something very special and unique about these times in our lives because it puts our daily needs very quickly into proper spiritual perspective. That day at the Wall, I was finally welcomed home by another veteran who understood my anguish. He accepted and comforted me, allowing me to cry with all my heart. It started the healing within. It was the beginning of my journey to write this book. I was finally opening up in sobriety to the reality and the horror I experienced in Vietnam. I had no inclination or reason to drink over it now. I could face it head on, putting the pieces of the puzzle together as it was revealed to me.

By 1991, I was practicing the art of a writing and had written an outline of *Widowmaker* and one sample chapter. Ten years earlier, I could barely read a paragraph, let alone write one.

In August of 1992, America went to war with Iraq. President Bush vowed "to wipe away the stigma of Vietnam with the heroism of the Persian Gulf war." My kettle was getting stirred. I began having flashbacks and nightmares once again. On January 16, 1992, our armed forces attacked Iraq. Later that morning, I got a call from a local television network asking me to appear on the afternoon news to talk about the effects of the war on Vietnam veterans. As I sat in the newsroom preparing for the broadcast, the anchorman said that 11 Marines were just killed in hand-to-hand combat. I could feel the snakes squirming in my gut. Then, he said we were going to drop 1,000-pound bombs on the dug-in Republican Guard troops of Iraq. What a waste! I found myself relating to the enemy like the first time

I tried to shoot my first man. I could momentarily feel the enemy's pain and could see their faces so clearly, taking on images of my own past. They looked frightened and I wondered if they would have much time to think about the danger they were in beneath the hot desert sand. These are the moments when the snakes squirm inside your belly so hard it burns through to your skin. Your thoughts begin to race uncontrollably, sensing Old Man Death is coming for you. I couldn't rejoice in our plan to massacre 100,000 Republican Guard troops—seasoned grunts to be exterminated like sand fleas. President Bush's adulation of this atrocity was making me sick.

As I drove home from the interview, Widowmaker began to transform into this book. I could see and feel the effects that combat had on me and I felt compelled to put my experiences down on paper. "The Black Magic Carpet" was the first chapter that spilled out of my soul and onto the pages of this book. The other chapters followed slowly as 25 years of repressed memories were unlocked. I cried many times in the still of the night, and quit writing a thousand times for fear of failure. However, I have felt a tremendous responsibility to not let the memories of Vietnam and the brave young men who fought alongside me fade away. We had fought and died in an unconscionable war that we all would just as soon have forgotten. I tell my story for those who are interested in learning more about the grunt's experience of living through this particular war. It is also for those who still doubt our courage, innocence, shame and sinfulness, love of country, and our humanness. It's a true story, as best as I recall—a story that I hope will force us to think a little about our heritage, and that we are a nation built not only on greatness, but also on shame. History is what we must never forget. It will guide us through the process of change based on a humble knowledge of our past. This war was not a waste so long as it prevents other boys from fighting other wars in faraway places in the world. The history of Vietnam must be constantly challenged, for truth or history will repeat and young Americans will continue to die.

From 1964 to 1973, 2,100,000 men and women served in Vietnam. That was exactly 24 percent of the 8,444,000 who were in active armed forces during those years, but only 8 percent of the 26,000,000 Americans who were eligible for military service. The vast majority of Americans who were eligible but didn't serve were exempt by reason of physical, psychiatric, or moral failure; or they were given deferments because they were college students, teachers, fathers, engineers, or conscientious objectors. Many of these men still carry a stigma of guilt for not having served. All of our generation of men and women were Vietnam era veterans because this war touched all of us.

Of the 2,100,000 men and women who served in Vietnam, about one in ten men served in the infantry. There were 58,151 brave, young men killed in combat in Vietnam. It is estimated that twice that many committed suicide after returning from the war zone. There were a total of 211,454 reported casualties representing nearly half of the young men that served in the infantry in Vietnam. Ninety-one percent of Marines wounded were either privates or corporals. More than half of Marine casualties were teenagers. Along the DMZ, most casualty rates were around 90 percent. In my battalion, there were about 800 grunts that hit the beach in December 1967. Two months later, there were 753 casualties. Uncommon valor was common among all of us. The DEROS, or "date of estimated return from overseas," was 13 months for the Marines. DEROS was not usually an issue for the majority of us because we lived on death row from day-to-day. None of us ever thought that it would be this way. War usually grabs the young and inexperienced, low-income, and uneducated boys from the culture. Vietnam was certainly an example of this notion.

Some statistics suggest almost half of the incoming prisoners in this country from 1970 to 1976 were Vietnam veterans. There has been a disproportionate amount of divorce, unemployment, homelessness, mental illness, legal problems, and chemical dependency occurring within our rank and file. Just ask any vet, mental health worker, policeman, or doctor about this. Wartime Post-Traumatic Stress Disorder is an illness that is treatable, but also *incurable.* Audi Murphy once said that you never get over war—you learn only how to live with it occasionally.

There are still some real-world sights and sounds that send shivers down my spine. The beautiful night surf, rolling onto a beach, carries with it the frightful memory of the Riviera. Christmas is tempered with the reality of fallen comrades. An Asian waiter will remind me of the dead NVAs staring blankly from a bunker. Low-flying aircraft will cause me to stop and wonder about the swooping Phantoms carrying the dreaded palm. Helicopters' clapping thunder reminds me of the red phone dribble—"Charlie four, we're in desperate need of a Zulu!" The beauty and stillness of a mid-summer night carries with it the sounds of a night ambush and the reflection of spooks and the bogeyman. Old Man Death still plays a part in my life, but now he must bow to God's authority.

I have learned to hold my head up when talking about Vietnam and admitting that I'm a Vietnam veteran. A 20-mile run is always dedicated